BROOKLYN BRIDGE PARK

BROOKLYN BRIDGE PARK A DYING WATERFRONT TRANSFORMED

Joanne Witty and Henrik Krogius

Photographs by Henrik Krogius except where otherwise credited

Empire State Editions
An imprint of Fordham University Press
New York 2016

ESE

Fordham University Press has no responsibility for the persistence or accuracy of URLs for external or third-party Internet websites referred to in this publication and does not guarantee that any content on such websites is, or will remain, accurate or appropriate.

Fordham University Press also publishes its books in a variety of electronic formats. Some content that appears in print may not be available in electronic books.

Visit us online at:
www.fordhampress.com
www.empirestateeditions.com

Library of Congress Cataloging-in-Publication Data

Names: Witty, Joanne, author. | Krogius, Henrik, author.
Title: Brooklyn Bridge Park : a dying waterfront transformed / Joanne Witty
    and Henrik Krogius.
Description: New York : Empire State Editions, an imprint of Fordham
    University Press, [2017] | Includes bibliographical references.
Identifiers: LCCN 2016016998 | ISBN 9780823273577 (cloth : alk. paper)
Subjects: LCSH: Brooklyn Bridge Park (New York, N.Y.)—History. | Parks—New
    York (State)—New York—History. | Waterfronts—New York (State)—New
    York—Planning.
Classification: LCC F129.B7 W59 2016 | DDC 974.7—dc23
LC record available at https://lccn.loc.gov/2016016998

Printed in the United States of America

18 17   5 4 3 2

First edition

CONTENTS

Color photographs follow page 178

to the memory of Eileen Dugan and Dennis Holt

FIGURES

PREFACE

Brooklyn Bridge Park is one of the largest and most significant public projects to be built in New York in a generation. It transformed a working industrial waterfront that had served New York's commercial needs for nearly three centuries into a new public use for the twenty-first century.

When we first thought about writing this book, construction of the park was well underway but far from complete. We both have a long history with the park. One of us spent sixteen years as a key player helping to bring the park about, and the other covered the unfolding saga from its inception in the mid-1980s as a journalist and supportive member of the community. We thought it was an interesting and important story to chronicle while it was still fresh in our minds and those of the other significant players, and we set about interviewing as many of those players as we could.

The more we talked to participants in the park's development, the more we realized that the story was much more than a chronology of events. It was a story of grassroots organizing and community planning to form a consensus around a common vision for the park. It was also a story about the difficulty of maintaining that consensus against the forces that threatened it and the controversies and criticism that seem to accompany every major public undertaking. It was the story of government at its worst and its best, the conflicts among public officials and public agencies and the impact of politics, but also the merits of excellent design and talented people. Perhaps most of all, it was the story of hard work and perseverance over more than three decades.

To tell that story properly, we had to tell it in detail and to weave all its elements into a tale that would be comprehensive and accurate. Fortunately, we were present at many of the events and meetings we describe. We used our own memories, of course, but we mainly relied on contemporaneous notes and documents, and an archive of newspaper articles and blog posts that captured every twist and turn in the story and served as real-time bulletin boards for participants. When possible, we consulted others who could confirm or deny our impressions. We interviewed more than sixty people. The aim was to document, fully and accurately, the level of participation and energy around the creation of Brooklyn Bridge Park by so many individuals over so many years.

Still, the story was complex and not easy to tell. Despite its broad and growing appeal, the park's creation was lengthy, messy, and often contentious. Legitimate issues were raised along the way, and even now that it is successful the park has its critics. The height and bulk of new buildings on the park's periphery was always an issue, as were the crowds that are drawn to the park and flow through Brooklyn Heights on warm-weather weekends. Feelings about gentrification, commercialization, development, class, race, and government ebbed, flowed, and sometimes boiled over. We have tried to present these issues accurately and fairly.

Some would argue that, during the long process, individual voices were sometimes drowned out. But those knowledgeable about how cities are made would probably agree that we have come a long way from the days of the formidable and imperious Robert Moses. The route by which the park was created, however rocky and circuitous, began with public advocacy and advanced through public planning. Allowing a community's voice to be heard while grappling with economic and political reality is a challenge. The story of the creation of Brooklyn Bridge Park suggests ways to address this challenge.

And New York City is not alone. There are many shorelines in need of a makeover, and cities around the world are struggling to reimagine, enliven, modernize, and monetize ailing or abandoned waterfronts. Although each situation is unique, elements of the Brooklyn Bridge Park story can be applied to important economic and planning issues elsewhere.

To preserve the history and tease out its lessons, we have tried to be comprehensive, to chronicle the inside deliberations as well as the public actions. Although we have tried to be complete and factual, we are not entirely neutral. We are reminded again and again that the alternatives would have been far worse. Had no public project arisen on the site, it might now be occupied by a wall of luxury high-rise housing or other commercial structures. It is hard to dispute the fact that a sweeping waterfront park that offers jaw-dropping views of a great skyline is a boon to a congested city—that sweet-smelling air, the bracing scent of the sea, and the seductive sound of water lapping at the shoreline provide moments of calm and respite. The economic boom that the park reflects and reinforces is a benefit to the whole region.

We like the park; we are glad it is there. We like it especially because it reflects the multitude of hands and minds that were applied to its creation. It is not precisely the park that any one person would have made, nor could it be. When we walk through the park, we do not see the things we might have done differently. Instead, we are struck by its utility, its beauty, and the continuing marvel of its very existence.

The park is a marvel but not a miracle. People imagined it, and people built it, sometimes in conflict but often in harmony. In this book we tell their story. It is said that if you like sausage you should not watch it being made. But if you do not, you will miss the chance to look behind the curtain, to see people with their sleeves rolled up and hard at work, to learn something we think you will find interesting and amusing and important.

BROOKLYN BRIDGE PARK

John Street (residential)

Environmental Center

Jane's Carousel

Empire Stores

Tobacco Warehouse

Fulton Ferry Landing

Pierhouse (hotel)

Pier 1

Pierhouse (residential)

Pier 2- sport courts, roller rink, swings and multi use field

Pier 3

Pier 4 Beach

Marina

Picnic Peninsula

Pier 5- multi sport fields and fishing

360 Furman (residential)

Pier 6 Development Sites

Pier 6- playgrounds, beach volleyball and flower field

Manhattan Bridge

Brooklyn Bridge

INTRODUCTION

Stretching 1.3 miles along the East River waterfront, Brooklyn Bridge Park is a dog-leg right, moving from south to north and turning sharply east, with the massive Brooklyn tower of the bridge standing at the bend. The site is narrow, hugging the shore, and much of it is squeezed between the waters of New York Harbor and the steep bluffs of Brooklyn Heights. To add to the challenge of creating a park on the site, a roaring two-level expressway is cantilevered off the bluffs adjacent to the park site and washes it in sound eighteen hours a day. On the waterside, the shoreline is punctuated by five irregularly spaced piers jutting into the harbor like an enormous, gap-toothed smile, a sixth pier having collapsed into the river in 2008 (see Figure 0-1). These piers offered a broad canvas but a serious challenge to the park's designers—featureless, flat, and, as park planners would discover, largely unable to support structures or even significant plantings.

These piers and the shoreline under the bridge had a long history as a focus of commercial activity followed by a sharp decline into obsolescence and decrepitude. In their final years as a maritime center, the Brooklyn piers were modernized and enlarged in an effort to keep up with the times, but the flow of commerce moved on to other, more modern venues. The site was left without its historical purpose or even its historic charm, and it was not at all prepared for its future.

The piers under the Brooklyn Bridge were not the only waterfront sites that needed a new purpose. By the 1970s and 1980s, most of New York's working piers had ceased working. The same could be said for waterfronts in many large cities. Historically, waterfront sites grew up without much planning; when they grew old, however, they became a planning challenge.

In the case of the Brooklyn shoreline, the government planners who controlled the site did not start out by thinking about a park. Instead, mesmerized by the views of and the proximity to Manhattan, they thought about development—a conference center, perhaps, a trade center or office buildings, but primarily housing. New York is a city of apartment houses, and the demand for housing always seems to exceed the supply. The owners of the piers and the adjacent upland were mostly public agencies—instruments of the city and state government—but they thought that the highest and best use of the site would be a sale to private developers. There was little doubt the developers would fill the site with luxury condominiums and co-ops.

The planners who were thinking about commercial and residential development on the shoreline had plenty of precedent in New York. Already, twin residential towers had risen on the Manhattan side of the East River at Thirty-Fourth

Figure 0-1 (opposite). Brooklyn Bridge Park Plan, 2015.
(Brooklyn Bridge Park Corporation.)

Street, literally and accurately called Waterside. The quaintly named South Street Seaport, actually a mall designed to attract tourists, had been developed at a pier head just across the river from the Brooklyn piers, and Battery Park City, a dense mixture of high-rise housing and commerce based on the "new town" model, was rising on landfill in the Hudson River. There had even been an ambitious plan to build a convention center supported by piling and extending hundreds of feet into the Hudson River near Forty-Second Street until questions of cost and practicality forced the choice of a more conventional site.

When commercial development of the Brooklyn piers was first suggested in the 1980s, the residents of Brooklyn Heights mobilized to oppose it. The principal engine of opposition was the Brooklyn Heights Association, universally known as the BHA, a savvy, well-funded, and well-regarded representative of the neighborhood. Looking for less-intensive uses of the property, the BHA ultimately came to the idea of a park. The public planners, primarily the Port Authority of New York and New Jersey, which controlled most of the piers, saw the idea of a park as a giveaway of valuable public land, as did the once-powerful longshoremen's union, desperate to hold onto jobs.

The battle was waged inconclusively for over a decade. Neighboring communities joined the BHA and formed a coalition to oppose development and advocate a park. Local opposition to the Port Authority was vigorous and effective, but a practical park plan and a way to fund it proved elusive. The Port Authority was prevented from developing the site, but the park did not move forward.

Then, local elected officials joined with members of the local communities to form a new organization called a Local Development Corporation (LDC) to explore whether and how the Port Authority might be induced to shed its money-losing waterfront piers in favor of a park.

The LDC in turn reached out to Brooklyn communities and carried out an open process of public planning, a democratic process that became a model for other public projects but that was unusual in its day. That process produced a plan—a more active, more varied, and more modern park than earlier plans—and that plan ultimately produced a park. The park is thus a rare example of private citizens initiating, planning, and achieving an important public purpose.

The plan created by the community was necessary but not sufficient to move the park forward. The local communities could not fund the park or carry out its construction. Those tasks required government support in a time of fiscal austerity. In government, as in all other walks of life, there is no deal until someone writes a check. Making that happen relied heavily on pluck and luck, on political skill to seize a rare political opportunity. Obtaining a commitment of significant funding from the city and the state was the true turning point for the park, and we will tell the story of how that happened in Chapter 8. After that, the park became a practical project, not just a pipe dream.

The path forward from that point was neither short nor straight. Even after a general consensus was reached, there followed more than a decade of wrangling over control of the project, over estimates of maintenance costs, over the actual size of the park, over how many activities should be provided, over the roles of two sets of community-based advocates in directing the park's development, over the competing desires and visions of different parts of the community, and over the park's governance. Many side issues were raised, and the courts were kept busy.

Over much of this period the project drifted as larger events preoccupied City Hall and Albany. Simply put, the park was not a sure thing. When Michael Bloomberg was elected mayor, the state and the city finally agreed on a vehicle to spend the available money and begin to build the park. Then they agreed on another vehicle to give the park a permanent home in the city government and a promise of new funding to accelerate its progress.

But the story of Brooklyn Bridge Park is far more complicated, nuanced, and interesting than that bare description suggests. Underlying the simple truth that in many respects the community achieved its dream are the dynamics and tensions of real life—of a community that never spoke with a single voice; of a community that is actually a multitude of neighborhoods, more often divided from their neighbors by geography and history than united by a common interest, much less a common vision; of groups within those neighborhoods that often focused on the things that were missing from a plan rather than the virtue of carrying it out.

In huge, complicated cities like New York, controversy goes with the territory. A former mayor of New York once said that giving out $100 bills in Times Square would provoke at least five different objections. Fortunately for the park's supporters, most of the arguments about the park that seemed very loud in Brooklyn were harder to hear across the water at City Hall.

On the government side, too, the story is about conflict and competition, but in the end it also became a rare example of cooperation between the city and the state. Because this story is about New York, it played out amid the constant tension between governors and mayors and the people who report to them. Because this story is about elected officials, it is also about elections, term limits, legacies, and personalities. All these elements played a role, often hidden, in moving the park forward, backward, and sideways, and their influence continues to be felt.

There were also local elected officials—state and federal legislators, council members, the borough presidents—whose crucial role in the early years moved the park plan past the starting line. Then the cast of characters changed, and a new group of officials played a very different role in the endgame. Once again, to the park's good fortune, by the time new local legislators wanted to change or delay the project Mayors Bloomberg and de Blasio and Borough Presidents Markowitz and Adams had become committed to it, but how this part of the story will end is not clear.

The park also represents a rare example of using a guaranteed source of private funding to maintain a public work. A condition of government support for building the park was an understanding that it pay for its own upkeep by generating revenue from the site, what we have called the Grand Bargain, which turned out to be housing. Some people steadfastly maintained that the public nature of the park would be compromised by having private development within its perimeter (actually, on its periphery). Others saw in the arrangement not only the necessary requirement for getting the park built but also a model for how to create and maintain other parks in a time when tax-supported public funding had become scarce. This controversy, too, continued long after it seemed to be resolved.

Once the government took over, things inevitably changed. The benefits of government commitment to the park were many—a focus of time and resources, fidelity to the master plan, and insistence on standards of excellence in design and execution. But, in government hands, the pace of decisions quickened and by their nature they were made with much less community participation than before. This was not an easy transition for the community to make, although it was a necessary condition to getting a park.

For those who study city planning or follow community activism, there is a profound irony here. In the beginning the government and the community were at loggerheads, with the government proposing a major private development with a little park and the community, represented by the Brooklyn Heights Association, countering with a major park and a little private development. Ultimately, the community won the battle—a great park came to occupy more than 90 percent of the site—but many felt they had lost the war. The government agreed to build and help fund the park, but that meant it became a public project. Even though the park was housed in a novel not-for-profit corporation that existed and operated outside of normal government channels, and even though community members sat on its board, the park in its final incarnation was answerable to the mayor, not the community or the BHA.

Two successive mayors were willing to build the park largely in accord with the master plan the community had developed, but they had issues of their own. The administration of Mayor Bloomberg felt strongly that the community had to hold up its end of the bargain to permit private development that would pay for the park's upkeep. That meant housing, some of it occupying tall buildings. Tall buildings and controversy go hand in hand; opponents would wage a two-front war, at the ballot box and the courthouse.

Bill de Blasio, who followed Mayor Bloomberg, upped the ante by adding a requirement for affordable housing. Even though the final pair of buildings on Pier 6 would be shorter and include more public amenities than called for in earlier plans, opposition from some quarters only grew. There was also confusion and consternation about the height of buildings on Pier 1 after Superstorm Sandy.

All of this put the Brooklyn Heights Association in a difficult position. The BHA was the author of the park idea and had been a staunch supporter, but some of its members were furious. A community organization can rarely stand above the fray, and the BHA joined a series of lawsuits against its own creation.

In a sense, David (the Brooklyn Heights Association) had defeated Goliath (the government, originally in the form of the Port Authority), but somehow that victory left Goliath (in the form of governors and mayors) in charge of the battlefield.

But the "battlefield," after all, had become a park. If it was not entirely the tranquil, sylvan park that often commemorates an actual battle (and that had been in the mind's eye of many early advocates of the park), it was an active, ambitious, award-winning, and well-used urban park, an amenity for the communities around it, and a symbol of Brooklyn's resurgence. It has taken its place among the great parks of New York and, to judge by its many foreign visitors, the world.

If well maintained, the park may last forever, but it is not finished as we write; if it is like other great parks, it never will be. Consider what follows the first chapter of its life story.

ONE
THE STAGE

The docks are covered with long rows of barrels of sugar and molasses while the ground is almost sticky with the spilled sweets.

—*Brooklyn Daily Eagle*, 1873

For much of its history, the working waterfront in Brooklyn was one of the busiest in New York, which, by the twentieth century, made it one of the busiest in the world. The piers lying just south of the Brooklyn Bridge were once at the heart of this great commercial activity, but their importance declined over time, and a serious problem arose when the ships and their cargoes grew too big. The Port of New York Authority (later renamed the Port Authority of New York and New Jersey) had acquired narrow "finger" piers from the New York Dock Company in 1955 and replaced them with wider piers whose sheds could accommodate greater loads.[1] For about a quarter of a century these would suffice. Then they, too, would be rendered obsolete.

The coming of containerships and the vast agglomeration of large boxes they carried finally put an unsustainable strain on these piers. Modern containerized shipping needed both large expanses of land to stack those boxes and easy access to roads and rail to move them. Wedged against the bluff that gave Brooklyn Heights its name, the piers in the shadow of the Brooklyn Bridge could offer neither. By the last quarter of the twentieth century, it was clear that something would have to fill the space when the ships were gone.

The residential community of Brooklyn Heights was laid out into twenty-five-foot row house plots in the early decades of the nineteenth century to attract commuters from Manhattan as well as those engaged in commerce on the bustling Brooklyn waterfront, and the neighborhood retains the low-rise, low-density character of its origins. It was not only New York's first suburban subdivision but also its first historic district.

For many years the Heights existed comfortably above the piers that lined its waterfront, protected by the bluff and later by the Brooklyn-Queens Expressway from the rougher life of the dockworkers below. But the demise of shipping presented an unforeseen threat. The land was too valuable, the view of Manhattan and the New York Harbor too spectacular, to suppose that it could lie empty. How would redevelopment on the piers be connected to the community? How would it affect its character? And who would decide?

Brooklyn Heights was not a historic district by accident; its residents had campaigned for the designation because they were proud of their unique community and energetic in its preservation. When the specter of change appeared, they mobilized quickly to investigate and influence it. As it turned out, the Port Authority that controlled the piers was just as conscious of its own unique status and just as determined to carry out its mission. A conflict over the use of the piers developed quickly and persisted for years. To many in the Heights, the Port Authority seemed an irresistible force bent on mischief. To many at the Port Authority, Brooklyn Heights seemed an immovable object, opposed to progress and indifferent to commercial reality.

Of course, nothing really stands still, and the waterfront stretch that became Brooklyn Bridge Park had been undergoing change since the early days of its settlement by Europeans. Originally a beach between Wallabout and Red Hook, it became the site in 1642 of Brooklyn's first ferry service. A Dutch farmer named Cornelius Dircksen provided rowboats for Long Island farmers to transport wheat, tobacco, and cattle to the Manhattan market across the East River.[2] In the colonial period, a small rural town grew up around the landing consisting of houses, inns and taverns, distilleries, and other small commercial enterprises.[3]

Later, this particular patch of waterfront played a key role in the Revolutionary War. After defeating the British in Boston, General George Washington brought a large force to New York. His goal was to prevent the British from controlling the New York Harbor, and he occupied the commanding bluffs that would later become the residential communities of Brooklyn Heights and Cobble Hill. The British, moving their own force from Boston to Staten Island and then to southern Brooklyn, outflanked Washington, defeating him in one of the largest engagements of the war.

Rather than pressing their advantage, the British prepared for a siege of Washington's forces, by then backed into the northwest corner of the bluffs. On the night of August 29, 1776, Washington saved his army and perhaps the American cause in a daring and stealthy evacuation, moving his forces down to the ferry landing at the foot of Brooklyn Heights and thence across the narrow stretch of water to Manhattan. The battle and its aftermath are little remembered in Brooklyn, but the circumstances that gave rise to them—the view of the harbor and the proximity to Manhattan—play a key role in our story.

Big changes came to the Brooklyn waterfront in the early nineteenth century. In 1814 Robert Fulton, developer of the first practical steamboat, brought steam ferry service from Fulton Street in Brooklyn to Fulton Street in Manhattan.[4] This quick, cheap, and reliable transportation opened the way for greater development of Brooklyn as a place to live and work as well as a place from which to commute, and greatly facilitated the development of Brooklyn Heights.

Slips along the Brooklyn waterfront were filled with boats loading and unloading cargo. Henry Stiles recorded in A History of the City of Brooklyn that in 1824, "On the 1st of July, there were lying at the wharves of the village, 8 ships, 6 hermaphrodite brigs, 10 brigs, 20 schooners, 12 sloops. Total 56, being 17 more than on July 1, 1823."[5]

The trade increasingly involved the production of spirits. Statistics for 1850, Stiles wrote, "show that 6 distilleries, rectifying establishments and a brewery, employing altogether 179 persons, and consuming grain and fuel to the value of $993,300 annually, produced during the same period 5,459,300 gallons of whisky, valued at $1,364,925, besides $40,000 worth of slops and swill."[6]

To facilitate these operations and their attendant shipping, wharf construction and some landfill was required. In an 1832 letter preserved in the Pierrepont Family Papers at the Brooklyn Historical Society, a contractor agrees to "specification for building two lines of wharf. Front line will be Eight feet high. Seven feet wide with Blocks for Receiving Stone every Forty feet apart. Said blocks to be seven feet running back fourteen feet from the line."[7] These wharves were among the many constructed in this period, along with warehouses needed as the Manhattan shore became more crowded.

Hezekiah B. Pierrepont, a successful distillery owner, was the leading developer of Brooklyn Heights. He saw clear business advantage in increasing ferry traffic to and from Manhattan. While there were ferry terminals at either end of the Heights, his interests were concentrated off Montague Street in the center of the neighborhood. He had the idea of cutting through the Brooklyn Heights bluff to create a ramp connection to the wharves below, accompanied by an arch to allow unimpeded passage along the Heights. Foreshadowing the future, delays and litigation attended Pierrepont's project.[8] Pierrepont died in 1838, but the incline was not completed until 1849 and the stone arch overpass was finished in 1853.[9]

Pierrepont did not live to see it, but his plan achieved its purpose. New ferry service began in 1853 from Montague Street to Wall Street in Manhattan, made possible by the new ramp down to the landing (see Figure 1-1). Later, cable cars ran up the ramp and continued on Montague Street to Brooklyn Borough Hall (see Figure 1-2). This access to the waterfront was continuous for more than one hundred years, only ending when demolition for the Brooklyn-Queens Expressway began in 1946.[10]

Figure 1-1. The Wall Street Ferry Company operated its service between Montague Street and Wall Street. The Pierrepont Stores are to the right in this pre-1884 lantern slide with passengers and goods on their way to the ferry by horse and buggy. (Brooklyn Museum Archives. Lantern Slide Collection [S10]: Views: Brooklyn, Long Island, Staten Island; buildings. View 24: Montague Street. Wall Street Ferry from Montague Terrace.)

After the Civil War, business in Brooklyn was booming and a string of new brick warehouses was built along both sides of Furman Street. Stiles notes that Martin's and Harbeck's Stores, handling coffee, hides, molasses, and East India goods, were completed and occupied as of May 1, 1867;[11] like the Montague Street incline, all these buildings are now gone.

Some nineteenth-century structures did survive. In what is now the DUMBO neighborhood, running along the waterfront between the Brooklyn Bridge and the Manhattan Bridge, the Tobacco Inspection Warehouse was built on Water Street to store tobacco arriving from Virginia, Kentucky, Tennessee, and the Midwest. And, by 1868, Nesmith & Sons, a Manhattan-based firm, had begun to build the Empire Stores warehouse complex on land between Plymouth, Main, Water, and Dock Streets. The Empire Stores held a wide variety of merchandise, including sugar and molasses from Puerto Rico, animal hides and wool from Argentina, palm oil from Liberia and Sierra Leone, rubber from Belize, and American manufactures awaiting shipment to England and Mexico. Schooners and three-masted barks lined the Plymouth Street shore while workers loaded and unloaded them.[12] These structures, battered by the passage of time, would remain standing until the modern era and play a part in our story.

Workmen moved, stored, and inventoried freight arriving from all over the world. "The docks are covered with long rows of barrels of sugar and molasses while the ground is almost sticky with the spilled sweets," a *Brooklyn Daily Eagle* reporter observed in 1873.[13] "Through the low doors of the warehouses you catch glimpses of piles of boxes, tiers of hogsheads and bales of goods." Fifteen years later the *Eagle* recorded a ship's cargo of live animals from South America: "100 parrots, 123 mon-

Figure 1-2. By 1900 a rail terminal abutted the ferry terminal and would function there for 75 years. The Brooklyn Bridge did not kill ferry service; the subways would do that.

keys, 2 catch-a camels, a mountain hog, a sloth and several armadillos."[14] Another report the following year told how crowds were watching the unloading of a ship at the Empire Stores said to have African boa constrictors as cargo that escaped and ate some of the other cargo of monkeys. Officials joked about the duty payable on the eaten monkeys.[15]

By the late nineteenth century Brooklyn had become the country's coffee and sugar capital. This was facilitated by Arbuckle Brothers, located since 1871 on John Street, which conceived a process of importing, roasting, and grinding coffee beans that were packaged into one-pound bags and distributed throughout the country. Other coffee processors could be found along the Brooklyn waterfront, but "by 1907 about two-thirds of New York's incoming coffee was stored in New York Dock Company's warehouses" on what is now part of Brooklyn Bridge Park (see Figure 1-3).[16]

Over time ownership of Brooklyn's commercial waterfront was consolidated, leaving only a few big players. In a foreclosure sale, the New York Dock Company acquired the assets of the Brooklyn Wharf and Warehouse Company, which had been owned by many of the old Brooklyn merchant families, and took control of all the warehouses stretching from the Empire Stores south to Red Hook's Erie Basin.[17] The fer-

ries survived the opening of the Brooklyn Bridge in 1883, but not the start of subway service in the early 1900s. Freight shipping thrived into the late 1970s. At its peak, the New York Dock Company was the world's largest private freight terminal. It built a ten-story, million-square-foot warehouse that dominated the site; the building, later known as 360 Furman Street and eventually One Brooklyn Bridge Park, would be converted to condominium housing as the park was being built.

Meanwhile, famed city planner Robert Moses finalized plans for the Brooklyn-Queens Expressway in 1943, having at first created a scare that it would cut through the heart of Brooklyn Heights. For reasons both practical and financial,

Figure 1-4. Construction of the Brooklyn-Queens Expressway's triple cantilever section with the Promenade on top was underway in 1948. The Promenade would be completed to its full length in 1951, and the expressway would open in 1954, dramatically changing the edge of Brooklyn Heights and cutting off Montague Street's access to the waterfront. (J. Brunelli / Brooklyn Historical Society.)

Moses ultimately opted for a highly engineered, three-tiered, and cantilevered structure built into the side of the bluff supporting the Heights, for which construction began in 1946. Atop the cantilever, in response to pleas that he place a "cover" on the highway on which private rear gardens could be restored, he instead built the planted Promenade overlooking the harbor, not for private use but open to the public (see Figure 1-4).[18] Its splendid views, stretching from the Brooklyn Bridge to the Statue of Liberty and beyond, soon attracted locals and visitors alike.

As the twentieth century progressed, maritime activity in Brooklyn declined but endured. As long as the ships carried what was known as "break bulk" cargo (individual items, bags, barrels, and crates), the piers below Brooklyn Heights could be adapted to handle the volume.

While the expressway was under construction, the Port Authority acquired the Brooklyn piers from the New York Dock Company.[19] As a bistate agency, the Port Authority was careful about balancing its projects between New York and New Jersey. Since it was developing substantial maritime facilities in New Jersey, the move to Brooklyn was probably designed to demonstrate its commitment to the New York side of the harbor. The Port Authority turned the Furman Street waterfront into part of its Brooklyn Marine Terminal and replaced most of the narrow, "finger" piers with wider ones (see Figures 1-5, 1-6, and 1-7). These larger piers could even deal with the early containerships (see Figure 1-8). However, as containerships grew in size and the number of containers multiplied, the Port Authority found itself compelled to shut down Piers 1–5, the Heights piers, closing them to normal cargo operations by 1983.

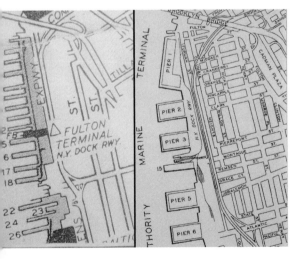

Not everyone accepted the proposition that maritime use of the piers had ended. Local 1814 of the International Longshoremen's Association, which represented the dockworkers in Brooklyn, opposed any disposition of the piers that would permanently preclude their maritime use. The union's political power was waning, but it had not disappeared en-

Figure 1-5. Port Authority maps from 1956 and 1969 show the change from many narrow, "finger" piers to fewer wider piers. Pier 15, not altered because it rested over a subway line, is renumbered Pier 4, with the railway platform remaining beside it. (Wolf Spille.)

Figure 1-6 (top). Freighters lay along the "finger" piers below Brooklyn Heights in the spring of 1953. The sun would soon go down on those piers, as their replacement by wider piers would begin later in the decade. Figure 1-7 (bottom). A photo of a wider Pier 3 shows a Manhattan skyline that has begun to change from the "classic" tapering silhouette that preceded it.

tirely, and the Port Authority was unlikely to act without considering the union's interest.[20]

Even so, once the Port Authority concluded that the Brooklyn piers were obsolete, the agency began planning for their disposition. First, Port Authority staff contacted city officials and created a working group, the Brooklyn Piers Task Force.[21] Relations between the Port Authority and the city were often strained, but on this issue the agency would need help from the city if the eventual plan called for private development of the piers.

In 1984 the Port Authority also reached out to residents who were active in the influential Brooklyn Heights Association. Rita Schwartz, a Heights resident and the Port Authority's director of government and community relations for New York, made the contact. In Schwartz's recollection, she asked Tony Manheim, then president of the Brooklyn Heights Association, to put together a group to discuss the piers over dinner with the expectation that the event would mark the beginning of a dialogue about their future use.

Here the stories begin to diverge. Schwartz remembered the initial dinner as extremely contentious; the residents Manheim had assembled questioned her and her agency's motives, made many demands, and showed little interest in an exchange of ideas. Schwartz said subsequent attempts to engage her neighbors—

there were at least three meetings—had similar results.[22] She was treated as an outsider, she said, not to be trusted, rather than a member of the community who sent her children to the same local private school they did.

Otis Pratt Pearsall, a litigator and noted preservationist from an old and distinguished Brooklyn family, had lived in Brooklyn Heights since the 1950s and was deeply involved in its civic life. Perhaps due to his role as orchestrator of the campaign that led to the Heights being designated the city's first historic district in 1965, he was invited to the meetings arranged by Manheim. Pearsall remembered them differently, describing them as offering simply the "appearance of community outreach." According to Pearsall, he and his allies outlined four goals: "Safeguarding the world-famous views from the Promenade, maximizing park and recreation, avoiding a direct link through Montague Street to anticipated Downtown development that might endanger [our] fragile historic district,[23] and promoting maritime activities and facilities such as the docking, repair and servicing of tug, fire, and police boats and other water craft."[24]

Fred Bland, a young architect with the well-regarded preservationist firm of Beyer Blinder Belle who would later serve as president of the Brooklyn Heights Association and as a member of the New York City Landmarks Preservation Commission,[25] was also present and described the process this way: "We all went around the table. My memory of all of this was that almost everybody said, 'It shouldn't be residential.' I didn't have such a strong thought as that. Of course, nobody said it should be a park; that was not at all in the offing at this point."[26]

Whatever the tone, there was clearly no meeting of the minds. After these meetings, the Port Authority staff came away believing that Brooklyn Heights residents wanted only to talk and not to listen. The Heights representatives felt similarly about the Port Authority. With disposition of the piers seemingly inevitable, the agency moved on with the work of the Brooklyn Piers Task Force, whose report was due by the end of 1985.

With Piers 1–5 no longer viable for maritime trade, with the Port Authority determined to dispose of them, and with residents of Brooklyn Heights equally determined to play a decisive role, the real story of this book begins.

Figure 1-8. Containers were stacked along the upland in 1979 during the brief period that Piers 1–6 had container shipping business. By the early 1980s the ships had grown too big, the containers too numerous, and the space too limited.

TWO
ALL HELL BREAKS LOOSE

If our view had prevailed, we might have had park twenty years ago.

—Otis Pearsall, on his early willingness to accept
some housing to provide revenue for the park

This was not the first time that Brooklyn Heights was threatened by the Port Authority meddling in its front yard. In the spring of 1953, when the Promenade had been open to the public for less than three years, the Port Authority wanted to replace the nineteenth-century warehouses along Furman Street with new seventy-foot commercial structures, reaching twenty feet higher than the Promenade. These structures would have completely blocked the magnificent views of the harbor, the skyline, and the Brooklyn Bridge. A public uproar, rare for its day, ensued and succeeded in bringing about changes. A fifty-foot height zone opposite the Promenade was soon established, and new maritime buildings constructed below the Promenade would have to stay below it.[1]

Even so, the Heights did not take the views for granted or relax its vigilance. After a sustained effort, the city's only "Special Scenic District" was created in 1974, defining an invisible "view plane" along a line extending 2,300 feet from the edge of the Promenade roughly into the middle of the East River. No new structure would be allowed to pierce that plane (see Figure 2-1).[2]

As time went on, the question changed from expanding the maritime structures to dealing with their increasing obsolescence. By the mid-1980s, the ships were gone and the Brooklyn piers were underused and forlorn. While some maritime use would continue farther south—the Port Authority built a small container port in Red Hook—there was no maritime future for the piers under the Promenade.[3] Once the Port Authority determined that they could not function as working piers, the question became what to do with them.

It must have been tempting to see the piers, along with the "upland" or mainland property adjacent to them, as parcels for real estate development. Developers like to use the word "incomparable" to describe their properties, but, viewed simply as real estate, the Brooklyn piers were indeed incomparable. Close to both Manhattan and public transportation, they boasted one thing that no Manhattan property would ever have: unsurpassed views of Manhattan itself, framed on one

15

side by the Brooklyn Bridge, one of the most venerated structures in the United States, and on the other side by a panoramic view of New York Harbor, punctuated by the exclamation mark of the Statue of Liberty.

So long as waterborne commerce was essential to New York, these views belonged to those who worked the docks. Once it was possible to think of other uses for the waterfront, it was hard for developers to ignore its commercial value. While the view plane protected the view directly across to Manhattan and thus prohibited tall buildings below the Promenade, it was still possible to imagine substantial commercial development that would respect the view plane. Moreover, because of the way the view plane angled out at either end of the Promenade, it did not fully protect views (or limit development) at the northern and southern ends of the site.

The temptation to develop the site was particularly strong in a period of fiscal austerity. Simply put, the piers were a liability, an added cost, without prospect of significant continuing revenue, in a period when costs were being cut wherever possible. The imperative to sell them arose from the desire to get out from under the obligation to maintain them and, it was hoped, to monetize their considerable value to invest in the Port Authority's core missions. One way of getting the piers off the Port Authority's hands was to get them into private hands.

Ultimately, that is precisely what happened in the form of Brooklyn Bridge Park, which is operated by a not-for-profit organization that receives no government operating support. However, most parks are purely public projects that require public capital funds to build them and public operating funds to maintain them. That was one reason the Port Authority had

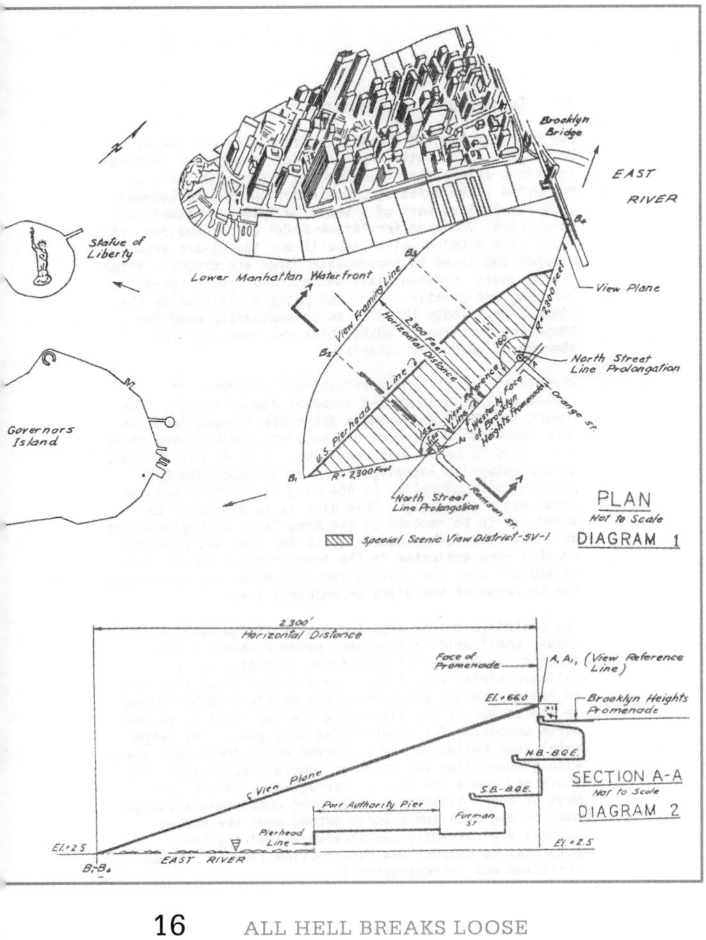

Figure 2-1. A diagram of the 1974 "scenic view plane" depicts protected views from the Heights Promenade. No structure could pierce an invisible plane that extended from the Promenade roughly to the middle of the East River. (New York City Zoning Resolution.)

so much trouble with the idea of turning the piers into a park. A park was a public project. The Port Authority wanted no part of that obligation and saw no one else willing to assume it.[4] Stephen Berger, then the agency's executive director, said he would have given the piers to Orin Lehman, the charming and well-liked commissioner of New York State Parks, Recreation, and Historic Preservation, but the state thought that even "free" was too expensive.[5] So did the city government in those days; the city's parks commissioner had too many other underfunded parks to take on a new one.

As Berger recalled it, he did want to shed the Brooklyn piers as extraneous to the Port Authority's main mission, but they were not often on his radar screen. He was far more concerned with larger issues, like the region's three major airports, the Port Authority Trans-Hudson rail line, and improvements to the mammoth container ports in New Jersey.[6]

To the extent that the Port Authority did think about the Brooklyn piers, it considered them a liability. This attitude is central to much that followed: the piers were expensive to maintain. The water under the piers is an estuary, or a tidal strait, partly salt and partly fresh, and the pier structures were subject to the corrosive effects of water and marine animals. Without costly underwater maintenance, the supports would fail and the piers would fall into the water as Pier 4 did while the park was under construction. Ironically, as the ecological health of the East River improved, the number of wood-devouring marine animals increased, and the risk of collapse accelerated.

As a public agency, the Port Authority was not automatically opposed to a public use for the property, but it did not see one on the horizon. As a result, selling all or a substantial part of the site to private developers seemed the most practical solution. Moreover, if the piers were to be sold to private parties, the Port Authority would be criticized if it sold them for less than their true market value. Because of the piers' unique nature, the Port Authority could not be sure what that value was. The only way to find out was to test the market, and that is exactly what the Port Authority proposed to do.

The city government, which was eager to stimulate economic development, especially in Brooklyn, was also attracted to the site's development possibilities. To consider these possibilities, the Port Authority and the city worked partly together and partly in parallel.

In the city, jurisdiction over economic development was divided among several agencies, including the City Planning Department, an agency that combined urban planning with development, and the Public Development Corporation, an agency focused on projects that facilitated economic activity. Both fell under the supervision of the deputy mayor for finance and economic development, at that time Alair Townsend, who would subsequently become the publisher of *Crain's New York Business*.

Together with the Port Authority, these city agencies produced a joint report called "Brooklyn Piers 1–6: A Framework for Discussion." Throughout the park's gestation, documents often carried qualified names like "framework," "preliminary," and "illustrative," the government equivalent of stretching out tentatively to touch a stove that might be hot.

Separately, the Port Authority commissioned the Halcyon Group, a Connecticut-based consulting firm, to assess and test the market for private development.

During the preparation of these studies, the Port Authority contacted the Brooklyn Heights Association. The mayor's office reached out to the association as well.

Both the joint "Framework for Discussion" and the Halcyon report were in draft form by the end of 1985 and in final form shortly thereafter.[7]

The framework listed planning criteria by which development could be judged. Most of the conclusions were unobjectionable, but the suggestion that Brooklyn Heights and the piers should be reunited visually and physically met with alarm.[8] As it turned out, this issue proved to be divisive, both within Brooklyn Heights and between the Heights and other communities near the piers.

The Halcyon report made a specific recommendation. It proposed a conference center devoted to international trade as the anchor for the site, surrounded by commercial, retail, and residential development. Taken as a whole, the report suggested a dense concentration that would completely fill the development envelope created by existing height limitations and exploit the openings at either end of the site where there were no limitations. If Halcyon had done any market testing to determine the feasibility of such a center, it was not mentioned in the report.

Viewed in hindsight, these documents were thin, unsophisticated, and, in the case of the Halcyon report, unrealistic. They did not significantly advance the discussion. But the Brooklyn Heights Association read them as the opening salvo in a campaign to overwhelm its community and commercialize the piers. The organization was determined to fire back.

To counter the anticipated impact of these studies, the Brooklyn Heights Association invited a panel of experts to discuss the development of the Brooklyn piers at its annual meeting in February 1986. Held before a large audience in the historic Church of St. Ann and the Holy Trinity, the discussion was moderated by Kent Barwick, president of the Municipal Art Society, a frequent ally in the BHA's fight to preserve its neighborhood character. The panel comprised Barbara Fife, a former head of the Parks Council's waterfront committee; Michael Zisser, chair of Pratt Institute's Department of City and Regional Planning and president of the New York Metropolitan Chapter of the American Planning Association; Roger Starr, member of the *New York Times* editorial board and a former New York City Housing Development administrator; the prominent architect David Childs of Skidmore, Owings & Merrill; Robert Campbell, architecture critic for the *Boston Globe* and a former Heights resident; and the city planner Edward Logue, widely known for his work in New Haven and Boston and for his role as president of the New York State Urban Development Corporation.

The panel exceeded the BHA's expectations, ripping apart the Halcyon report and the "Framework for Discussion," with all participants agreeing that neither was the type of study that was needed. The Halcyon report came in for the worst criticism as putting market analysis ahead of planning. One panelist compared the trade center concept to a Disneyland.[9]

Apparently Carl Geupel, one of the report's authors, took the panelists' comments personally and fired off a letter to Logue, Campbell, and Earl Weiner, then president of the Brooklyn Heights Association, challenging the "view that physical planning should take precedence over economics and market planning," adding that such planning "has filled the shelves of city offices with expensive, ineffective plans." He said that the view plane "significantly reduces the value of resources held by the citizens of the States of New York and New Jersey to the benefit of a small, but well-connected and influential neighborhood." In an addendum to the copy of the letter sent to Logue, Geupel accused the panel of "pandering to a privileged audience" and Heights residents of a "last-one-in-slam-the-door attitude."[10]

To the community this was incendiary stuff. Former Brooklyn Heights Association president Tony Manheim explained to Geupel that, had he been present at the meeting, "at least some of your concerns and misperceptions would have been allayed." While saying the BHA would welcome further discussion, Manheim argued that "a strong case can be made that the unique attributes of this site (both its strength and its limitations) should yield a development concept—dare we use the phrase a Master Plan?—that calls for uses that can go nowhere else."[11]

Robert Campbell's reasoned response defended Brooklyn Heights, saying that "the willingness and success of communities in fighting for their right to survival and self-determination has been the healthiest force in American urbanism of recent years, and has counteracted to some extent the incredible depredations so often wrought, in the name of some social or economic abstraction, by architects, bureaucrats and developers."[12]

But in the 1980s it was difficult for Brooklyn Heights to shed the government's perception that it was an elitist group trying to protect its own interests. The Brooklyn Heights Association realized that it would be in a much stronger position if it broadened its base and presented a positive vision for the piers instead of simply opposing suggestions from developers and the government.

In October 1986 Earl Weiner of the Brooklyn Heights Association named Scott Hand, a lawyer and former BHA president, to cochair a committee on the future of the piers with Otis Pearsall and Tony Manheim as vice-chairs. The new committee had forty-five members, including representatives from other neighborhoods, the local community boards, the Municipal Art Society, and the New York Landmarks Conservancy. The planning firm of Buckhurst, Fish, Hutton & Katz was retained, as Hand put it, to "analyze the site, not only from the perspective of Brooklyn Heights and adjoining communities, but also from a regional context, and [to] come up with an overall plan."[13]

The Buckhurst, Fish report, titled "The Future of the Piers," was presented to the public on February 24, 1987.[14] It made no specific recommendations, but rather set forth six goals and criteria:

1. Preserve and enhance a unique view
2. Maintain maritime uses
3. Enhance public access to the waterfront
4. Ensure environmentally sensitive development
5. Provide character, quality, and scale compatible with surrounding historic districts
6. Provide uses appropriate to the local and regional context.

"The Future of the Piers" concluded with four illustrative plans for development possibilities that fell within the goals and criteria set out in the report. These plans were:

Scheme A: Continued Maritime Use. Continued or enhanced maritime development of the site, primarily support services, repair, and docking, as well as a possible marina. The study acknowledged that this might be impractical, given the declining demand for maritime use.

Scheme B: Pure Park. Development of a major public park without accompanying private development. The report acknowledged that this approach required major capital investment as well as significant, continuing maintenance, and that meeting these costs would require a source of substantial public or private funding.

Scheme C: Moderate Mixed-Use Development. Development of a park, a marina, and a hotel/conference center with corporate condominiums. This option was described as "a relatively high-risk venture" that would probably not cover its maintenance costs.

Scheme D: Mixed-Use Development with Housing. Development of a park, a marina, a conference center, and housing. The final proposal described a balance of private and public development that could occur within the site's planning and design criteria. Of this, the report stated, "The major addition to the program exploits the safest market opportunity for the site: the potential for private residential development."[15]

Since significant maritime use was impossible, Schemes B and D became the "bid" and the "ask," the Brooklyn Heights community advocating essentially "pure park" and the Port Authority wanting to rid itself of the piers in a plan that was sufficiently self-financing to guarantee they would not be a continuing burden or returned as damaged goods. In the early days compromise might have been possible, but the parties spent much of their time moving to and then holding extreme and incompatible positions. The hope of an early deal soon faded.

The Port Authority made clear its position immediately. Although Philip LaRocco, Berger's chief deputy for economic development, promised to take the Buckhurst, Fish study into account, the Port Authority wanted to go even further than Scheme D. Rejecting the first three options in the report as unrealistic and unachievable, the Port Authority thought the fourth option was not ambitious enough to be self-sustaining.

Eventually the Port Authority issued a draft document stating that "an economically feasible density had been determined" for the site—up to 2.3 million square feet of housing and 700,000 square feet for commercial uses. Low-rise buildings would fill the piers, with taller, fifteen-story buildings at both ends, just outside the view plane.[16] The Port Authority had a preliminary plan prepared by the architects Beyer Blinder Belle. It also sought expressions of interest from developers, eighteen of whom were said to have shown interest.[17]

The mission of the city's Public Development Corporation was to stimulate economic development. According to Hardy Adasko, a longtime PDC official, "We were begging for development" in Downtown Brooklyn. And he added, "Into the Giuliani administration and really into Bloomberg, it was inducing development, not controlling it."[18]

These interests were not shared by Brooklyn Heights, and the Public Development Corporation was viewed with suspicion as a coconspirator of the Port Authority. On September 26, 1987, at a forum cochaired by State Senator Martin Connor, himself a Brooklyn Heights resident, Pearsall accused the PDC of secret planning, saying the Brooklyn Heights Association "had not heard a peep from them" since they had been apprised of the Buckhurst, Fish report. He also perceived "gall" on the part of officials who thought the view plane did not apply to city and Port Authority zoning prerogatives. And Borough President Howard Golden complained that the Port Authority had not involved his office in planning decisions. "We're only a cheering section," he lamented.[19]

Although the city and the Port Authority had been working together, the city set its own timetable and announced that a developer would be chosen by the summer of 1988.[20]

At this point the narratives of the parties diverge again. According to Pearsall, the Port Authority decided to "sidestep the BHA and its piers committee" by taking its plan instead to the local community board. Pearsall described this approach as "an elaborate stratagem" for "end running" direct discussion with the Brooklyn Heights Association.[21]

Another participant recalled events differently. According to William Vinicombe, an active member of Community Board 2 and later its chair, under the New York City Charter proposed land use changes must first go to the relevant community board before further action can be taken. He thought the Port Authority was simply following proper procedure.[22]

According to the Port Authority, taking its plan to the community board was a means of making contact with all the relevant communities, not avoiding it. Rita

HARBOR PARK

A MARITIME AND PUBLIC USE DEVELOPMENT ON THE BROOKLYN PIERS

Schwartz, who sought initial contact with the Brooklyn Heights Association, recalled that she asked the community board to develop a mechanism for community-wide input, and the board responded by creating its own nineteen-member Piers Subcommittee, as distinct from the BHA's piers committee with a confusingly similar name.[23] The Piers Subcommittee had six BHA appointees as well as representatives from surrounding communities, some not within the community board's borders.

The subcommittee's process took most of a year, during which the Port Authority continued to argue for private investment, economic activity, and job creation, with park and recreational uses taking a backseat. In contrast, the Brooklyn Heights Association favored Scheme B from the Buckhurst, Fish report, which called for a project that was fundamentally all-park, with private development limited to incidental uses.

Realizing that a physical representation of this idea would be more powerful than words, the Brooklyn Heights Association engaged the landscape architect Terry Schnadelbach to produce drawings of a mix of passive green space with recreation and income-producing commercial facilities emphasizing maritime uses (to be known as Harbor Park) (see Figure 2-2). Schnadelbach described the vision as an "American landscape" of "natural elements, long beautiful curves, shaded sitting areas, waterfalls, and fountains for kids to get wet."[24] His inspiration, he said, came from the idyllic Hudson River School painters and from Frederick Law Olmsted, the designer with Calvert Vaux of Central Park, with a little Robert Moses thrown in.[25]

John Watts, a yachtsman, bond expert, and active member of the Brooklyn Heights Association, estimated that the project would cost $122 million, of which he expected the proposed restaurants, skating rink, marina, and other leased facilities to generate $86 million in capital, leaving the public cost at $36 million.[26]

Within days the Port Authority rejected the Harbor Park proposal. Karen Burkhardt, of the Department of City Planning and a consultant to the Port Authority, presented four alternatives, each with a different ratio of residential development to public space but all with fifteen-story residential buildings at either end of the view plane (see Figure 2-3). "From our perspective," said Eileen Daly, the lead project director for the Port Authority, "a park, even with some commercial use, would not provide a return."[27]

Despite their preference for a pure park, a number of representatives of the Brooklyn Heights Association were ready to negotiate with the Port Authority to find a middle ground. Pearsall recalled that he and Scott Hand, the group's recent president, and possibly former president Tony Manheim, were actually prepared to support a plan that combined a park with revenue-generating activities, including housing.

According to Pearsall, he and Hand were on a course to propose a combination of elements from the menu created by its own report: the "Pure Park" of Scheme B, enhanced by the hotel/conference center of Scheme C and portions of the 750 units of housing added by Scheme D. "We were prepared to accept no more housing than the two towers" at Pier 6, Pearsall remembered.[28] They were not immune to the argument that twenty-four-hour "eyes on the park" as a security measure could only be guaranteed by a residential presence. Interviewed in 2013, Pearsall also said it was obvious that the modest commercial activity proposed for Harbor Park would not come close to generating the needed income. He said that he and Hand found the Port Authority "not crazy," but open to a possible deal, adding, "If our view had prevailed, we might have had park twenty years ago."[29]

This plan was derailed at a meeting of the Brooklyn Heights Association piers committee after an impassioned speech by Benjamin Crane, a corporate lawyer with Cravath, Swaine & Moore and BHA member who argued forcefully for a pure park. Pearsall and Hand were apparently surprised at how quickly they lost control of the decision-making process and especially by Manheim's swift change in direction to support Crane.[30]

In many ways the two sides were talking past each other. The Harbor Park plan did have the virtue of foresight—ultimately a park was built on the site—but it was not a compelling plan, and the actual park came to differ greatly from the one described in this early plan. Moreover, the park's proponents did not have the resources to build or operate a park or a practical idea of how to get them. The park required a public sponsor to build and operate it. Even if the Port Authority or the city had thought the Harbor Park was a good idea, neither could or would fund it.

In fact, the Port Authority was marching in the opposite direction. Reluctant to make further investments, and having neither the mandate nor the desire to manage a park, it was trying to exit the scene. The city government also had its own priority for the site—to foster economic development—and it had, if anything, fewer resources to devote to a park in Brooklyn than did the Port Authority. No other public funding was on the horizon.

The absence of funding did not deter the Brooklyn Heights Association. If people want the government to do something they see as a public benefit and within the proper scope of government, then surely, they think, the money can be found. The fact that the government has competing claims on its scarce resources is seen as a political problem, not a practical one.

Moreover, the idea that the government should do something became a conviction that the government must and will, even if it takes time. The Brooklyn Heights Association, founded in 1910, was famous for its endurance and, at least locally, respected for its political clout. Notwithstanding the willingness of Pearsall and Hand to compromise, the fact that the Port Authority and the city did not regard Harbor Park as a practical or economically viable solution did not alter the community's position. The Harbor Park plan, or something similar, would be the community's choice for years.

Nonetheless, financial viability did become an issue during the community board process. The argument was framed as the Port Authority's desire to make a buck at public expense versus considering whether the Harbor Park plan was economically feasible. John Watts presented the financial analysis on behalf of Harbor Park, argu-

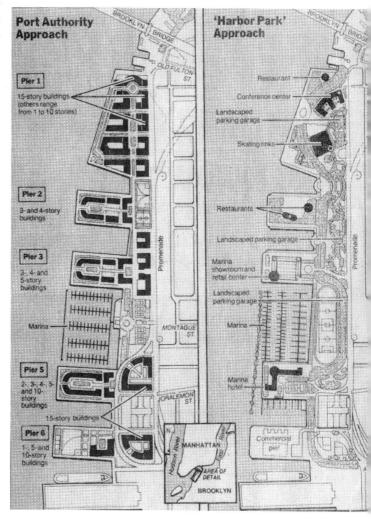

Figure 2-3. *The New York Times* of August 19, 1988, highlighted the difference between what the Port Authority and the Brooklyn Heights Association envisioned for Brooklyn's waterfront. Housing dominates the plan on the left, green space the plan on the right. (*New York Times*, © 1988.)

ing that a combination of federal, state, and city funds, along with proceeds of a bond issue and commercial lease revenues, could finance the park.[31] For its part, the Port Authority saw no reason to expect any government capital or any issuance of bonds.

Another sticking point for the Heights and other park supporters was the Port Authority's proposal to restore the Montague Street access to the piers that had been lost when the Brooklyn-Queens Expressway and Promenade were built. This was strongly resisted by some Brooklyn Heights representatives who feared such a move would create a thoroughfare disrupting their community. On the other hand, Heights residents who lived on Joralemon Street were equally concerned about traffic on their street, the only street in the Heights with direct access to the potential park site. Left unresolved, this issue would arise again.

In the end, the Piers Subcommittee of Community Board 2 was asked to choose between the Port Authority's dense development plan and the BHA's Harbor Park. When the subcommittee voted in November 1988, it was not much of a contest. The vote was unanimous in favor of the BHA plan, a result that was repeated at the full committee and at the community board itself. Who would not want a large public park in a borough with the least parkland per capita in the city, especially if it was not their responsibility to pay for it? While the Port Authority plan was defeated, the large public commitment required to support the alternative was not in evidence. The votes in the community board process did not move the project forward.

After four years of studies and meetings, misunderstandings, and missed chances, the parties seemed locked together like sumo wrestlers, unable to move. In fact, a repeat of this scene would be pretty much the story of the park for the next decade.

At the end of a tumultuous year, Hand and Pearsall decided to bow out "rather than dividing the ranks," Pearsall said, adding, "We were not going to be spoilers." Still, he acknowledged, "When we departed there were bad feelings."[32] On January 9, 1989, Hand issued a memorandum saying that "it seemed appropriate for new leadership to take over the Piers effort." He said that the architect Ted Liebman would cochair the Brooklyn Heights Association's piers committee, with Manheim continuing as vice-chair and Watts serving as a new cochair. Hand also pointed out that "many other communities and groups, both within and without Brooklyn, have lined up behind the Harbor Park concept in the form of a Coalition which itself will pursue its realization."[33]

THREE
THE MANHEIM YEARS

Government is great at making announcements that don't happen.

—New York State Governor George Pataki

The idea of creating a park on the piers now enjoyed considerable support from the neighboring communities, and there was an organization that assumed the mission to carry it out. Tony Manheim, who had been involved with the issue from the outset, became the point man for the group that would soon call itself the Brooklyn Bridge Park Coalition.[1] He set about trying to move the levers of power to get the park built and, in any event, to prevent any development that would preclude it. He would work tirelessly, only to meet repeated frustrations. In the process, he came to be thought of as a founding father of the park.

Manheim grew up on Gramercy Park in Manhattan, the son and nephew of partners of the investment firm Lehman Brothers, and he had worked for more than two decades as an investment banker for the small but respected firm Allen & Company. He had a commanding manner and a voice that projected; he wore colorful suspenders and a nautical cap (see Figure 3-1). As a sailor himself he knew something about boats; John Watts, a Texan and a sailor, described him as "aggressive," the kind of sailor who would single-hand a boat where others would sail only with a crew.[2] He was admired for his forcefulness and determination (some called it arrogance), and he was fearless in approaching public officials at all levels of government. Manheim was a natural leader, and he devoted enormous time and energy to the job.

Free office space for the Coalition was provided in a vintage shop front at 76 Montague Street, where Wolf Spille, holder of a German shipmaster's license, had established a marine brokerage and placed a large anchor in front of the premises. Captain Spille, as Manheim liked to call him, had named the building Sirius House. There, on its second floor, Manheim mapped the Coalition's campaign with the help of Barbara Brookhart, a community activist deeply involved with the nearby Carroll Gardens neighborhood and Community Board 6.

Anywhere from thirty-three to more than seventy community, civic, and special interest groups were at various times participants in the Coalition, but as a practical matter its work came down to the volunteers Manheim and Brookhart.

They wrote letters, made phone calls, met with public officials, and presented arguments at public meetings in favor of a park as the most desirable use for the stretch of piers.

Manheim faced a daunting task. Alexander Garvin, the well-known city planner, has described four components of any successful public project: politics, funding, function (by which he meant a practical plan), and form (meaning design and aesthetics). But politics and funding were the key ingredients.[3] From his own experience Garvin knew that you could have a great design but it would go nowhere if the political stars were not aligned, if there was not a capable and motivated funder, and if the plan was not grounded in a realistic, buildable reality. As it turned out, Manheim generated a lot of local support, and he kept the Port Authority from carrying out its own scheme. But he never developed a plan that a critical mass of politicians and government officials would support and fund.

Manheim and Brookhart advocated a park that was mostly green, a park for sitting in or walking through (or, as some critics suggested, for viewing from the rear windows of the brownstones that lined the Promenade).[4] Manheim, the sailor, saw some maritime uses at the water's edge, and plans included playing fields that could be used by local schools strapped for outdoor space. Still, the park they sought was largely passive rather than active, a place for reading, not roller-skating.

Not everyone shared the Coalition's vision for the park, and not all of the skeptics were employed by the Port Authority. Even the esteemed group that had

criticized the Halcyon report did not agree on what might be better uses for the site. Robert Campbell, for example, found a green, park-only scheme "boring."[5] Roger Starr favored maritime uses.[6] Some thought a modern park should emphasize active recreation. Some thought including tennis courts and a marina but no basketball courts was elitist and set the wrong tone.[7]

Then there was the issue of money. Manheim recalled later that he never objected to revenue-

Figure 3-1. Tony Manheim (right) and Cobble Hill's Roy Sloane (left). (Collection of Joanne Witty.)

generating uses on the site; he claimed the real difference of opinion involved what kind of uses and how much money they could generate. He always thought a marina, restaurants, and an executive conference center would be part of the mix. But even if these uses would have generated sufficient revenue to support a park (which, as it turned out, they would not), some government entity still had to agree to build it. Despite his best efforts, none would comply.

A constant throughout this time was the Port Authority's wish, intermittently but consistently expressed, to divest itself of the piers. "Real estate like this will not stand a vacuum," State Senator Martin Connor said. "There's a vacuum, somebody will fill it."[8] In November 1989, near the end of Stephen Berger's tenure as chief executive, the Port Authority shook things up by announcing it would sell its share of Piers 1–5 to Arthur Cohen, part of a group that had previously acquired the still privately owned uplands of Pier 4 at auction, and Larry Silverstein, later to be a major figure in the rebuilding of the World Trade Center site, for $1 million.[9]

The deal and the price tag brought howls of outrage. Local City Councilman Abe Gerges complained that the down payment of $150,000 was less than the price of a studio apartment, and he offered to write a check for the property himself.[10] Other local elected officials were equally outraged: Assemblywoman Eileen Dugan, State Senator Martin Connor, and Council members Gerges and Stephen DiBrienza vowed to try to block the sale.[11]

Tony Manheim wrote to Hugh O'Neill, assistant executive director of the Port Authority, "Rather than turning the site over to a private consortium . . . for four years at an annual rental of a bit over a penny per square foot, we believe the duly elected public officials whose mandate and vision are broader and whose responsibilities are longer range, should assume control of the planning process."[12] That was a sentiment Manheim would later have cause to regret.

At the time, Mario Cuomo was governor of New York State. Early in his career he had represented community groups in Queens opposed to projects that would have an impact on their neighborhoods. He gained prominence when he mediated confrontations involving residents, city authorities, and developers involving several projects in that borough. Perhaps he was influenced by this experience when he considered the Coalition's opposition to the sale of Piers 1–5. In any event, Governor Cuomo intervened with the Port Authority, which agreed to abandon its proposed sale and solicit broader interest through a request for proposals.[13]

In the meantime, the Coalition obtained financial information from the Port Authority that appeared to show that the agency was not losing money on Piers 1–5, as it had claimed, but instead was clearing $300,000 from current leases. Manheim saw what he described as "very good news" in those figures, and Assemblywoman Dugan said the information "takes away the great urgency that the Port Authority seems to have in dealing with the piers."[14]

The Port Authority was then coaxed into sponsoring a joint study with the New York State Urban Development Corporation (which became the Empire State Development Corporation) and the City's Public Development Corporation (later the Economic Development Corporation), conducted by the planning firm of Carr, Lynch, Hack & Sandell, to investigate financially viable plans for the waterfronts of Manhattan's West Side and Brooklyn.[15]

Manheim saw this as "a step in the right direction" and took comfort in a letter from Cuomo supporting values that "include open space for active recreation and parkland, view preservation and enhancement, and permanent career-path jobs."[16] But a careful reading of the letter suggests the governor did not support an all-park plan; the project would "include open space," not *be* open space. Councilman Kenneth Fisher clearly remembered Cuomo at an event on the piers with community leaders and elected officials: "'I know what you want,' Cuomo said, but he never used the word 'park.'"[17] Another professional politician, Martin Connor, drew a similar conclusion from a similar experience with Governor Hugh Carey: "He said, 'Yeah, good idea.' They were like, 'The governor's on our side.' Carey, he said, 'Yeah, yeah, yeah.' Come on. That's like the Irish shake-off—'Sure, yeah, yeah.'"[18]

In any event, the cheering stopped on January 10, 1991, when Gary Hack, a principal of Carr, Lynch,[19] told a public meeting at St. Francis College that the Coalition's plan was not financially feasible. He presented five alternatives with varying degrees of open space but all with greatly increased commercial space or housing.[20]

Feeling pressure to compromise, the Coalition was prepared for some modifications of its plan, but the Carr, Lynch alternatives did not admit of enough park. On behalf of the Coalition, Tom Fox, as executive director of the Neighborhood Space Coalition and president of the Hudson River Park Conservancy,[21] along with Cobble Hill leader Roy Sloane, argued that long-term revenue from park tourism would make up for any short-term gaps seen by the consultants.

Fifteen months later, on April Fools' Day in 1992, another push came from the Port Authority in the person of its new executive director, the former deputy mayor Stanley Brezenoff. Brezenoff said Pier 1 required $5 million in emergency repairs while structural problems with other piers required an additional $5 million. His solution was the immediate sale of the piers for development. "It isn't a question of negotiation," he said.[22]

Once again there came a chorus of protest from Brooklyn's elected officials. "This is not something that is going down easy," Assemblywoman Dugan lamented to *New York Newsday*. Congressman Stephen Solarz protested, "I believe it is terribly shortsighted to go forward with the sale of an invaluable public asset simply in order to avoid the need for capital expenditures."[23]

Once again the state, this time in the person of Vincent Tese, a close political associate of Governor Cuomo's and chair of the Urban Development Corporation, called on the Port Authority to hold back. For the first time, a concrete idea for removing the Port Authority from the equation was proposed. Tese suggested that a public benefit corporation or a subsidiary of UDC be created to plan for the site and reimburse the Port Authority for emergency repairs. Brezenoff indicated a sense of relief, provided "that the property be put to good use, that it not be a drain on our budget, and that our capital expenditures be reimbursed." Manheim voiced confidence that the state officials "have become persuaded that our public-use concept can work" after finally taking a close look at the Coalition's ideas.[24]

Beating back the Port Authority was one thing; getting agreement on a park plan was another. In an effort to narrow the debate, Howard Golden, Brooklyn borough president from 1997 to 2001, convened a series of meetings at Brooklyn's Borough Hall, a grand, Federal-style building that had been the city hall before an independent Brooklyn became part of a unified City of Greater New York in 1898. Participants included State Senator Connor, Assemblywoman Dugan, and Councilman Fisher, along with representatives of the Coalition and other key players interested in the park.

Golden was not a frequent participant in these meetings, but Marilyn Gelber, who worked for and represented him, urged the parties to identify points of agreement rather than focus on their differences. "Brooklyn was still struggling at that point," Gelber said. "We struggled for resources, we struggled for attention. It was pretty clear to me that a totally fragmented set of players would get nothing because that was Brooklyn's history."[25]

Drawing on her experience as a city planner, Gelber encouraged all the local players, including elected officials, to endorse a common set of planning principles to govern the development on Brooklyn's downtown waterfront.[26] The group began with the principles proposed by Buckhurst, Fish in 1987, adding and subtracting until they achieved a consensus around thirteen propositions. Within a few months the state, the city, local officials, the Coalition, and many other local and citywide groups officially signed a statement that has always been referred as the "Thirteen Guiding Principles."[27] These principles came to be regarded as sacrosanct.

The first principle stressed comprehensive planning of the entire stretch from the upland of Pier 6 at Atlantic Avenue (but not the pier itself, which was still used for shipping) to the Manhattan Bridge. This principle reflected a desire for an extended park that went well beyond the area covered by the Brooklyn piers. The southern end of the park would be south of Pier 5 and connect directly with Atlantic Avenue, a major thoroughfare that divided Brooklyn Heights from Cobble Hill. To the north, the park would extend to (and ultimately beyond) the Manhattan Bridge (whose arching structure gave the DUMBO neighborhood its name).[28] By planting the flag so far north, a claim was staked to the area between the Brooklyn and Manhattan Bridges that came to be called the "interbridge area." The interbridge area waterfront represented a hodgepodge of uses and owners, including land and buildings owned by the city, an empty lot belonging to Con Edison, and a small, neglected, and little-used state park.

In addition to claiming an enlarged footprint, the first principle said the park should be subject to a comprehensive plan. Given the multiplicity of public owners and uses of the site this was a radical idea, but it proved a good one. It was fortunate that the site was largely in public hands. While the public entities that controlled the site were often at odds, they shared a mission to serve a public purpose; if too much of the site had been in private hands, its unification would have been far more difficult.

The unification of different elements of the park would create a grand canvas on which planners could paint with broad strokes. It also provided a rallying cry that ultimately allowed control of the park to be extracted from competing owners and ideas, and placed at the disposal of a single institution whose only interest was to design, build, and maintain the park.

A second important principle was a "fiscally prudent plan." Commercial development was acknowledged as a means to enliven the area and provide security—to ensure the presence of people and services when the park itself was not in heavy use—and to finance the park's operations and some of its capital costs. Housing and office use were discouraged but not precluded. The recognition that the park could and should be self-sustaining became critical in the campaign to obtain public funds to build the park. A Grand Bargain was forged that provided public capital to build the park in exchange for revenue-generating uses to maintain the park.

Other principles focused on full public participation in the planning process, protection of scenic views, maximum open space for active and passive recreation, and creation of jobs.

Agreement on the Thirteen Guiding Principles was a milestone. But it did not resolve thorny underlying issues that had plagued the project from the beginning: consensus on the mix and proportion of uses, how that mix would be paid for, who would make decisions, and who would be in charge. By their nature the principles would accommodate many different approaches, and a number were indeed proposed.

One approach to these issues came from the administration of Mayor David Dinkins, which was working on an ambitious plan published as the "New York City Comprehensive Waterfront Plan: Reclaiming the City's Edge." The plan covered all 578 miles of New York City's waterfront. A waterfront management advisory board was created, supervised by the City Planning Commission. To allay fears about the loss of Brooklyn autonomy over the development of its own piers,[29] Wilbur Woods, director of waterfront planning for the City Planning Department, said, "I don't think one would want to set up something that would impose conflict" with local plans.[30]

As it turned out, the citywide plan devoted only three sentences to the Brooklyn waterfront, but they revealed the city's priorities: "Both the Brooklyn Piers and Fulton Ferry can be redeveloped. The State Parks Department has recommended reuse of the Empire Stores Warehouses. Proposals being prepared for the Port Authority–owned Piers 1–5 should consider the inclusion of housing, mixed uses, recreation, open space and marina development."[31] Brooklyn Bridge Park was not mentioned.[32]

The state government also got into the act, with a grant of $300,000 toward preservation of the post–Civil War Empire Stores on the "interbridge" site in DUMBO. As the state saw it, those warehouses would have a mix of retail and cultural uses, while the smaller, adjacent Tobacco Warehouse would serve experimental theater groups.

Then another vision for the waterfront emerged from a surprising quarter. Borough President Golden had sponsored development of the Thirteen Guiding Principles, but he did not embrace the Harbor Park concept promoted by the Coalition. Instead, he produced his own plan, called the "Brooklyn Harbor Market." Rather than sponsor a plan for a sylvan community park, he was interested in uses he thought would appeal to a broad swath of Brooklyn residents and bring economic activity to the area. He proposed a vision that retained the industrial character of the site, with more activity and more crowds than the Coalition's plan. Concerned about jobs and the local economy, he imagined a bustling market where "vendors will sell ethnic foods from knishes to kielbasa and from roti to ravioli; fresh foods including fish, fruits and vegetable; and goods that are prepared on-site such as baked goods, beer confections, arts and crafts."[33] A "Brooklyn Harbor Trust" to oversee this project would be appointed by the governor, the state legislature, the Brooklyn borough president, and the City Council.

At a meeting of the Community Board 6 waterfront development committee, Marilyn Gelber explained that, while the plan would include dedicated parkland, "The point is not to develop this to its highest commercial value, but the point is to be prudent." She said the Harbor Trust would include heads of pertinent state agencies and Brooklyn civic and business representatives, and she encouraged them to endorse a common set of planning principles to govern Brooklyn's downtown waterfront development.[34] Tony Manheim remarked of the Golden plan, "We would like to see it a little more greener, maybe a little more quieter."[35] A few weeks later he distanced the Coalition further from Golden's idea, saying, "The borough president would like to see a hard-surface South Street Seaport kind of place, whereas we want something softer and more park-like."[36]

The borough president's plan reflected sharp and significant disagreement with the Coalition's thinking. The Coalition, and by extension the Brooklyn Heights Association, supported a park for its own sake—that is, as a relatively pastoral, relatively passive source of pleasure and recreation, an amenity for the surrounding residential communities. The borough president was proceeding from a very different starting point. He saw the waterfront as still possessing the power to support and generate economic activity, which, in the context of Brooklyn's serious economic problems, was among his highest priorities. He saw the park site as part of an economic zone that started in downtown Brooklyn and swept in an arc to the piers. If the piers could no longer support maritime activity, perhaps they could support other forms of commerce and job creation.

His idea of a crowded market may have sounded odd, even whimsical, but it proved prescient: by the turn of the century Brooklyn would become a borough full of artisanal producers of high-quality, low-volume food and consumer goods, increasingly dotted with small shops, restaurants, and open-air markets where these goods were produced and sold. In Brooklyn Bridge Park, one of the most popular early attractions was Smorgasburg, a three-season outdoor festival of local food resembling a Renaissance fair and drawing thousands of visitors on summer weekends. For many supporters of the Coalition's original concept the crowds were too large, but Howard Golden was probably smiling.

In retrospect, Golden's plan made another, larger point that was also missed by many of the park's supporters. The large sums of public money required to build a park on the piers were not going to become available for a neighborhood park, even if the community was powerful and the site commanding. When Golden connected the idea of a park to the idea of economic development and the idea of a wider and more general public benefit, he was suggesting a connection that would justify and encourage the necessary expenditure. The wholehearted and generous support of the park by Mayor Bloomberg's administration was explicitly driven by the park's role in encouraging Brooklyn's economic development.

Councilman Ken Fisher explained the park's connection to economic development this way: "The Bloomberg model was that price was not New York's value proposition. Talent was. The way you attract talent is by creating places for people to live, work, and play. You can do that on the waterfront more easily, (a) because it was desirable, and (b) because in a lot of neighborhoods not many people lived there so you weren't going to run into as much opposition."[37]

Though Fisher's last point did not apply to Brooklyn Bridge Park, the others did. From the beginning the park was seen as an important step in reviving Downtown Brooklyn. Later on, the park was designed and celebrated as a democratic destination, but it was also an amenity for those who could afford to live in the relatively high-rent districts that abutted the park. It was an amenity not only for those who enjoyed the view but also for young people looking for active outdoor recreation, for young families looking for play space, for landlocked schools looking for sports venues, and for a growing crowd of new arrivals to the borough who brought their friends or their families to the park and said with pride, "This is why I moved to Brooklyn."

Like many cities, New York attracted talented people with its energy and excitement, but it needed to hold onto them. Living close to the center in Manhattan had always been attractive, but Manhattan was fearfully expensive and not a place where everyone wanted to raise their children. The waterfront of Brooklyn and Queens provided an alternative, and for many, parks helped seal the deal.

Moreover, as the city's economy turned increasingly to high-tech, new media, and cutting-edge start-ups, location decisions for new businesses became less a matter of access to Manhattan's anthill of lawyers, bankers, and corporate headquarters and more a matter of where creative people wanted to spend their working day. Hip and vibrant but still relatively low-rise and low-rent, parts of Brooklyn became an office park. On the flanks of Brooklyn Bridge Park the Empire Stores, a long block of nineteenth-century warehouses, would come to be renovated and filled with such tenants.

Finally, Golden's plan reflected his concern as an elected official for all of Brooklyn, not just the communities near the piers. Likewise, the mayors and governors who controlled the public purse and ultimately funded the park were elected by a much larger constituency. While Brooklyn Heights had considerable political influence and had blocked the Port Authority for years, a park that stretched for nearly a mile and a half and cost hundreds of millions of dollars could be justified only if it were likely to be used by the whole of Brooklyn, perhaps the whole of New York. That was not the park that the Coalition had in mind, or the one that many of its supporters expected.

When Golden proposed his piers plan, the Brooklyn Heights community was focused on the many signs that seemed to suggest their own plan was moving forward. But the state did not create the Urban Development Corporation subsidiary that Tese, the agency's chairman, had suggested, and hopes for $11 million to stabilize Piers 1–5 were dashed when voters defeated a state bond referendum in November 1992.

Still, a hopeful air pervaded the floating Bargemusic at Fulton Landing, where the Coalition held a reception on March 5, 1993, with several elected officials in attendance. The reporter Dennis Holt observed in the *Brooklyn Heights Press*:

> Assembly Woman Eileen Dugan arrived for the meeting—
> "a terrific assemblywoman" Manheim called her, "but she's
> not the best sailor in the world"—and she departed early
> feeling queasy on the unsteady flooring. But State Senator
> Martin Connor said he spoke for both of them in working

to get the state and its Urban Development Corporation
moving on the piers' project. He said they had met recently with Vincent Tese who heads the U.D.C. and is also a
vice chairman of the Port Authority. "Vincent Tese, stop
the Port Authority giving away the piers to developers,"
Connor had just observed, when a large wave from a passing vessel rocked the barge and the clatter of a falling tray
was heard. "You have to be very careful when you mention
Vincent Tese," he added, to general laughter.[38]

In September 1993 there seemed to be a deal to transfer the piers from the
Port Authority to the Urban Development Corporation. A reported purchase price of
$10 million was to be repaid in fifteen years from revenues derived from develop-
ment, and the UDC would pay the Port Authority $1.8 million annually to manage
operations on the piers. "UDC will continue to work with local officials and the community to create a feasible plan to open and maintain Piers 1 through 5 for public
use," Tese said.[39]

But once again there was a hiatus. The transfer of title was put off. In Governor Cuomo's 1994 State of the State message, the Brooklyn piers got a mention but
hardly the ringing endorsement for a park many had expected. "The UDC will take
the lead in implementing a plan developed by the city and Brooklyn Borough President Golden's office and long supported by Assemblywoman Eileen Dugan to create a mixed-use development on the Brooklyn waterfront, at Piers 1–5," the governor said.[40] It was unclear what the governor had in mind by a "mixed-use development," but his reference to the Golden plan seemed to reflect a focus on generating
economic activity. There was no mention of a park and no reference to the Coalition's plan.

Yet again, good news came at the end of the summer, just in time for the
election. At a meeting within the cavernous Brooklyn Bridge anchorage, a state
official told a gathering of more than one hundred people that the title transfer
would be completed in two months. But Manheim was getting cautious. "Tonight
is a milestone in many senses," he said, "but the mile marker reads zero."[41] Still, a
real surge of optimism flared early that November. Dennis Holt, a veteran observer
of the Brooklyn scene, wrote in the *Brooklyn Heights Press*:

> No Hollywood producer could have contrived a better set-
> ting.

A single microphone and a single podium stood in front of a temporary wooden platform, all framed by the soaring Manhattan skyline between Pier 1 and 2.

Clouds were swept overhead by a brisk wind showing patches of blue, and the sun would bask the setting with the subtle light that November brings. But it wasn't a November air; the warmth was more like early October.

The crowd, like a cast of extras, trickled in during the late morning of Saturday, November 5, until it numbered more than 200; an expectant crowd, some with children, some with dogs.

No Hollywood casting director could have produced a better set of stars, at least for this occasion: the Governor, Mario Cuomo; the Mayor, Rudolph Giuliani; the Borough President, Howard Golden (see Figure 3-2); a front row of other elected officials, three from the City Council, Ken

BEFORE THE VOTE: Governor Cuomo, flanked by Mayor Giuliani and Borough President Golden, appeared at the Brooklyn Heights waterfront last Saturday for the joint announcement of a task force for development of land along the piers. Cuomo's defeat in Tuesday's election casts doubt on the project.   Photo by Leon Daniels

Piers 1-5 Task Force: A Last Moment in the Sun for Cuomo

Fisher, Joan McCabe and Steve DiBrienza; State Senator Martin Connor, and Assemblyperson Eileen Dugan.

What brought all these people together to this essentially unused part of Brooklyn's waterfront was exactly that: a dream to bring a large part back to life, Piers 1–5, as a public place, a parkland setting.

The event signaled the apparent implementation of a major step toward realizing that dream: the creation of a public/private task force under the leadership of Vincent Tese of the State's Urban Development Corporation.

That was before the voters went to the polls.[42]

Three days later Cuomo was voted out of office, to be replaced by the Republican George Pataki. A disappointed Manheim (though himself a registered Republican) said the Coalition had overcome adversity before, adding, "We will simply have to redouble our educational and advocacy efforts and get to meet the new players when we know who they are."[43]

To promote renewed interest in the project, several community meetings were held, moderated by Edward Rogowsky, a Brooklyn College professor and member of the City Planning Commission. Ed Logue, who had so bluntly denounced the earlier Halcyon study done for the Port Authority, told one session that the Schnadelbach plan was as good as any he had seen, but that it was crucial to persuade Governor Pataki of its feasibility.[44]

Logue was only partly right. The first person who needed convincing was Charles Gargano, the new chairman of the Empire State Development Corporation (formerly the UDC) and vice-chairman of the Port Authority.

Wearing his hat as vice-chairman of the Port Authority, Gargano favored disposing of the useless piers as a drain on port resources.[45] In the meantime, he and the other Port Authority commissioners pressed Lillian Borrone, director of the agency's Port Commerce Department, to squeeze as much revenue as possible out of the piers while things played out.[46]

Wearing his other hat, as chair of the Empire State Development Corporation, Gargano concluded he had no interest in completing the transfer of the piers from the Port Authority, which he viewed as taking on a liability with neither a plan nor any funding in place. Gargano saw the Brooklyn piers as part of a larger plan for the harbor. For him, pride of place in that plan would be Governors Island, the for-

Figure 3-2 (opposite). Governor Mario Cuomo (center) is flanked by the new mayor, Rudolph Giuliani (left), and Borough President Howard Golden (right) at a waterfront ceremony on November 5, 1994, to announce a task force for developing the land along the piers. Three days later Cuomo lost his reelection bid. (Leon Daniels / *Brooklyn Heights Press*.)

mer military facility close to the Brooklyn shoreline, which the federal government was willing to turn over to the state if a practical use for it could be developed.[47]

Governor Pataki, who was Gargano's boss, agreed with him. As he recalled in an interview, "What we didn't want to do was deed it over and see it sit there as a junk heap with weeds, as the West Side Highway was a junk heap for twenty years owned by the state. We wanted to make sure the resources were there to turn it into a park that was a public asset." And he added, "Government is great at making announcements that don't happen. Government is great at having grandiose schemes that never get off the shelf."[48]

Wearing his various hats, Gargano was Pataki's appointee with primary responsibility for dealing with Brooklyn Bridge Park. As it happened he was no stranger to Brooklyn's borough president, Howard Golden, whom he knew growing up in Brooklyn. Later, armed with an engineering degree and a master's of business administration, Gargano became a partner in a successful Long Island–based construction company. He was a prolific fund-raiser for Republican candidates, including then State Senator George Pataki when he ran successfully for governor. Because of their history, Golden was particularly disappointed that Gargano did not give him a hearing before making a decision and told him so. Assemblywoman Eileen Dugan and State Senator Martin Connor jointly wrote to Gargano, stating that a sale of the piers for private development would be "totally unacceptable."[49]

By then Borrone had begun negotiating a ten-year lease of the centrally located Pier 3 with the Strober Brothers building-supply company to satisfy the need for revenues to cover pier expenses.[50] David Offensend, an investment banker and then president of the Brooklyn Heights Association, wrote to Port Authority Executive Director George Marlin, "The long-term nature of the lease being proposed, which extends way beyond the period when we would hope to begin construction of Brooklyn Bridge Park, constitutes a privatization of Pier 3, represents a piecemeal approach to the entire site and offers no community benefit to enhance the use of the waterfront."[51]

At the same time, the Coalition had asked the Port Authority's permission to use part of their property temporarily for public recreation (often referred to as "interim use"). A rendering of a hedged-in area was circulated to garner public support.

Borrone said she thought she had no choice but to go forward with the Pier 3 lease to generate revenue for pier repairs. She also felt she had no choice but to deny the Coalition's request for interim use of the Pier 2 upland. She did not want the liability headache or potential conflict with paying tenants of allowing the public on the piers. She also believed that interim use would diminish the pressure to find a lasting solution for disposal of the piers.[52]

Faced with this defeat, the Coalition sued to block the lease. The case was dismissed but showed that litigation was never far from anyone's mind.

Things were finally beginning to happen on the piers, but it did not look like a park. "I thought we had the development pretty well stymied through the local elected officials," said David Offensend, who was at one point vice-chairman of the Coalition, "but that would have a half-life, that they could only stonewall for so long." Offensend thought the precise character of the park was less important than its existence. "Let's just get a park before they do something really stupid in that space," he said. And he saw the virtue in making it self-sufficient and safe through some form of private development.[53]

The Coalition, under Manheim, had also moved in this direction. The Coalition had come to accept, at least implicitly, the notion that any park project would have to generate enough revenue to cover maintenance and operating expenses. With that in mind, the Coalition refined the plan with Schnadelbach into a somewhat different concept that devoted much more space to boating, including a three-hundred-boat marina filling all the space between Piers 3 and 5, with services related to boating consuming most of Pier 3. A boatel, catering hall, restaurant, and boatyard filled Pier 5. On Pier 2 were two enclosed National Hockey League–sized skating rinks and on Pier 1 an executive conference center. Even parking was included.[54]

In an attempt to prove that its plan was financially feasible, the Coalition commissioned an economic viability study for what it defined as the piers sector of Brooklyn Bridge Park. The study's lead consultant, the Praedium Group, did a market assessment for the proposed uses in the plan and projected annual revenues, declaring, "Private sector interest in the site coupled with projected market demand supports the development concept envisioned in the Plan."[55]

That optimistic report proved to be too little, too late. Borough President Golden and other local officials had given up on the Coalition as a partner and decided to take matters into their own hands. In December 1997 they announced the formation of an entity that would ultimately be the engine of the park's development, the Downtown Brooklyn Waterfront Local Development Corporation, which came to be called the LDC. The LDC was to work with the Port Authority on the disposition of Piers 1–5.[56]

Initially this entity confused and confounded the public. The Coalition was visible, popular in the community, and energetic; the Port Authority's plans had been frustrated and it seemed the park was making progress with public officials. This startling development guaranteed wide attendance at a "town hall" meeting of the Brooklyn Heights Association held in the First Unitarian Church on January 13, 1998. As Dennis Holt reported in the *Heights Press*:

> After a strong plea from John Watts, Chairman of the Co-alition, that his group should be a member of the LDC, the large audience that nearly filled the sanctuary roared its approval.
>
> Later, City Councilman Ken Fisher asked the audience if they really believed local elected officials would "sell you out" over park development for the piers, and most people raised their hands "yes."
>
> A stern Fisher then laid it on the line:
>
> "I must tell you, although everyone else has been danc-ing around the truth, that your elected officials have no confidence in the Coalition. The Coalition is not account-able to anyone. The proposed Local Development Corpora-tion is accountable to everyone in this room and to me."[57]

Greg Brooks, Gelber's successor as Howard Golden's chief of staff, added that many organizations that were part of the Coalition would have representation on the LDC board and there was no need of an "advocacy" group to be part of it.[58]

Contending in an open letter that "the Coalition should be included and should participate in its own name," Watts, as its chairman, together with Maria Favuzzi as vice-chair and Manheim as president, also argued that keeping the Co-alition only in an outside "watchdog" role "would deprive the planning effort of the knowledge and expertise that has been developed over so many years."[59]

A follow-up editorial in the *Brooklyn Heights Press* noted that Watts ulti-mately acquiesced to Fisher's offer to appoint him as his representative on the LDC board "as a way to keep the coalition's voice alive in the deliberations ahead." The editorial concluded by observing that the Coalition showed "no intention of going quietly into the night," and that "Manheim has arranged for it to set up a new Furman Street office and, curiously, there is even talk of adding an executive director."[60]

That executive director was in fact appointed before 1998 was out. Tensie Whelan, previously executive director of the New York League of Conservation Voters and involved in other park and environmental enterprises, quickly set about developing an "activist network" ostensibly to advance the Coalition's original mission "to get the park to happen." These ambitions would set her on a collision course with both Manheim and the Local Development Corporation.[61]

Whatever lay ahead, the days of Tony Manheim as central to the planning effort were over. He had held out for a park at times when there seemed no hope for it; he had made the park seem desirable to the community and possible to public officials, but he could not field a plan that officials found practical and financial feasible. He wore out his welcome even among a number of his own park campaign associates. Still, the existence of Brooklyn Bridge Park owes a great debt to his zeal and devotion. He could not make it happen on his terms, but it would not have happened without him.

FOUR
A NEW GAME WITH A FRESH TEAM

This is a real opportunity. But make no mistake about it, we
have to seize that opportunity as a community.
—State Senator Marty Connor on the need for community
agreement on a plan for the park

Martin Connor, who had been president of the West Brooklyn Independent Democrats, Brooklyn's first reform club, became a state senator in 1978. In 1995 he was
chosen as the minority leader of the Senate, the year his fellow senator, the Republican George Pataki, became governor. His district included Brooklyn Heights,
where he lived. He had been helpful in keeping the Port Authority at bay, and he
had been an early supporter of the park.

The New York State government was run largely by the governor and the
majority leaders of the two houses of the legislature, an arrangement described as
"three men in a room." But in those days, especially in the State Senate where the
numbers were close, the minority party had influence. As Hardy Adasko, by then a
senior vice-president of the city's Economic Development Corporation, recalled,
whenever they moved up to five men in a room Connor was there.[1]

Connor's image, as a large imposing figure with a reputation as a fearsome
election lawyer, belied the easy familiarity of "Marty," as he was called, and his ability to keep people in stitches with his stories of how politics really works. Connor's
relationship with the new governor went back to Connor's days as an associate at
the Wall Street law firm White & Case while Pataki was at the equally white-shoe
firm of Dewey Ballantine. They played basketball and touch football against each
other in leagues for young lawyers. When they were in the legislature together,
Connor had enjoyed a good relationship with Pataki despite their political differences. A phone on Connor's desk connected directly to one on the governor's desk.
Given the right circumstances, Connor thought, the new governor would be open
to a Brooklyn Bridge Park plan.[2]

Assemblywoman Eileen Dugan, Connor's Brooklyn partner in the legislature,
had just died of breast cancer at age fifty-one. Irish by descent, Dugan had lived in
Carroll Gardens, a largely Italian enclave south of Brooklyn Heights. Her devotion to
the community was well-known.[3] An ally of Connor's, she was a member of the
Independent Neighborhood Democrats of Carroll Gardens, and she had served in
the Assembly since 1980.[4]

Dugan had been a member of the Democratic Party leadership in the Assembly, which commanded a substantial majority, and had been the first female member of the powerful Ways and Means Committee. She had obtained an appropriation of $1 million in the state budget earmarked for the Downtown Waterfront Task Force, a creature of the Brooklyn borough president's office. Shortly before her death, Dugan asked Connor to make sure the money would be used for Brooklyn Bridge Park.[5]

Satisfying that request would not be easy. At that moment prospects for a park looked bleak. The Coalition had not produced a credible plan, and the Port Authority was renting out part of the site. All parties concerned were growing frustrated.

If there were any hope of breaking the logjam, Connor and the other elected officials had to solve two problems. First, without a concrete and practical plan for a self-sustaining park, there would be no park at all. The three important governmental players—the city, the state, and the Port Authority—had to be persuaded that building a park was not only possible but also preferable to any other plan for disposing of the piers. While local officials might influence the major government players, they were not the decision makers; ultimately, authority over purse and park rested with the mayor and the governor.

In addition, local officials knew that the communities surrounding the park site were deeply divided over the park (see Figure 4-1). Though nearly everyone who lived near the site would benefit from the park's construction, opinions over what had been proposed were sharply divided. A long history of neighborhood rivalry also infected the process. The local officials knew that resolving the differences would be difficult, and yet they had to be resolved for the park to progress. As Connor said at the first public planning meeting in 1999, "This is a real opportunity. But make no mistake about it, we have to seize that opportunity as a community."[6]

Brooklyn Heights, which sat immediately above the piers, is a landmarked district of brownstones, old residential hotels, and relatively small apartment buildings. Heights residents felt most directly affected by possible development of what they regarded as "their" waterfront. The Heights also had a long history of marshaling political and financial resources to influence public policy, primarily through the Brooklyn Heights Association.

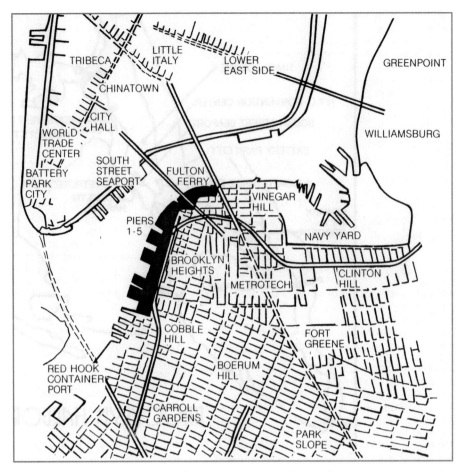

Yet Brooklyn Heights was by no means monolithic. Some wanted a passive, green park with very little activity. Others accepted the idea that the government was unlikely to build a park that did not serve a wider audience. Residents who were willing to live with more park activity nonetheless worried about protecting the Heights from crowds and traffic. Over time, these opinions hardened into convictions, and some people were thought to prefer no park at all if they could not get the park they wanted.

Because the Brooklyn Heights Association supported the idea that the park would need to be self-sustaining, its leaders felt a need to counter an image of BHA obstructionism that was held by many outside the Heights. "Today's board of governors clearly does not view all development as anathema," Deirdre Carson, the association's latest president, told the group's annual public meeting in February 1999, "nor does it wish to alienate decision makers by constantly taking positions without regard to the facts or distinctions which may be fairly drawn among projects."[7] Nevertheless, the membership could not agree on what was required; many hoped that a small hotel, a restaurant or two, and a few concessions would be adequate.

Although much of the Heights was isolated from the piers by the bluff and many wanted to keep it that way, the southern part lacked similar protection. In particular, those living along Joralemon Street, which ran down to the waterfront and passed under the Brooklyn-Queens Expressway, were afraid that their street would invite hordes of visitors heading to the park. They did not think the Brooklyn Heights Association was protecting their interest in maintaining the quiet of their picturesque cobblestone street.

In addition to geography, Brooklyn Heights could be divided in other ways. In the view of Ken Fisher, the neighborhood's councilman from 1991 to 2001, the Heights was home to at least four overlapping "neighborhoods": a relatively small group, many of them bankers and lawyers, that Fisher called "Brooklyn Heights Brahmins," who were deeply conscious of the community's identity and interests and who formed the active core of local organizations; a larger group who lived in the Heights by the accident of birth or because it was an attractive neighborhood but who were less involved in community issues or institutions; a scattering of artists and writers, including luminaries such as the author Norman Mailer; and a "courthouse" crowd, both local lawyers who wanted to be near the state and federal courts in nearby Downtown Brooklyn and small business owners and others who had a reason to be in this particular neighborhood.[8] The developments surrounding the park would become a focus for the first group and would frequently command the attention of the other three.

Farther south lie Cobble Hill, Columbia Street, and Carroll Gardens. These neighborhoods, previously collectively called South Brooklyn, also contained many charming brownstones but were more recently gentrified. They were also home to many working-class families, fewer than in the past but still a significant number. Many residents were of Italian descent, and the commercial streets were well-known for their concentration of ethnic merchants and restaurants.[9]

Since these communities, which lay south of Atlantic Avenue, did not border directly on the proposed park, their residents worried more about having good access to it and about the traffic the park might generate through their neighborhoods. They spoke often about the importance of equal sharing of the prospective burdens between the Heights and other communities.

Their resentment of the Heights went back at least to the late 1940s, when the six-lane Brooklyn-Queens Expressway was constructed in a reviled "ditch" that tore apart their neighborhoods while the Heights was spared. Furthermore, the Heights received the benefit of the cantilever construction for the BQE at the edge of the bluff that made possible the third-of-a-mile Promenade above the express-way. And Brooklyn Heights clearly did benefit from the establishment of the scenic view plane, a limitation that protected the views from the Promenade. No other neighborhood in the city had similar protection.

At the northern end of the Heights, where the Fulton Ferry Landing district fans out from the intersection of Furman and Old Fulton Streets, residents were worried about the fact that they were at the same grade as the park site at what would be the park's front door, and they feared that they would be overwhelmed by park traffic.

DUMBO lies just beyond Fulton Ferry Landing, also at grade with the pro-posed park; it became known as the "interbridge" area because it lay largely be-tween the Brooklyn and Manhattan Bridges. It was hoped that the DUMBO water-front could be included in the park, but the land was controlled in part by the city and in part by the state's Office of Parks, Recreation, and Historic Preservation.

Much of inland DUMBO, a collection of nineteenth- and early-twentieth-century manufacturing buildings, was owned by a real estate developer named David Walentas, who had purchased them, cheaply as it turned out, in the 1980s. By this point Walentas had begun to convert the buildings into residential use. There were not many people living in DUMBO—primarily artists and other pio-neers living in loft buildings without proper certificates of occupancy—but Walen-tas envisioned another SoHo, a progression from artists' studios to art galleries to fashionable (and expensive) shops and restaurants, with a corresponding rise in real estate values.[10]

As soon as Walentas started executing his plan to convert his buildings to residential use, there began a long running battle with the Brooklyn Heights As-sociation, which consistently opposed his efforts to change DUMBO.

Northeast of DUMBO lies Vinegar Hill, a tiny historic district where Brooklyn Navy Yard workers used to live. This neighborhood brought the least baggage to the park planning process, perhaps because of its isolated and tangential location.

Internal divisions and issues among these communities increased the difficulty of achieving consensus beyond the already great political problems involved in get-ting government sponsorship of a park. Local officials, trying to pull everyone to-gether, were acutely aware of these underlying strains.

The local officials, however, did have two important tools. One was the power to call a meeting, to get representatives of the competing communities to sit down in the same room and confront the same set of facts. The other was the power of the purse. The $1 million legacy from Assemblywoman Dugan proved the basis for having the communities come together around a single, practical plan that could then be used to win further funding. The Dugan money would eventually be leveraged to obtain an extraordinary $400 million in public funds, dramatically changing the face that Brooklyn turned toward the world.

Still, in the fall of 1997, the process had stalled and a good outcome was hard to imagine. The local officials concluded that new players and a new entity needed to be brought in to make the best of the legacy Dugan had entrusted to Senator Connor. They decided to create an unusual entity controlled neither by the government nor by any particular community, but rather one that was autonomous and positioned to earn confidence from all sides (or perhaps to be disavowed by all if it failed).

The technical basis for such an entity was found in Section 402 of the New York State Not-for-Profit Law that allows the creation of a self-governing body to serve a public purpose simply by incorporating it. Known as a Local Development Corporation, or LDC, this body could be established without passing any legislation or securing approval from any public body, and it could legally accept the $1 million appropriation to conduct studies and draw up plans. While certain regulations governed the expenditure of public funds, an LDC was largely autonomous and empowered to make its own decisions. It could also permit representation by all the interested groups and allow them to share in the decision-making authority.

But no one had any idea of how this would work when, on March 19, 1998, a certificate of incorporation was duly filed in Albany to create the Downtown Brooklyn Waterfront Local Development Corporation.

The elected officials carefully considered the composition of the LDC's board of directors. It would have fifteen members, and each elected official could appoint one member, except for the borough president, who could name two. This meant there were six appointees from the officials. The other nine directors were chosen by the community groups, the two pertinent community boards, and the Brooklyn Chamber of Commerce. The Brooklyn Heights Association got the right to name two directors, while Cobble Hill, Vinegar Hill, Columbia Street, and Fulton Ferry Landing got one each (DUMBO did not yet have an official neighborhood organization). The community boards and the Chamber of Commerce also got one each.

The LDC's formation, publicly announced in December 1997,[11] provoked considerable consternation, especially within the Brooklyn Heights Association. The Coalition immediately called foul not only because it believed it was heir to Dugan's $1 million but because it was excluded from participation altogether. The Coalition portrayed the LDC as a sham set up to fail in order to justify letting the Port Authority do what it wanted with the piers. The exclusion of the Coalition, the bearer of the park torch, was seen as proof of this.

After a town hall meeting in January 1998 to sound out opinion on whether the Brooklyn Heights Association should participate in the LDC at all, the association held a meeting of its own board. David Offensend, a former BHA president and the Coalition's current vice-chair, urged the association to cede to the Coalition one of its two seats on the LDC. A newly elected BHA board member questioned why the association should want to give away a seat to an intermediary that local officials clearly distrusted. The influential Otis Pratt Pearsall, a former BHA governor, threw his support behind the "new guy." In the end, the board elected Offensend and that new member, Henry ("Hank") Gutman, as the association's representatives to the LDC.[12]

John Watts, the chairman of the Coalition, took Councilman Kenneth Fisher's seat.[13] Assemblywoman Joan Millman, who had replaced the late Assemblywoman Dugan, chose Marcia Hillis of DUMBO to compensate for the fact that the neighborhood lacked its own seat. (When Hillis later dropped out, Millman chose Franklin Stone, president of the Cobble Hill Association, as her replacement.) Senator Connor picked Joanne Witty, a recent Brooklyn Heights Association governor, lawyer and environmental activist (and coauthor of this book). Congressman Edolphus Towns chose his chief of staff, Karen Johnson.[14] Borough President Golden named Greg Brooks, his chief of staff, and Jon Benguiat, his director of land use planning.[15]

The four community organizations besides the Brooklyn Heights Association that were given power to appoint were smaller operations without the association's membership numbers, staff, or resources. For balance, two were from areas north of Brooklyn Heights, two from south. Fulton Ferry Landing on the north picked Allen Swerdlowe, an architect and outspoken Coalition board member. Vinegar Hill picked an artist and accomplished amateur gardener, Per-Olof Odman, who was soon replaced by Michael Winikoff, a technology consultant with no prior connection with the park issue. Cobble Hill on the south picked Roy Sloane, a graphic designer, former president of the Cobble Hill Association, and a former member of the Coalition. Columbia Street picked Madelaine Murphy, a member of Community Board 6.

Community boards in New York City are advisory bodies on many matters, including land-use policy. Board 2 to the north and Board 6 to the south were given seats to increase input on park planning from communities beyond those directly represented on the LDC board. Community board approval carried more weight than did that of the neighborhood associations because boards answered to a larger and more diverse population. The elected officials believed that Brooklyn Bridge Park had a far greater chance if it was seen as a park for all Brooklyn and not just for a few relatively affluent nearby communities.

Community Board 2 covered Brooklyn Heights, Fulton Ferry, DUMBO, Vinegar Hill, Fort Greene, parts of Boerum Hill and Clinton Hill, as well as two large public housing complexes—Farragut and Ingersoll—in Downtown Brooklyn and Fort Greene, respectively. William Vinicombe was an active member of Community Board 2 and its designee on the LDC board. "Think about CB2," he said. "We had one of the strongest and richest neighborhoods in the city, and, at the same time, we had the poorest. All in one. And that dynamic was constantly being played into everything."[16] The public housing was physically separated from the brownstone communities by the Manhattan and Brooklyn Bridges and their wide approach roads, and for the same reason they would be separated from the park.

Community Board 6 covered Cobble Hill, Carroll Gardens, the Columbia Street Corridor, Gowanus, Red Hook (including Red Hook Houses East and West, another large public housing complex), and Park Slope. That meant there would be representation of views from a broad swath of Brooklyn, which helped foster the notion of a widely welcoming park. Board 6 chose Alric Nembhard, who was later replaced by Pauline Blake, a former chair of CB 6.

Finally, the Brooklyn Chamber of Commerce named its president, Kenneth Adams, to the LDC board. His first priority was to revive stalled momentum for Downtown Brooklyn redevelopment, raising money for and creating the Downtown Brooklyn Council. The business community realized that the park could be an important boost for a revitalized downtown core and therefore lent its support to the park's creation. An effective politician, Adams helped hold the center in the LDC's councils. He subsequently became head of the Empire State Development Corporation and leader of the state's economic development efforts.

The LDC's success was by no means a foregone conclusion. It faced the difficult task of achieving credibility with the outside world while figuring out how to work productively among its own members. One complication was that three of its fifteen members were also members of the Coalition: John Watts and David Offensend, the Coalition's chair and vice-chair, respectively, as well as the architect Allen Swerdlowe. To the extent that the LDC and the Coalition were inevitable competitors, the three Coalition members had divided institutional loyalty.

Despite tensions, a cohesive center of gravity coalesced early and productive work began quickly. In an important sign that the elected officials did not intend to dictate the rules governing the LDC or its specific tasks, the corporation wrote its own bylaws and created its own work plan.

To insure that it would not be wasting its time, the corporation decided that it needed a formal agreement with the Port Authority, in which the agency promised to support and not undermine the LDC's work. After more than a decade of poor communication and demonization, many members of the group approached this possibility with skepticism. As it turned out, Lillian Borrone, the Port Authority's director of port commerce, was receptive to an agreement that the LDC would conduct studies and set a timetable in exchange for a commitment that the Port would not try to dispose of or develop the piers in the meantime. Borrone proved as good as her word, and everyone was so relieved that no one stopped to consider why this had been the case.

For one thing, as maritime use of the piers was fading further into history and the piers themselves were growing costlier to maintain, the pressure to dispose of them was increasing. In these circumstances, as Borrone later explained, she saw the LDC and its backing by local officials as a real chance finally to dispose of the piers and put them to better use. Since the community seemed capable of preventing her from acting unilaterally, the development of a practical plan that had community support seemed the only way she could carry out her own mission.[17]

Borrone did have a positive reaction to the LDC. As she said later in an interview, "The coalition folks who I always thought were trying to do the right thing for their community, but just weren't always listening to what we were saying to them, were tough in the sense that we might approach with ideas and we'd always get a negative reaction rather than a positive reaction. I think when the LDC came, was talking and working with us, it was more communicative, more understanding, more collegial."[18]

In the interview Borrone took the thought a step further: "If the borough president's office and we, the Port Authority, and the state and the city had been able to sit in the same room, like we often did, and put our cards on the table openly, saying, 'Here's what we are trying to achieve, each of us. Now, where's the common interest?' maybe we would have managed to do something more openly and more successfully sooner."

In any event, timing and circumstance came together. Moreover, at about the same time, the Port Authority reached an agreement with the dockworkers' union that guaranteed them work in Red Hook, the waterfront area to the south of the park's piers, in exchange for ending their opposition to the disposition of other piers. The combination of a political agreement and a union agreement opened the way for serious consideration of the park.[19]

Even at this early point in the LDC's life, it was clear that as a group it was working well. It forced representatives of the most interested communities to meet and cooperate under the watchful eyes of the borough president's two representatives. Faced with difficult personalities, historical neighborhood grudges, competing institutional interests, shifting alliances, and fears of compromise, the group nonetheless managed to come together sufficiently to get things done.

Reflecting on that period, Coalition vice-chairman David Offensend said in an interview:

> I thought it worked pretty well. I think that, generally
> speaking, all the key voices were at the table, which was
> useful, even if they didn't all feel they had the right repre-
> sentation. Fortunately, the LDC's greatest strength was
> that they had the whole force of authority of the five elect-
> ed officials who put it together, and it represented the
> commitment by those five elected officials to push for a
> park here. So not only did it bring these various neighbor-
> hood voices at least around the same table in the same
> room, but, in a funny way, it made the elected officials
> even more committed, because they had skin in the
> game.[20]

That consensus was reflected in the process for selecting officers. Roy Sloane of Cobble Hill had taken the lead by circulating a slate of candidates and discussing the names with board members. Joanne Witty, a Heights resident with experience in government who was appointed by Connor, was proposed for president, Greg Brooks (appointed by Golden) for vice-president, Kenneth Adams (the Chamber of Commerce appointee) for treasurer, and Hank Gutman (appointed by the Brooklyn Heights Association) for secretary. Ultimately the proposed slate was accepted because members felt that the individuals chosen were competent and fair-minded. The acceptance of the slate was another sign of mutual trust growing among the corporation members.

Though creation of the corporation was something of a Hail Mary pass by the elected officials, it proved successful. By acting together they signaled that the former process had run its course, and they forged a new path forward. The path they chose brought the relevant stakeholders together at the table as decision makers. This empowered the participants and led them to take seriously their responsibilities for Brooklyn Bridge Park. A broadly representative, bottom-up process changed the rhythm, the substance, and ultimately the outcome.

FIVE
STRANGE
BEDFELLOWS

I don't know what Allen and John are up to, but it's not the LDC.
—Michael Winikoff, Vinegar Hill representative on the Local
Development Corporation board

Once the Local Development Corporation was created, many people assumed that the Coalition had been replaced and would simply disappear. Some thought the Coalition should just die a quiet death. Some worried that the Coalition was redundant at best, destructive at worst. But the Brooklyn Heights Association had given birth to the Coalition and found it hard to give up its child. Offensend, the Coalition's vice-chair, argued that an independent advocacy group like the Coalition was still needed, and the BHA concluded it had too much invested to abandon the Coalition completely. Thus, the Coalition remained in business.[1]

The Coalition's first restructuring step was to bring in a paid part-time executive director, Tensie Whelan, who had left the New York League of Conservation Voters with a reputation for institution building. Early on she identified as an impediment Manheim's continued service as the volunteer president. Manheim, who was also a Coalition board member, insisted he be officially removed, which he was, awkwardly ending his tenure with the organization.[2]

Since the Coalition's planning function had been taken over by the LDC, and the Coalition's role as park advocate would be somewhat moot until the LDC produced a park plan, Whelan was looking for a way to rebuild the Coalition. David Walentas (see Figure 5-1), the real estate developer struggling to develop DUMBO, provided the focus.

As the Local Development Corporation was beginning its planning process, Walentas floated a new version of a plan he had previously proposed for the interbridge area. In effect, Walentas proposed that he become the developer of the DUMBO waterfront (having already become the de facto developer of inland DUMBO by buying most of the real estate). At the time, the DUMBO waterfront was largely derelict. Walentas proposed to clean it up, fill it with commercial activity, and provide some public amenities.[3]

The centerpiece and signature element of his plan was a hotel designed by the cutting-edge French architect Jean Nouvel that jutted out over the East River with a glass-floored bar allowing patrons to see the tides changing below (see Fig-

Figure 5-1. Developer David Walentas in his DUMBO office in 2000.

ure 5-2). The plan included a marina, a skating and performance space, a movie house, shopping, and parking.

In addition, the plan called for renovation of the Empire Stores and the Tobacco Warehouse, both owned by the State of New York and controlled by its Parks Department.

The Empire Stores actually consists of a combination of seven buildings containing more than three hundred thousand square feet that were built and used as warehouses in the nineteenth century. Its profile as a commercial building of its period is unmistakable—the famous New York photographer Berenice Abbott took evocative photographs when it was still in use—but by this point the structure was empty, unused, and unstable. Because of its origins the structure had few windows and little interior light; because of its age the supporting columns were made of wood and closely spaced. It was a tempting but challenging target for adaptive reuse. The state had tried in the past to attract developers for the Empire Stores. Walentas was the only bidder and had been designated the site's developer.

The Tobacco Warehouse was even more of a relic and in some respects more of a challenge. Owned for a time by the Lorillard tobacco family, whose company, P. Lorillard, was eventually controlled by the Tisch family of developers, it was a customs collection shed for tobacco brought into New York for processing. At some point the Tobacco Warehouse lost its roof, its upper floors, and any practical purpose. It was originally constructed as a five-story building, but it had been cut down to two stories and part of its exterior had been demolished when the Brooklyn Bridge was built.

By the time Walentas issued his plan the structure was nothing more than a concrete floor enclosed by crumbling, freestanding walls pierced by arched open-

ings that had once been windows and doors. It was picturesque but in danger of collapse (see Figure 5-3). The New York State Parks Department had little money to maintain, much less transform, the building.

There was also a state park on the DUMBO waterfront, the grandly named but woebegone Empire Fulton Ferry State Park. As the landscape designer Cindy Goulder remembers it, that park had its beginnings in 1977 when a dozen civic leaders calling themselves the Empire Stores Preservation Committee persuaded Governor Hugh Carey to use his discretionary funds to buy what was described as "the Empire Stores buildings, grounds and waters" from Con Edison on behalf of the state.

This move established a park on the interbridge waterfront, a site that would later be incorporated into the larger Brooklyn Bridge Park. According to Goulder, this action "was the beginning of community-based planning for the Brooklyn Bridge waterfront." Members of the committee included Brooklyn Heights Association President George Silver and his predecessor, Scott Hand, Brooklyn Heights Press publisher J. Dozier Hasty, along with Peter Stanford, president of the National Maritime Historical Society and an original spark plug for the creation of South Street Seaport, and Michael ("Buzzy") O'Keeffe, who would gain fame as the owner of the River Café. State Senator Martin Connor lent a hand in obtaining state funds.[4]

The committee disbanded after attaining its immediate objective, but Stanford convened a public meeting in August 1978 to promote his vision for what he called an "East River Renaissance." A local waterfront planning group was then formed, called the Fulton Ferry Renaissance Association, signifying the revival of ferry service as part of its aims.[5]

Once created, the Empire Fulton Ferry State Park was not well cared for by

Figure 5-2 (opposite). A 1999 rendering of the hotel in DUMBO proposed by David Walentas shows it extending well over the East River. (Two Trees Management.)

the state. Senator Connor recalled a day he and his wife went down to the park and found knee-high grass. When told by the lone park ranger that he had no gasoline for the mower and no budget to buy any, Connor handed the ranger fifty dollars so he could cut the grass. Walentas proposed to rework the park, offering a design by the landscape architect M. Paul Friedberg that included space for a vintage carousel being restored by Jane Walentas, the developer's wife.

At a time when there was no tenable plan for the Brooklyn piers and not even the hint of a funding source, Walentas was proposing to redevelop the DUMBO waterfront with his own money; later he said that he was trying to catalyze some broader action on the waterfront.

Though critical of the plan as a whole, the *New York Times* architecture critic Herbert Muschamp hailed the hotel as brilliant architecture in a city more recently filled with mediocre design, but the Brooklyn Heights Association and most of the local communities were appalled by the scheme.[6] Walentas was widely seen as seeking to remake DUMBO according to his personal vision and asking the government to help him do so. As it turned out, this plan was never adopted or approved by either the city or the state.[7]

While the plan was unlikely to move forward, Walentas did have a toehold. His earlier designation as the developer of the Empire Stores was still in effect although he had been unable to advance the development. The state was empowered to lease the property for twenty years, but Walentas needed a forty-nine-year lease as collateral for financing, and legislation to permit such a lease had been blocked by the local legislators Joan Millman and Marty Connor.

There was also confusion over the future of Empire Fulton Ferry State Park. The state parks commissioner, Bernadette Castro, had little interest in the idea of a unified Brooklyn Bridge Park and was focused on improving and keeping the dilapidated state park she already "owned." She was therefore believed to be interested in the private funds offered by Walentas, although without the legislation being blocked by Millman and Connor she lacked the power to help him.

Still, many local residents saw Walentas as a threat, regarding his plans as out of scale, out of sync, and out of touch with the surrounding communities. Walentas was a developer whose private holdings would benefit from his improvement of the public space. This made him a natural target.

Even though the Walentas plan had no official support, it seemed too brash and too visible to ignore. Until the city or state formally vetoed it, many park advocates felt apprehensive.

The Local Development Corporation was also concerned about the Walentas plan because the corporation wanted the unified park to include the interbridge area in a single, comprehensive plan. However, by a quirk of its history, the LDC's funding at that point was limited to the Brooklyn piers. While awaiting new and unrestricted funds, the LDC could not work actively on a plan for the area covered by the Walentas plan.

Tensie Whelan, the Coalition's executive director, saw here an opportunity to infuse new life into her organization, and she was creative and capable in the effort.[8] Walentas became a rallying cry to raise money from the Brooklyn Heights Association, private foundations, and the public.[9] With the concurrence of the BHA,[10] the Coalition launched a spirited attack on Walentas and his plan. To provide an alternative to the Walentas proposal, the Coalition hired the Pittsburgh architect Ray Gindroz to create a separate plan for the interbridge area.

For many on the Local Development Corporation this was a frustrating development, particularly because it undermined the notion of comprehensive planning for a unified park, the first of the Thirteen Guiding Principles. On the LDC board, Allen Swerdlowe and John Watts worked openly to support the Coalition's agenda, which led Vinegar Hill representative Michael Winikoff to remark, "I don't know what Allen and John are up to, but it's not the LDC." Some corporation members from the south were also unhappy with what they saw as an organization seeking to further its own interests at the expense of the park.[11] Cobble Hill had earlier resigned from the Coalition, concluding that it was not effective.[12]

It all proved to be a passing storm, and one that cleared the air in important respects. Prior to these events, the Local Development Corporation had petitioned the state for additional funding and for the right to use the money to plan for the entire park. Shortly after the Coalition hired its planner, the LDC did receive new and unrestricted funding from the state. Eventually Ray Gindroz joined the LDC's planning team under chief planner Ken Greenberg and focused not on the interbridge area but on the connections between the park and surrounding communities. This agreement required months of negotiation between the LDC and the Coalition, which did not conclude until Albert Butzel, a Manhattan-based environmental lawyer, replaced Tensie Whelan as head of the Coalition.[13] But ultimately the LDC was acknowledged as the sole planning entity for the park.[14]

Meanwhile, the Coalition focused on promoting the park and organizing free programming inside its precincts. When construction of the park was well along, the Coalition renamed itself the Brooklyn Bridge Park Conservancy, continuing its focus on popular and recurring programs. From early on, it ran a program of outdoor movies in the summer. It sponsored yoga, book readings, nature tours, environmental education, kayaking, and other free activities. It held two fund-raising events each year and generated enough money for its own operations and its programs.

Other major conservancies in New York City raise private funds for both capital and operating expenses. The Central Park Conservancy, for example, has invested nearly $700 million into Central Park, pays for most of its operating expenses, and, under a contract with the city, manages the park. Similarly, the Friends of the High Line has raised substantial sums for capital improvements and has day-to-day control over the park. The Prospect Park Alliance has also raised capital, and its head is the park's administrator.

The role of the Conservancy in Brooklyn Bridge Park has been much different. The vast majority of the park's $400 million capital cost has been paid by city and state government, and its operation and maintenance have been funded by the development sites. However, the cost of recreational, educational, and cultural programs are not covered, and the Conservancy has marshaled private resources for these activities that are important to the park. As the spotlight of government attention and support shifts to other parks and other priorities, the role of the Conservancy may increase in the future.

The Conservancy was and is popular with the community residents and organizations that supported it for so many years, and the park would not exist without the group's tireless advocacy in its early years. Because of its public-facing role, some confused the Conservancy with the government-sponsored organizations that actually designed, built, and operated the park. Much later, when residents were upset about the height of Pier 1 buildings, the Conservancy lost donors who were under the impression that their donations contributed to building the park.

The Local Development Corporation was created by local government officials to replace the Coalition, and it gained credibility with the mayors and governors who held the purse strings. It also established credibility with the community with its commitment to public planning and with the park plan it produced. When new governmental entities were eventually created by the mayor and the governor to advance the master plan developed by the LDC, four board members of the LDC were appointed to the board of the state agency and three of them—David Offensend, Hank Gutman, and Joanne Witty—later joined the board of the Brooklyn Bridge Park Corporation, the city-sponsored body that became the park's ultimate home. The LDC itself remained in existence to carry out certain legacy functions, but its public role ended when the governments took over.

In fact, the LDC and the Coalition/Conservancy had quite different roles. There was a place and time for them both to contribute.

The fight over the Walentas plan ended quickly. In December 1999, seven months after Walentas unveiled his plan, Joseph Rose, chairman of the City Planning Commission, publicly repudiated it. "The revitalization of the waterfront in a way that creates a public amenity is the city's goal," he said.[15]

Still, in some ways, Walentas helped to unlock the potential of Brooklyn as the place to be, and Brooklyn helped to unlock the value of his real estate investments. In the course of fifteen years, Brooklyn became enormously fashionable and his DUMBO real estate rose rapidly in value, making him reportedly a billionaire.[16] Thwarted in his efforts to build a waterfront hotel, Walentas subsequently built a block-square apartment complex close to the Brooklyn Bridge.

Walentas and the park planners were often at odds. Walentas did not get to develop the DUMBO waterfront; instead, the unified park incorporated the interbridge area, and

Figures 5-4. Images of DUMBO when it was still a working waterfront in the 1950s and later when Jane's Carousel had been installed in the new park. (Henrik Krogius, opposite, and Sven Krogius, this page.)

the plan adopted for it was very different from the Walentas plan (see Figure 5-4). Years later, when proposals for the Empire Stores were solicited yet again, he was not chosen as the developer,[17] but by its very existence the park enhanced the value of his adjacent properties. The carousel that Jane Walentas restored (known as "Jane's Carousel") was donated to the park along with an agreement to care for it for thirty years. The Walentases also made a contribution of $4 million to renovate and incorporate the old Empire Fulton Ferry State Park into Brooklyn Bridge Park.

The carousel, which sits prominently on a spit of land just north of the Brooklyn Bridge,[18] is housed in an elegant pavilion designed by Jean Nouvel, who finally got a building on the Brooklyn waterfront. He gave the structure glass walls so riders and their horses could look out and the world could look in. Visible from Manhattan, gleaming in daylight and glowing at night, the carousel has become a well-known symbol of the park.[19]

SIX
PUBLIC PLANNING

An inclusive planning process was central to our vision for the park.

—Joanne Witty, Local Development Corporation president

Shortly after its creation, the Local Development Corporation concluded that the best way for its fifteen volunteers to manage the large task ahead was to hire help.

Rather than hire a staff, the LDC decided to look for professional consultants who already had experience with complex public-private projects. The idea was to bring on a team for a temporary period to create and carry out a planning process while helping the group avoid rookie mistakes.

The candidate search came down to two finalists. One was a team headed by Harvey Schultz and Martha Holstein. The two knew Brooklyn well—Schultz had been the borough president's chief of staff—and were respected for their work in state and local government.[1] The second team came from the firm of Hamilton, Rabinovitz and Alschuler, known as HR&A, one of the leading firms advising public and private clients for projects in which private capital is used to carry out public policy.

The LDC would have been well served by either firm, but it chose HR&A, which had wider and deeper experience. Its presence was expected to add to the LDC's credibility.

John Alschuler, the head of the New York branch of HR&A, led the team (see Figure 6-1); his partner, Candace Damon, was second in command. Given that the LDC was a group of volunteers with no experience planning a large public project, their firm's advice was both specific and strategic. They advised the LDC about what kinds of planners they would need, how to find them, how to get the best people interested, how to choose among them, and how to manage them. When public meetings were held, the firm set them up, made sure that people knew they were taking place, and initially ran them. They helped the LDC communicate with the public and make its way through the forest of government agencies and authorities.

The Local Development Corporation and HR&A agreed on the need for a public planning process, but on this score the LDC was out in front of its advisers. Because the board of the LDC represented so many different communities and points of view, it knew that a fully democratic and public process was the only way to reach a consensus on a specific plan. Even at this early stage the LDC leadership knew that difficult choices would have to be made. Those choices would be in-

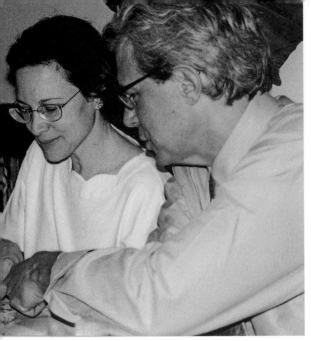

formed by what the public wanted out of a park, but public opinion would also have to be informed about the constraints as well as the possibilities.[2]

Still, a broad and comprehensive public planning process was fraught with risk. It could easily produce a cacophony of incompatible desires or a utopian but unaffordable vision. It could produce, as it did, competition and controversy. That would be a huge problem for a park project: what public official would support, much less spend public money on, a project mired in controversy?

New York had a rich history of community planning, in part thanks to its network of community boards, originally known as community planning boards, created in 1963. To encourage even more civic engagement, revisions to the New York City Charter in 1975 added Section 197a to create a community-initiated process, especially involving land use and zoning. This provision was designed to empower communities to take a hard look at their neighborhoods, assess the local needs of different populations, and agree on guidelines and recommendations for change, instead of reacting on an ad hoc basis to the proposals of outsiders.

However, the 197a process turned out to be weak. Quality planning requires resources that the community boards and other groups generally lack. They have no funds to hire staff or consultants. Planning is a long and complicated process, and maintaining continuity in leadership and participants over a long period is difficult. The City Planning Commission has adopted only thirteen 197a plans, and the next step, implementation, is even harder. The plans lack the force of law, and city agencies are free to ignore them, contributing to community frustration.

At the same time that the Local Development Corporation was hiring planners and gearing up for an expansive community planning process, Brooklyn's Community Board 2, with jurisdiction over the entire park site, was completing a draft 197a plan for the "Old Brooklyn District" comprising Vinegar Hill, Farragut, Bridge Plaza, DUMBO, and Fulton Ferry. That plan covered a wide range of issues, such as economic development, transportation, historic preservation, land use and zoning, the environment, art and culture, and community facilities. In the section on open space and waterfront access, the plan endorsed the idea of developing the Old Brooklyn waterfront as part of the proposed Brooklyn Bridge Park, in accordance with the Thirteen Guiding Principles, and added specific recommendations to satisfy local community needs.

Although this plan was never adopted, simply going through the process of developing it did a great deal for the people who lived and worked in the Old Brooklyn District. Collaboratively, they assessed the district, identified the needs of the different communities who lived there, and recommended ways to protect their neighborhoods and make them stronger.

Fresh from that exercise, many eagerly joined in the community planning process for Brooklyn Bridge Park to make sure their views were represented. They would not be responding to a project that was already "cooked," one they could change at the margins at best. The Port Authority wanted to rid itself of its piers but, having failed to accomplish that goal, it seemed willing to consider the possibility that a community planning process might produce a better result.

"An inclusive planning process was central to our vision for the park," recalled Joanne Witty, president of the Local Development Corporation. In a sense, community input was its DNA. The board was chosen precisely so the membership would represent the diversity of communities neighboring the park site. Their differing and frequently conflicting views did play a role in the park's development. Still, the LDC felt from the beginning that only public planning would engage a broader community and produce a plan that would garner the necessary widespread public support. Therefore, the LDC laid out a public planning process that was broader and deeper than anything with which anyone was familiar.

This was also a shift from what the Port Authority expected the Local Development Corporation to do. In fact, the Port Authority wanted to test the market before settling on a plan. The agency had wanted to issue an RFEI (request for expressions of interest) to let prospective developers suggest what they would be interested in doing. The LDC, by contrast, thought the proper course was to create what came to be called a master plan, which would be based on an overall vision of the park. To create the master plan, a series of questions would be addressed: for example, what kinds of park uses were desirable and achievable, what kind of park would fit into the site, and how would the park relate to the surrounding communities? The LDC thought private capital would ultimately help pay for the park, but it wanted the outlines of the park to determine what could be offered to private parties, rather than the other way around.

Before the Local Development Corporation could talk to the public about a park plan, it had to hire planners. With the assistance of HR&A, the LDC published a request for proposals for a master planning team that could carry out the necessary studies and point the way to a credible plan. The LDC members knew they needed three kinds of professionals: planners, designers, and engineers. Planners were the big-picture thinkers who would help develop a program for the park and determine how it related both to its surroundings and to Brooklyn and the rest of the city. The designer, probably a landscape architect, would help develop a more specific design for the park. Engineers, required for any project, were especially critical for a project that would be constructed on piers and along the waterfront.

The request for proposals generated many different responses from teams as far away as Switzerland and Japan, signifying that professional planners took the project seriously.[3] "The outreach helped build some initial visibility for the Corporation and the park," recalled Candace Damon of HR&A, adding, "What an extraordinary diversity of strength and approaches we had from the respondents."[4]

In a few months the LDC had organized itself, secured substantial funding, negotiated a "standstill agreement" with the Port Authority, persuaded the agency that it could and should carry out a planning process, and attracted the interest of leading planners in the field. All this was accomplished after years of deadlock by a group of volunteers who were more a parliament than a board representing many neighborhood constituencies.

As it considered the planning team proposals, the LDC concluded that the choice would be guided by the character of the park the corporation wanted to build, the team that could best handle the tricky community process, and the team leader who would be the best salesman for the project.

In interviews some of the teams came across as more corporate, leaning toward buildings and hard edges. Others were talented designers but lacked experience in large-scale projects. The noted architect Robert A. M. Stern impressed but was paired with a weak planning group. The well-known landscape architect Laurie Olin was a member of one team but not its lead.

By the end of August 1998 a majority of the LDC board agreed on Urban Strategies, a Toronto-based group headed by Ken Greenberg.[5] The firm's work on urban spaces had included waterfronts in Toronto, Detroit, Hartford, and Charleston. Greenberg impressed most of the corporation's board as a good listener with a calm presence conducive to winning community consensus. On his team was the landscape architect Michael Van Valkenburgh, who had just stepped down as chair of landscape architecture at Harvard's School of Design. His relatively new firm had already done interesting work in Columbus and Pittsburgh, and his presence was a chief reason several LDC members voted for Urban Strategies.

Without a broadly supported plan for a park that was attractive and accessible to everyone, the LDC knew that the government would not adopt and fund it. The planning process would in any event have to go well beyond the single twenty-four-hour cram sessions that had preceded a few New Urbanism projects of the recent past. Even some of the professional planners were unprepared for the extensive community process the corporation had in mind.

As it turned out, Ken Greenberg, the LDC's master plan team leader, was perfectly suited for this job. He was comfortable in a process that was not top-down but more community driven, and he had an intuitive sense about the group dynamics of such a process, which he described as "collective soul searching." He wanted participants to see the biggest possible picture of what the park could be and the opportunity open to them. He was low-key, he asked questions before he gave answers, and he knew how to listen. People responded well to him.

Broad outreach for the planning sessions was essential, and attendance was encouraged through mailings, e-mail, newspaper advertisements, posters, and word-of-mouth by way of community boards and other organizations. Three groups of three meetings were scheduled and were held in many different locations to make them accessible to as many people as possible.

The first set of sessions was designed to hear people's uncensored ideas for the park. In subsequent sessions, practical limitations and needs for trade-offs would be discussed.

Greenberg kicked off the sessions with a message that sounded inspirational at the time and proved prophetic. "We are not going to re-create a nineteenth-century park," he said. "We are going to create something new and of our time. We want to start a discussion of what it takes to make a great park in the new millennium."

An estimated six hundred people crowded in for the first three sessions. At least four thousand would participate before a plan was finalized. The young, the old, mothers with children, empty nesters, singles, runners, bicyclists, dog owners, all manner of sports enthusiasts, musicians, educators, preservationists, local merchants—all had their stake in a future park. So did local schools, colleges, and cultural institutions. All would have a chance to express their views and hear new ideas.

Unanimity was neither expected nor desired. In fact, Greenberg said, he wanted to get people out of their comfort zones as they thought and spoke to one another about the park in sociological, physical, and financial terms. Participants broke into working groups small enough so that everyone could speak. Ideas were recorded on large sheets of paper. Those groups broke apart and re-formed with other participants, each led by a professional member of the team. The groups eventually reassembled to report on what was said.

One focus of discussion was whom the park would serve. This question extended beyond individuals with their particular desires to questions of whether it would be primarily for local residents or for all of Brooklyn, the whole city, or tourists. Significantly, those attending included representatives from groups outside the immediately affected communities, such as the Alliance for Downtown New York (a Manhattan group), the Brooklyn Museum, the Brooklyn Academy of Music, the Regional Plan Association, the City Planning Commission, Catholic Charities, and the Bedford-Stuyvesant YMCA.[6]

Another focus of discussion was access to the park and how to traverse the 1.3-mile stretch of land. The park was seen as isolated, with direct access limited to Atlantic Avenue at grade on the south, Joralemon Street passing under the Brooklyn-Queens Expressway (see Figure 6-2), and Old Fulton Street at grade level in the middle. The area adjacent to the interbridge area, including DUMBO, was at grade level with the park site and therefore more accessible. Although there were several subway stops within a ten- or fifteen-minute walk, it was thought that the topography and distances would discourage park attendance.

But if the alternative were to come by car, that raised problems of traffic circulation, neighborhood disruption, and parking. Should cars be banned from the park itself? Should parking be provided? Would parking encourage more cars?

Some people worried that not just cars but also pedestrians would overwhelm the neighborhood. The fear of cars and pedestrians was widespread along Joralemon Street, with many residents wanting to prevent through traffic by blocking the foot of the street with bollards.

Figure 6-2. The Belgian block–paved Joralemon Street runs to the waterfront under the Brooklyn-Queens Expressway and offers the only direct street access from Brooklyn Heights to the piers.

Some wondered whether there could be a subway stop at the Brooklyn or Manhattan Bridge. Trolley cars and jitneys were suggested. What about ferry service or a link from the Promenade at Montague Street to the park?

Then there were questions about uses within the park. Should the park favor active or passive uses? Should it have single-use athletic fields? How much space does a baseball or soccer field take up, anyway? How much unprogrammed open space should there be for sunbathing and Frisbee, for example? What about indoor recreation spaces that could be used year-round?

And what about cultural uses? Were they even appropriate for a waterfront park, and if they were, should they be temporary, permanent, or a combination of the two? Should there be a place for concerts? Or would they create too much noise or light for the neighbors? A community of artists in DUMBO mounted shows in the state park; how should they be engaged? Should there be a place for public art? A museum outpost?

The relationship between built and open space was heavily discussed. What should be done with existing buildings on the site? Should the pier sheds be retained for indoor uses or torn down to create more open space? Should historic buildings be repurposed, and if so, by whom and for what? Did all the piers have to be retained?

And what about the water? Could it be used for recreation or some other maritime use, like a marina? Did waterfront currents and traffic make the location too dangerous or dirty for public access?

Still, the water had a powerful, even a spiritual effect on many at the meetings. Perhaps Mickey Murphy, a member of the Brooklyn Heights Association board, expressed it best. As Michael Van Valkenburgh remembered it, Murphy said, "I am retired. I live on a fixed income. I am old. I can no longer go to the country for vacations. I want to be able to go down to the East River at night and put my feet in the water and see the reflection of the moon."[7] Van Valkenburgh said he remembered her words because they changed his thinking about the park. Rather than be a border of the park and a barrier to its users along its entire length, he decided, the water should become a part of the park, as years later it did.

The session on financial feasibility grappled with difficult and important issues. Was it fair to ask the park to generate revenue to cover annual maintenance and operating costs? What other parks had to do that? What uses were most compatible and could they generate sufficient revenue? Which uses could potentially ruin the park by taking up too much space or prove incompatible with park uses such as destination retail? A hotel and/or conference center had been discussed for some time, but would such a project produce sufficient revenue? How many restaurants could the park support, and how much revenue would they generate?

The very likelihood that a park could be built and survive below the aging cantilever structure of the Brooklyn-Queens Expressway was questioned. The state's Department of Transportation was then studying the need for major reconstruction of the fifty-year-old cantilever, and there was the possibility that it might have to be closed for years with untold consequences for traffic and the park. On the other hand, some thought the rebuilding of that interstate highway would open up the possibility of federal funding for the park.[8]

Most people had seen the piers only from the Promenade. They were surrounded by chain-link fence and closed to all but tenants and Port Authority personnel. The Local Development Corporation and its planners decided that the public had to experience the site in order to be informed participants in the process, and so many guided tours of the area were offered.[9] People were surprised to feel its vastness and the impact of the water as well as the overwhelming sense of the land's industrial history.

But the waterfront strip was about as unpromising a site for a park as imaginable. Much of it was covered by concrete or contaminated soil, exposed to high winds, airborne salt, and storm surges. The noise of cars and trucks on the expressway was a constant drone; the regular passing of subway trains on the Manhattan Bridge sounded like jackhammers on steel. The challenge seemed daunting.

After digesting all they had heard at the first sessions, the planners distilled a set of what they called "Core Design Principles," twenty-three in all. A key principle was that a green spine must extend along the length of the park with a green heart at its center. Other principles dealt with specific design considerations, such as clearly defining the edges of the park, creating distinct places within the park, perhaps incorporating floating structures to acknowledge the river and its tides, and making structures within the park accessible on all sides. The planners also called for more access points to the park, more connections to the park by all modes of transportation, and links from the Brooklyn Bridge and the Promenade.

The Promenade connection, a contentious issue for many in Brooklyn Heights, would provoke considerable dispute. Another controversial premise was that there should be a clear visual connection between the two sections of the park at the Fulton Ferry "hinge." Implicit in this principle was the demolition of the 1937 Purchase Building, a two-story structure beneath the Brooklyn Bridge that was valued by preservationists for its Art Deco design and derided by its critics as featureless and ugly.

The new principles were outlined at the next set of sessions, held on January 23–24, 2000, at the New York City Technical College in Downtown Brooklyn. These principles were the basis of discussion in the same workshop format as the first group of sessions. The object was to move toward consensus on a framework that would let the team begin creating specific alternative park scenarios for the public to critique. As the reporter Dennis Holt wrote in the *Brooklyn Daily Eagle*, "Ken Greenberg of Urban Strategies Inc., the chief planner, spoke three times with 45-minute presentations each time and agreed that he had never spoken so long and so often any time before."[10]

The audiences were both repeat visitors and newcomers. Some of the principles were not controversial at all. Others were questioned. Residents from the south end of the park wondered how Atlantic Avenue could truly be a gateway if Pier 6 (then still in partial maritime use, with Quonset huts for cocoa beans at its base) was not included within the park's boundaries. Those residents were eager for considerable activity at their end of the park, advocating indoor recreation and a restaurant at Pier 5. The Brooklyn Heights contingent supported connections but not at Montague Street. What the planners referred to as the "green heart" of the park was a subject of comment, with some noting caustically its location below Brooklyn Heights and others worrying about it becoming a dead spot.

Issues of all kinds were raised and many suggestions were made, not all compatible with one another or even feasible. But reactions to the meetings seemed generally favorable.[11] The public was having a chance to give the planners their reactions and to hear back from the planners. The confrontation with an actual plan and its limitations was yet to come.

As the planning process continued, other wheels were turning. A boost to the planning process came in early 2000 when the Port Authority held a public signing of the memorandum of understanding long in the works between the agency and the LDC. In signing the agreement, which essentially gave the corporation an exclusive option on the piers until September 30 when its master plan was due, Robert Boyle, the Port Authority executive director, said, "While there is a potential for commerce on these piers, we believe there is also a higher and better use of this property." Boyle also pledged $5 million for pier maintenance in 2000. Finally, New

York Secretary of State Alexander Treadwell announced a $500,000 state grant to the LDC to continue planning.[12] This money, from the state's Environmental Protection Fund, came on top of $1.4 million in state funds that had already been secured by Connor and Millman.

Despite these encouraging developments, other events still posed dangers to the planning process. A city-state agreement to convert the former military base at nearby Governors Island into a public history park with open space, sports facilities, cultural attractions, and a hotel-conference center raised fears that future public funding and policy commitment would favor the island over the Brooklyn project.[13]

And a serious jolt came in March when, as part of its bid for the 2012 Olympic Games, the city proposed a plan for a 5,000-seat aquatic arena and a gymnastics training site at Pier 1, taking up a total of nearly five acres, plus a 12,500-seat volleyball court in the DUMBO section of the park site.[14] This was part of an initiative to create facilities that could be reused after the Olympics. These plans would become moot when the city lost out to London in the competition for the games, but it was another warning that the prospects for a community-planned park were hardly a sure thing.

Notwithstanding these diversions, the Local Development Corporation and its planners soldiered on. In the next step in the planning process, several alternatives would be displayed and hard choices would have to be made. The park could not have everything for everyone.

SEVEN
PUBLIC PLANNING CONTINUES

In my memory, no major public works project has received as much public input as this one.

—John Alschuler of HR&A, addressing a meeting scheduled by opponents of the park plan

At two public planning sessions in February 2000 the Local Development Corporation presented several alternatives for several distinct locations in the park. Each scheme was essentially a kit of different parts, and participants were asked to pick and choose which parts of each scheme they preferred. Groups moved from one to another station where professional planners explained the different schemes, their components, and the thinking behind each one. The scene was replete with maps, drawings, and a model that allowed the pieces to be moved. Because there were so many variables, the object was not to pick a single scheme for any one section of the park but to identify specific elements in different schemes that were preferable or objectionable.

Attendance was good and engagement high. There was an air of excitement, but that could not mask differences of opinion still in need of reconciliation. Jerry Armer of Cobble Hill, for example, "took issue with the concept of housing, either stretching down Furman Street or clustered around Pier 5 or 6." Sandy Balboza from the Atlantic Avenue Betterment Association said, "We don't want Atlantic to be the main auto artery to the piers." At the same time, a Brooklyn Heights resident worried that a connection from Montague Street to the piers "will attract more cars than Montague can handle as people drop off folks to go down to the piers."[1]

Once again, the Local Development Corporation and its advisers retired to consider what they had heard. But integrating the puzzle pieces into a draft master plan proved a challenge. If consensus could not be achieved among corporation members, the group would have failed. Without a consensus, the dream of a community-backed plan that could be sold to government funders would evaporate once again and perhaps forever.

Within the LDC the issue of access to the park was among the most contentious. Board members from Cobble Hill and other neighborhoods to the south thought that a bridge into the park from the Promenade at Montague Street was an important way to bring visitors to the middle of the park site. Some of the members from Brooklyn Heights cited cost and landmarks issues (the Promenade itself having landmark status) in opposing it but, most crucially, they believed that such a connection would have a profoundly negative impact on the neighborhood character.[2]

In fact, the idea of a Montague Street connection stirred animosities that were atavistic and almost tribal. Remembering how the Brooklyn-Queens Expressway had sliced through Cobble Hill but swerved around Brooklyn Heights, the neighborhoods to the south did not want Brooklyn Heights to have a veto over any feature of the park. Explaining his insistence on a connection at Montague Street, Roy Sloane, the corporation board member representing Cobble Hill, said, "Because you got the Promenade and we got the ditch." Hearing that, Hank Gutman, a board member representing Brooklyn Heights, later said he was thinking, "My God, now I understand why Serbs slaughtered Bosnians because of something the Turks did a thousand years ago."[3]

Another less controversial connection considered was one through the usually locked, below-grade Squibb Park playground near Middagh Street, which would provide a shortcut from the A and C subway lines at the High Street station and serve the northern part of Brooklyn Heights. Everyone agreed that a direct subway connection to the park would be ideal, possibly by way of an extension of the Clark Street platform serving the 2 and 3 lines, but further consideration was put off until its feasibility could be studied.[4]

Considerable discussion focused on gateways to the park. Pier 6 at the foot of Atlantic Avenue was still in maritime use, but the Local Development Corporation was promised access to the upland of that pier. Not quite sure what this meant, the LDC was cautious even as it was eager to stake a claim to the space. Because Atlantic Avenue was to be one of the three main entrances to the park, it had to be welcoming. In its existing configuration, pedestrians had to enter the area by passing under the expressway and navigating a dangerous maze of traffic ramps and turns; furthermore, the Quonset huts storing cocoa beans and a million-square-foot building owned by the Jehovah's Witnesses at 360 Furman Street prevented easy access to the park interior.

One possibility was to move to the Pier 6 upland an indoor recreation center contemplated for Pier 5, which would require a new building but might allay fears about traffic along Joralemon Street. Those living south of the park liked the idea of recreation but wanted green space to announce the park at a prominent Atlantic Avenue entrance. Without removing commercial uses on Pier 6 this would be hard to achieve. The LDC, therefore, decided to begin gently advocating just that by showing Pier 6 as green on the park plan.

The second major park entrance, at the foot of Old Fulton Street next to the looming Brooklyn Bridge, presented other challenges. The entrance opened onto Pier 1, which, unlike the other piers, rested mostly on landfill rather than piles. A hotel/conference center was proposed for part of the site, but the configuration was hotly debated. To make the hotel financially viable, it was suggested that long-term residential stays be offered. Possible spots for restaurants or banquet facilities at Pier 1 were also discussed. Despite the pressure to minimize buildings and com-mercialization and maximize the sense of park, the LDC wanted to avoid present-ing too little to generate the revenue needed to maintain the park. It would be easier to reduce those uses than to have to add them later.

Now that a draft master plan was about to be presented, alarm grew in some quarters. The park might become real! In Willowtown, a small enclave at the west-ern end of Joralemon Street, and in other parts of Brooklyn Heights and elsewhere, opposition mobilized. One Joralemon Street resident compared the crowds that would be coming down her street to "Napoleon's Grand Armée invading Russia in 1812."[5] Another hung pennants reminiscent of the Revolutionary War era that bore the words "Don't tread on me."

Not everyone in the vicinity shared such sentiments; Peter Flemming, a for-mer president of the Willowtown Association, eventually said publicly that he thought the traffic issue was overblown.[6] An editorial in the *Brooklyn Heights Press* noted that Joralemon Street residents would have the most convenient access to the park of any neighborhood.[7]

Some insisted that their opposition was based on more basic concerns, such as the park's financing. These critics said they were not opposed to a park but rather the proposition that it had to be self-sustaining.[8] Opposition to having the park pay for itself would continue well after the park was completed.

It was clear that objections would be raised to various possibilities men-tioned in the draft plan being readied by the Local Development Corporation for presentation in April 2000, and the corporation realized that it would need facts and figures to buttress its recommendations. For instance, it had to know how much it would cost to build a bridge to the park if people were to accept the practicability of that option. It also had to count the number of pedestrians moving along Joralemon Street and the number of cars traveling down Old Fulton Street to be able to persuasively counter fears about impacts. If the choices made by the LDC were not perceived as fair and reasonable, the group would lose its authority.

Before the Local Development Corporation had a chance to unveil its plan publicly, an impromptu preview of the draft master plan was offered on April 24, 1999, at Packer Collegiate Institute on Joralemon Street. John Alschuler of HR&A addressed a meeting originally scheduled by Joralemon Street residents to discuss their concerns.[9] Introducing the plan, Alschuler asserted, "In my memory, no major public works project has received as much public input as this one." By then, about fifty open sessions had been held at which people had commented on the plans and offered their ideas.

A week after Alschuler's presentation, the draft master plan was explained further at another LDC public session at Long Island College Hospital, standing at the junction of Cobble Hill, Brooklyn Heights, and the Columbia Street district. The roughly 150 people who attended were generally favorably disposed toward what they saw and heard, although one woman worried that the park would become "the destination of destinations" and would cause "psychic pollution."[10]

The plan they learned about that day was the product of an unusual collaboration involving professional planners, LDC board members, and the community at large. Among the elements shown on a map of the site were the three gateways at Atlantic Avenue, Old Fulton Street, and the space beneath the Manhattan Bridge; possible tennis courts, roller-skating, and other play areas on a parcel still owned by Con Edison at the park's north end; a naturalized cove at the existing state park; adaptive reuse of the Empire Stores and Tobacco Warehouse; a plaza below the Brooklyn Bridge where a truncated Purchase Building would serve as a visitor center; a hotel, restaurants, marina, pool, basketball courts, and space for temporary installations at Pier 1; open space recreation on Pier 2; an earthen amphitheater and fountain on Pier 3; fishing at what was left of Pier 4; and an indoor recreation center, with parking, within the existing shed of Pier 5 (see Figure 7-1).

A barrier designed to dampen noise from the expressway would run along the upland from Pier 2 to Pier 5. The upland of Pier 6 would allow pedestrian access to the park. Eighty-five percent of the site was devoted to open space and the rest to new or existing structures.

Figure 7-1 (opposite). The 2000 illustrative master plan, a product of public planning, was the conceptual framework for subsequent planning and design of Brooklyn Bridge Park. (Brooklyn Bridge Park Local Development Corporation.)

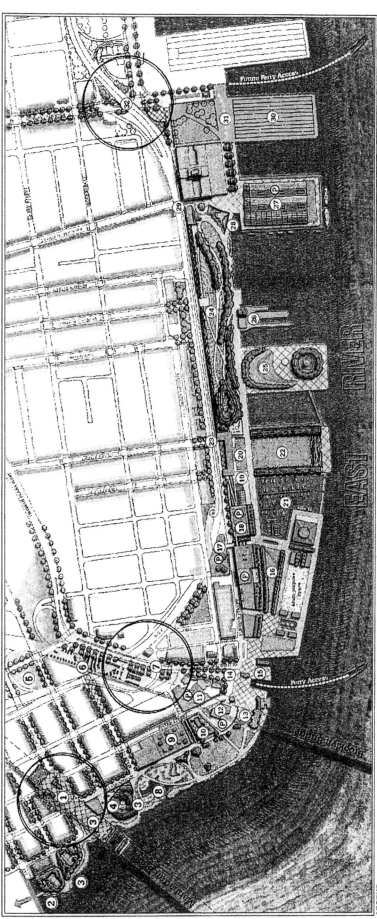

1. Manhattan Bridge Gateway
2. Allow for Eventual Northward Extension of Park
3. Tennis & Handball Courts, Skating, Half-Pipe, Playground
4. Community, Cultural & Educational Facilities
5. Improved Linkage & Streetscaping
6. Open up Main Street Pedestrian Underpass
7. Old Fulton Street Gateway
8. Renaturalized Cove
9. Empire Stores: Civic, Cultural, Historic, Educational & Mixed Uses

10. Tobacco Warehouse: Walled Garden and Cafe
11. Mixed Use Development incorporating Parking
12. Visitor Education & Information Center
13. Potential Future Stair to Brooklyn Bridge Walkway
14. Bus Drop-off
15. Fulton Ferry Plaza
16. Hotel, Civic, Cultural, Historic & Educational Venues, Restaurants, Marina Building (mixed use with public character), Fountain Pool/Skating Rink
17. Squibb Park and Connection
18. Rooftop Basketball

19. Public Pool
20. Park House, Cafe, Banquet Facility, Playground
21. Marina
22. Open Space for Recreation
23. Potential Future Connection to Clark St. Station
24. Contoured Landscape: Sound Attenuation Landscape, Maintenance Area below Mound
25. Tree-lined Fountain & Earthen Amphitheater
26. Fishing Piers Education Center/Restaurant
27. Active & Passive Recreation, Cafe
28. Rock-face Edge

29. Park Administration with Ground Floor Public Educational Uses & Entry Garden
30. Port Authority: Potential for Future Recreational/Cultural Programming
31. Temporary Elevated Pedestrian Access
32. Atlantic Avenue Gateway, Fountain, Bicycle Route, Potential Red Hook Transit Connection

 = Parking

Brooklyn Bridge Park Illustrative Master Plan

The first public reaction to this plan came from residents of Joralemon Street. A newly formed group called the Waterfront Development Watch unleashed an attack against the very idea that the park be self-sustaining. The group wanted a passive park without commercial development, but with additional points of access. It also wanted the foot of Joralemon Street sealed off against access to the site.[11]

A couple who had recently moved to Joralemon Street from Manhattan—he was a traditionalist architect, she had experience in publicity—took a lead in the opposition. The architect, Donald Rattner, issued a document titled "Report on Transportation and Access in the Proposed Plan for Waterfront Development at Piers 1–5, Brooklyn, New York."[12] The word "development" in that title would get picked up by a free-distribution local weekly whose publisher was a fellow resident of Joralemon Street. The *Brooklyn Paper*, which up to then had published straightforward coverage of local issues, would in the next several years reflect deep skepticism of the planning process for the park, putting quotation marks around the word "park" in its headlines and repeatedly suggesting that the project was more private development than public amenity.

Some of Rattner's criticisms had merit. He took exception to the forty-five-foot, stepped "bio-wall" sound attenuation barrier for the way it cramped views from the Promenade and for creating a dark corridor along Furman Street. However, his solution—to enclose the two cantilevered traffic decks of the expressway in translucent membranes—introduced new difficulties: not only the extraordinary cost and technical feasibility, but also the problem that the power to build such a structure lay with the state's Department of Transportation, not the LDC. Still, Rattner's point was valid, and the forty-five-foot sound barrier would later be lowered and become a planted earthen berm.

Donald Rattner's wife, Gabrielle, wrote letters and leaflets, organized letter-writing campaigns, placed news stories, and tried to enlist the governor and local officials in opposing the plan. Despite the publicity, the couple's point of view did not gain any real traction.

More constructively, comments and suggestions kept arriving through the website the Local Development Corporation had created to solicit additional exchange with and input from the public. The planners sought to produce a document—part text and part graphics—that could be understood by both the public and government officials. It would not be a blueprint for construction, and the project was certainly not financed. The corporation's document, the "Illustrative Master Plan for Brooklyn Bridge Park," was designed to unite the community behind a common vision, to attract the support of citywide civic organizations, to encourage the Port Authority to help see the project through, and to encourage the mayor and governor to provide funding. The presentation had to be compelling.

What resulted was a conceptual image, subject to further input and change, especially with regard to access and traffic. It contained financial projections of the money needed for construction, the estimated operating costs, and sources of revenue. At the time the estimated construction cost was $150 million,[13] projected to leverage about $400 million in private capital investment for the revenue-generating portions of the project.

The plan also covered governance and management of the park, along with sources of funds for its upkeep. Design guidelines were offered, but the wording left open the possibility of revisions. An enormous model of the future Brooklyn Bridge Park and its environs, built in Canada, was transported to Brooklyn and displayed at the Brooklyn Public Library and Borough Hall. Watercolor renderings of a day in the park that could be shown on video were commissioned.

After being seen and approved by New York Secretary of State Alexander Treadwell and the Port Authority's Robert Boyle, the master plan was revealed to the press on June 26, 2000. A few late changes were evident, among them a reduction of about half in the building coverage at the Pier 1 section (urged by the Coalition and the Brooklyn Heights Association) and the elimination of parking on the Pier 6 upland (the result of pressure from Cobble Hill). The elimination of parking meant that cars would not enter the park from Atlantic Avenue, and traffic would have to come along Furman Street instead. No final decision had been made about a Montague Street entry bridge, showing again the political strength of the Brooklyn Heights Association.

Overall, the plan was little changed from what had been shown earlier.[14] "This is a way station in the process, not the end of it," Alschuler said, noting that the plan still had to be shown to the governor and the mayor, who "need to agree on a common vision."[15]

The Waterfront Development Watch was not impressed. It sent a letter to Governor Pataki in which it complained that the LDC plans "do not provide for a public sanctuary so much as they radically and negatively redefine the meaning of the word 'park.'" "The Brooklyn Bridge Park proposal dissolves the vital boundary that separates a park from the everyday world by co-mingling commercial and purely private experiences," they wrote, exhorting the governor not to tarnish his reputation as a park advocate by "presiding over the dissolution of the park as people have known it for hundreds of years."[16]

Gabrielle Rattner warned of "a serious challenge to the plan if the promoters insist on its realization in its present form." Among many other objections, she contended that the open space in the park would amount to only a fraction of what the Local Development Corporation claimed. She also maintained that more than a thousand people from several neighborhoods had signed letters and petitions opposing the plan.[17]

Julian E. Barnes, a *New York Times* reporter who had been covering park developments, stirred further consternation when he wrote that some park opponents "have accused supporters, their own neighbors, of putting the character, peace and property values of Brooklyn Heights in jeopardy." "In response," Barnes wrote, "some park supporters have argued that concern over traffic, quality of life, crime and litter are code words that betray a fear of blacks and Hispanics from poorer sections of the borough [which] perpetuates Brooklyn Heights' elitist reputation."[18]

It was not just politics or grand policy that threatened to scuttle parts of the plan. Sometimes the plan stepped on toes the planners did not even know existed. One part of the plan, calling for a tidal salt marsh traversed by a curving boardwalk at the cove in DUMBO, was opposed by technicians in the state's Department of Environmental Conservation and its Parks Department. "You cannot exchange a marsh for a littoral area, which is the shore zone between high and low water marks," a parks spokesman explained somewhat opaquely. The marsh, which would have conflicted with the city's plan for a parking lot at the foot of Main Street, had strong advocates within the LDC, but others saw it as an expendable element, and it died quietly. Local landscape ecologist Cindy Goulder, who had been arguing for a natural edge there throughout the process, had won her point.[19]

Still, while criticism and controversy got press coverage, the merits of the park plan were winning important converts. Despite the opposition of some vocal groups in Brooklyn Heights, the Brooklyn Heights Association had resolved most of its own doubts about the plan. Deirdre Carson, the departing president, argued strongly for its adoption, a position reaffirmed by her successor, Neil Calet.[20] All the organizations represented on the Local Development Corporation supported it, as did many citywide civic and environmental groups.[21]

As corporation board member Franklin Stone said, the public planning process accomplished what it set out to do. "The community really did feel part of it and were enthused, and saw a lot of their ideas embodied in the park. It was an amazingly productive process. Whatever the rubs were, they were small compared to the overall achievement."[22]

Moreover, the support of civic organizations was matched by support from important governmental agencies. The Port Authority became increasingly supportive of the park effort and supplied the LDC with a new infusion of cash. More aid was expected from the state, and it arrived in due course. Still, the biggest question remained to be answered: would they really reward the plan with real money?

EIGHT
MONEY AND POLITICAL GAMESMANSHIP

Giuliani and Vallone are having their going-out-of-business sale
because of term limits.
—Kenneth Fisher, City Councilman from Brooklyn Heights, on the
opportunity to nail down city funding for the park

Having a master plan, even a draft master plan, represented a huge step forward, but how much was it worth? Public budgets were tighter than ever. Was there anybody who would pay for the park?

This had always been the fundamental question. In the best of times, spending public money on parks is a low priority when it is a priority at all. If you have to choose between putting police officers on the street, teachers in the classroom, or maintenance workers in the parks, that is not what politicians call a tough choice. By the time the master plan was completed, the country was in the midst of another recession, this one accompanied by the bursting of the dot-com bubble that laid waste to Wall Street as well as Main Street. Even New York's greatest parks were suffering. Did anybody have the resources and the will to build a new one?

In early 2000, in this grim economic and political climate, the Local Development Corporation held strategy sessions to determine how to sell the master plan to state and local governments. The need for funding was obvious, but because the price tag seemed too big for a single funder, the effort would be made to solicit support from the Port Authority as well as the city and the state. But even at this early stage such an approach led to another set of questions: Who would be in charge? Could the integrity of the plan for a single, unified park be maintained? And would the community continue to have a say in the outcome?

The question of park governance—who would run the park and how?—had been constantly before the corporation. Examples both inside and outside New York State had been studied. Early on, it seemed that Brooklyn Bridge Park might be created through the same legislation as Manhattan's Hudson River Park, the 4.5-mile strip of greenery, bike paths, and other uses stretching north from Lower Manhattan.

Complicating the issue of governance was the joint ownership of the park site. After the Port Authority transferred the piers to the state, about 70 percent of the site would be in state hands and the rest in the city's. Joint city-state entities, like Hudson River Park and Queens West, often found themselves embroiled in intergovernmental struggles and politics, and thus prone to paralysis.

It had long been assumed that the park would be built by a state agency, the Empire State Development Corporation. The agency had the power to override local zoning, so it could build a park on the piers despite their designation for commercial and manufacturing use. Such power was created when Nelson Rockefeller was governor to prevent local communities from using their zoning powers as a form of racial discrimination. By 2000 the power was only exercised with the approval of local government in circumstances where it provided a simpler and quicker means of rezoning than the local government could accomplish itself.

Perhaps even more important, ESDC had the power to capture all the revenue generated on the site. The Thirteen Guiding Principles envisioned that the park would be self-sufficient and that its revenues would pay for its operations. This was also a condition of public funders. But if revenues were to be raised by the park, it was crucial that they be captured by the park rather than siphoned off to meet other governmental priorities. If, for example, the title to the park had been held by the city or the state, the revenues would have gone directly to the general treasury and reached the park only if they were so appropriated in the normal budget process.

For the planners and park supporters, insuring that the park would be well maintained and insulating that task from the annual budget free-for-all was almost as important as building the park in the first place. Because the ESDC was an independent agency of the state and thus controlled its own funds without the need of legislative appropriation, it was a useful vehicle for this purpose.

Using the Empire State Development Corporation to build the park and collect the revenue might have made sense, but the ESDC was not an ideal designer or operator of the park, these being tasks with which it had no experience. The master plan envisioned a single, unified Brooklyn Bridge Park under a single operator. But if not ESDC, then who?

The Local Development Corporation was moving toward the idea of a not-for-profit entity that could provide a level of stewardship not expected of a government agency. Such an operator could also raise money privately for programming and other items. Ideally, this approach might keep the park from becoming a political football. The government funders proved unwilling to place the park entirely in private hands, but the idea of a not-for-profit corporation controlled by the city was ultimately adopted and would prove useful in many respects. Unfortunately, the structure did not succeed in keeping the park outside politics.

In the short run, especially tricky was how to approach the Giuliani administration. The fear was that the city would want to control the project and thereby alienate Governor Pataki, who was seen as the obvious candidate to take the lead and provide the bulk of the funding. Pataki's interest in open space was well-known, and he already had an existing park on part of the site. Furthermore, the Port Authority, over which the governor had considerable sway, owned Piers 1–5, the largest section of the park, and was expected to provide at least some of the capital funds.

Nevertheless, the city acted first, prompted by a strange confluence of political and personal circumstances. In 1993 a voter initiative established two terms as the limit for any elected city official, and by the spring of 2000 there was a scramble for the seats of those whose second terms would be up at the end of the following year. This group included Borough President Howard Golden; Ken Fisher, councilman from Brooklyn Heights, who began by running for mayor and eventually ran for Brooklyn borough president; Speaker Peter Vallone, who did run for mayor; and Mayor Giuliani himself, who would be leaving City Hall but who actively considered running for the United States Senate.

Fisher was a smart and talented politician.[1] He was concerned with substance and probably responsible for more legislation during his tenure in the Council than any of his colleagues. After deciding that his chances of being elected the next mayor were slim, he set his sights on the Brooklyn borough presidency race. His old mentor, Howard Golden, had already endorsed his deputy borough president for the job. This caused tension between Fisher and Golden that proved remarkably helpful to the park.

It was the time of year when New York City's budget for the 2001 fiscal year was being prepared. By then Golden was totally committed to Brooklyn Bridge Park, and his two representatives on the LDC, Greg Brooks and Jon Benguiat, had been working tirelessly to make it happen. To jump-start the project Golden had put $14 million in his own budget for fiscal year 2001. This was a handsome gesture, and Golden did not get adequate credit for it because of the events that followed.

As Fisher described it, "Giuliani and Vallone are having their going-out-of-business sale because of term limits."[2] By this he meant that, because of term limits, both of them would be leaving their current office, both would be considering a new office, and both would be eager to spend any funds under their control to reward old friends and make new ones.

Of his relationship with Vallone, Fisher said, "I passed important legislation, I did public hearings that made headlines, sometimes around the world. I made the Council look good." Concerning the mayor, he added, after starting out "with a very strong relationship with Giuliani, I went on the enemies list for some time. I got off the enemies list when Joe Lhota became first deputy mayor and needed me, and we made peace."[3]

Although the city's budget was tight, there was money available at the margins. Helped by his relationships at both the Council and the mayor's office, Fisher was ideally placed to capture capital money for his district and even some other districts.

As Fisher laughingly recalled, "One day a woman named Joanne Witty comes to see me, together with a planner by the name of Josh Sirefman.[4] They told me they wanted me to put some money in the budget to give the park a little momentum. I said, 'How much should I ask for?' I think it was Josh that said, '$5 million.' I said, 'I'm not going to ask for $5 million; I'm going to ask for $50 million!'" Amy Klein, a new Brooklyn resident who handled the capital budget for the Council speaker, was concerned about Brooklyn getting its fair share of capital dollars and gladly took Fisher's request for Brooklyn Bridge Park.[5]

Aware that the relationship between Giuliani and Golden at that point was "acid,"[6] Fisher used the borough president's $14 million budget allocation for the park as leverage. He called Deputy Mayor Joe Lhota, who, as a resident of Brooklyn Heights, already knew something about the park. According to Fisher, he said, "You're not going to guess what that son of a bitch Golden just did. He put $14 million in the budget for the Brooklyn Bridge Park. They are going to name it the fucking Golden Gate Park. You can't let him get away with this."[7]

A few days later, Lhota called back to ask Fisher whether he needed all the money in one year, and Fisher agreed to take it over four years. Later Lhota confirmed that the money was in the mayor's budget, which meant it was a done deal. Fisher promptly announced the funding to a crowd of several hundred at a fundraiser for the Coalition. "That was a pretty electrifying moment," he said.[8]

Welcome as these promised funds were, they raised serious questions—

namely, how would the money be spent? There was great concern about a piece-meal approach to the park. If the city started down its own path, it might be hard to pull the unified park back together. Renewed efforts were made to engage the state, and plans were made to brief state officials who were seen as important in the decision-making chain.

But the Port Authority proved the most valuable source of information and advice. Executive Director Robert Boyle, an old friend of the governor's, and his chief of planning and external affairs, Christopher Ward,[9] who would later be the agency's executive director, confirmed the obvious—that the city and state did not have a good working relationship. This meant that, in their judgment, the more the city became involved, the less interested the state would become. While the city had not approached the Port Authority about the piers, Boyle made it clear that his agency would never turn them over to the Giuliani administration. In the meantime he promised to promote the park to Governor Pataki and his senior staff.[10]

Money was also discussed. The Local Development Corporation would be out of action by the time the next stage of the master plan was complete and could not continue to advance the park without more money. Boyle agreed to provide $200,000 to the corporation to finish technical and financial components of the master plan, to outline the process for transferring the piers, and to help the LDC keep navigating the treacherous political waters.

Suddenly, in early January 2001, an opportunity appeared, not unlike the one that had allowed Ken Fisher to secure $50 million in the mayor's budget for Brooklyn Bridge Park. LDC President Joanne Witty learned that Mayor Giuliani was planning to feature Brooklyn Bridge Park in his State of the City address on January 8. She immediately called State Senator Connor, and the two agreed that this was a perfect moment to approach Governor Pataki.

Both thought that Brooklyn Bridge Park was a natural for the governor. His administration had shown an interest in helping Brooklyn in other ways and had helped fund the planning process; he himself had spoken publicly about the park. The question for Witty and Connor at that moment was how to get the park off the dime.

The relationship between Mayor Giuliani and Governor Pataki was no better than that between Mayor Giuliani and Borough President Golden. Giuliani seemed to enjoy throwing punches, but even under the best of circumstances New York City mayors and New York State governors rarely get along. Witty and Connor used this to their benefit. Connor, as Senate minority leader, picked up the phone in his office that gave him direct access to the governor. Once they connected, Connor told the governor of Witty's information from City Hall, arguing that the mayor, with only 16 percent of the park site, should not be permitted to snatch away Pataki's legacy by slapping a maple leaf (the logo of the New York City Parks Department) on the project.[11]

The governor was scheduled to deliver his State of the State address the next day, a Thursday, and was unable to get his announcement into the already-printed text. But Connor had gotten his attention. On Friday, January 5, 2001, the week before Mayor Giuliani's speech, Pataki issued a press release announcing that the Port Authority would provide $85 million to build Brooklyn Bridge Park. He also revealed that Con Edison had donated a 1.16-acre parcel at the north end of the site. Finally, he said, $2 million of additional money would immediately go to state parks for improvements to Empire Fulton Ferry State Park, "which will ultimately be folded into Brooklyn Bridge Park."[12]

The governor's action was widely reported, and it was assumed that a total of $150 million had now been jointly committed by the state and the city. The rivalry that underlay the development generally went unremarked on, except by Gregg Birnbaum of the *New York Post*, who wrote, "Governor Pataki yesterday gave a public pat on the back to the besieged Port Authority by announcing it will pump $85 million into a Brooklyn park—a move sources said was intended to embarrass Mayor Giuliani,"[13] and by Wendy Froede writing in the *Brooklyn Paper*, "Pataki's announcement, coming just a week after Giuliani launched fresh attacks against the Port Authority, appeared to some as a well-timed message to the mayor."[14]

But the euphoria that marked most responses to the news was not echoed by Donald Rattner of Waterfront Development Watch, who told the *New York Times*, "It validates what we believe is a flawed plan for the waterfront."[15] Only the *Daily News*, in an editorial, noted that the park still faced a big hurdle, that of resolving the problem of governance.[16]

Pataki had acted on most of the steps suggested to him by Connor and Witty on behalf of the Local Development Corporation.[17] He had acknowledged the community's vision for the park and come much closer than Giuliani to endorsing it. He had obtained needed money from the Port Authority and made a commitment to improving Empire Fulton Ferry State Park in a way consistent with the master plan.

However, Pataki was not ready to establish the entity that would build and operate the park without first trying to reach a joint arrangement with the city; without it the environmental reviews required for converting the piers to park use could not commence.

Giuliani, who earlier had shown no particular interest in the park, seemed eager to get his name on the project before his term ended. Now that he had included a budget item for it, his aides came to the Local Development Corporation seeking ideas for small items that were modest in cost and could be implemented before he left office at the end of December. The most obvious candidate for a quick and dramatic transformation was a lot at the foot of Main Street in DUMBO currently used for parking; the city needed only to cancel a month-to-month lease. The corporation's concern was that the city had never actually endorsed the master plan.

In fact, Joseph Rose, chairman of the City Planning Commission, signaled that the city would go ahead with the development of its own parcel in DUMBO regardless of the fate of the master plan. Rose indicated that this work should not conflict with the overall park aims, though it might not be bound precisely by what the Local Development Corporation and its planners envisioned. He contemplated a new organization to oversee the larger park development, a body whose membership would be determined by the governor and mayor.[18] But apparently the city and state could not come to terms on such a joint entity.

The city insisted on using its own Parks Department planners to design what it wanted on the Main Street lot. While refusing to use the 2000 master plan as its model, at least some at the Parks Department thought that they were furthering Brooklyn Bridge Park, and in consequence the city called its work there Phase I of Brooklyn Bridge Park. As proof of good intentions, Joanne Witty was invited to speak at the groundbreaking on a July day in 2001.

Witty had already enlisted Theodore Roosevelt IV, who served with her on the board of the national League of Conservation Voters and was the former chair of the Regional State Parks Commission, to try to persuade State Parks Commissioner Bernadette Castro to follow the master plan in carrying out changes in her section of park. Though she agreed to study their suggestions, Castro clearly did not want to lose the section's identity as a state park by submerging it into Brooklyn Bridge Park.

Still, state parks lost no time in gearing up to spend its $2 million in new funds announced by Governor Pataki.[19] Some money would go to complete the bulkhead repair and a planned new walkway along the water. Some would pay for cleaning up the cove, regrading paths, improving the lawn, and installing irrigation. There was also talk of converting the Con Edison lot for active recreation and soliciting university interest in creating tennis courts there. Although many of these initiatives were completed, the state never obtained title to the donated Con Edison site. As a result, the park would later have to pay Con Edison more than $9 million for what had been announced by Governor Pataki as a gift.[20]

Commissioner Castro was once again seeking to generate private investment to develop the Empire Stores. David Walentas had proposed, in collaboration with Polytechnic University (now NYU Tandon School of Engineering), to create a high-tech "incubator" in the Empire Stores for advanced students and faculty to explore entrepreneurial possibilities, leaving the first floor for retail stores and turning the roof into a garden and restaurant. Under the proposal, Brooklyn Bridge Park would be a one-third partner with Walentas's Two Trees Management Company and Polytechnic in a project expected to provide annual net income of about $290,000. State legislation would be needed for a forty-nine-year lease on the property.[21]

To the dismay of Polytechnic, which envisioned a benign, adaptive reuse of the warehouses, the Brooklyn Heights Association and the Coalition vehemently opposed the plan. They did not consider the educational use "public" enough, their reaction reflecting in part an old animus against Walentas.

Though not actively opposing it, the Local Development Corporation thought the proposal was premature. It was concerned that the revenues could not be assured to go for park maintenance since a governance structure was not yet in place, that design compatibility with the park was not guaranteed, that a separate environmental review required for the site might not fit in with the overall review for the park, and that the promised financial return was less than the master plan contemplated. The setback led Polytechnic to find another location for its incubator, and the future of Empire Stores would continue to bedevil park planning.[22]

Figure 8-1. The 2001 proposal by architect Donald Rattner for a grand stairway connecting Montague Street to the park was not taken seriously, with some likening it to the Spanish Steps in Rome. (Ferguson, Shamamian & Rattner / *Brooklyn Heights Press*.)

All this time, the Waterfront Development Watch had tried to derail the official park plan. Having from the first advocated a park entrance from the Promenade at Montague Street, Donald Rattner produced an actual and startling design for it, a monumental staircase wrapping around a subway ventilator building (see Figure 8-1).

Gabrielle Rattner, for her part, kept challenging the claims for the master plan; she contended that less than one-third of the site would be "green park" and that her group had collected more than one thousand signatures from Brooklyn Heights and other neighborhoods "objecting to the project's over-commercialization as well as needless reliance on automobiles."[23]

But by this point the plan for the park had gone too far to be derailed by the Rattners. As one more proof of that, Mayor Giuliani used the July 21 groundbreaking ceremony for the playground at the Main Street lot, the city's Phase I of Brooklyn Bridge Park, to announce a Phase II (see Figure 8-2).

In his remarks, the mayor said the city-owned Purchase Building, a two-story Art Deco structure beneath the Brooklyn Bridge (see Figure 8-3), would be removed and reassembled elsewhere, freeing the space to become a public plaza and fountain. The *Brooklyn Heights Press* argued for taking advantage of a sound, existing structure to use its expansive second floor as a popularly priced restaurant. The park master plan, in a compromise with preservationists, had called for a truncated section of the building to be kept for a visitor center; preservationists wanted to save it in its entirety.

The opposing viewpoint was most strongly expressed by Marianna Koval of the Coalition, who called the building "an enormous physical obstruction within Brooklyn Bridge Park" and urged its demolition to open up views and remove "a psychological barrier to the creation of one unified park."[24]

Testifying before the Landmarks Preservation Commission, whose permission was needed to tear down the Purchase Building, Witty demonstrated how the

building would be treated under the master plan. The hearing, as it turned out, took place a week before the September 11 attack on the World Trade Center, an event that effectively tabled the issue for the time being.

That event had an immediate consequence for the park. The city's Office of Emergency Management, which had been headquartered in the Trade Center complex, chose to use the Purchase Building on an interim basis while a less-vulnerable facility was constructed on the edge of Downtown Brooklyn. This gave the building a reprieve,[25] although ultimately it would be demolished.

In a symbolic gesture to commemorate the devastation of 9/11, the Coalition enlisted 160 schoolchildren to plant daffodil bulbs in two Twin Tower–shaped beds on a one-acre plot near Pier 4 (see Figure 8-4) that had been secured through talks with the Port Authority and the city. A large billboard would be placed by the Coalition at the foot of the two beds announcing, "After Winter, Spring."[26] Although this planting would not last long, it was the first visible suggestion of something like "park" along the piers section of the waterfront.

Figure 8-4. The first physical sign of park along the piers was a pair of tulip beds planted behind Pier 4 in 2002, their rectangular outlines recalling the destroyed Twin Towers that were missing from the skyline.

NINE
BREAKING THE LOGJAM

When I arrived . . . there were paper files, but there was nothing in them. I was led to believe that the environmental impact statement was complete, when in fact it had not begun.

—Wendy Leventer, the second president of the Brooklyn Bridge
Park Development Corporation

Despite the commitments of government funding, the months after the attacks of September 11 were a time when the community's plan for Brooklyn Bridge Park was almost entirely adrift and very much at risk.

In the long run the election of 2001 was a big boost to the park. Not only was Michael Bloomberg, who would become the park's principal benefactor, elected mayor, but Marty Markowitz was elected Brooklyn borough president. A long-serving state senator and already a prominent park supporter, Markowitz would also become a funder and, as he would say, chief "noodge" on the park's behalf.

In the short run, however, the park's path forward was neither clear nor easy. While Governor Pataki was in theory interested in carrying out the master plan, the state park agency was not. The city seemed determined to go its own way, building the Main Street playground to its own design standards and showing no interest in a unified park, much less a unified park organization. In contrast to the governor's support of the Local Development Corporation and the efforts of his staff to bring the parties together, the lack of progress in dealings with the city led to considerable frustration on the part of the park's planners. Indeed, the governor was tempted to create an expanded state park encompassing whatever land the state controlled, even if it was not contiguous.[1] Such a move would have ended hopes for a unified park, and in the process the community would have been deprived of its role.

It was widely believed that a Democrat would succeed Giuliani, but the primary field was crowded. Mark Green, then the public advocate, narrowly defeated Fernando Ferrer, the Bronx borough president, in a runoff election that left the Democratic Party divided. A weakened Green subsequently lost to Michael R. Bloomberg, who had changed his party registration to run as a Republican. Daniel Doctoroff, an investment banker, was among the first people Mayor Bloomberg appointed to lead his new administration. He had gotten an intense tutorial on New York City planning and real estate issues as head of the city's unsuccessful bid for the Summer Olympic Games of 2012.[2] He knew the park site from prior scouting for Olympic venues, but his early support of Brooklyn Bridge Park came from what he called a "comprehensive view of this harbor district which was going to be a critical part of the revival of both Lower Manhattan and Brooklyn." The district, he continued, would include "Governors Island, Brooklyn Bridge Park, Battery Park, the East River waterfront, and a handful of parks that would go up the East River on the Brooklyn side and to some extent into Queens."[3]

Joshua Sirefman, who had done important work for the Local Development Corporation as part of the team of HR&A consultants, was hired by Andrew Alper, new chair of the city's Economic Development Corporation, and went on to work for Doctoroff, the deputy mayor for economic development and rebuilding. Eventually he returned to EDC as its president. During this time he was the city's point person on Brooklyn Bridge Park. As Sirefman remembered it, Doctoroff said to him, "'Take this and run with it,' which was fantastic to then be in a position to make the park happen."[4]

Sirefman contacted Charles Fox,[5] who worked for the governor on energy, transportation, and environmental issues. Sirefman and Witty, on behalf of the Local Development Corporation, had spoken with Fox when they were trying to help get the city and state together. Now Sirefman was representing the city.

Fox recalled that getting the various parties together on Brooklyn Bridge Park did not involve a hard sell. Speaking of the governor, Fox said, "One thing that he always focused on was the concept of, during the Industrial Revolution, that American communities had turned their backs on waterfronts and made them into a backyard where they dumped things," adding, "That needed to be turned around."

"My sense of it is that the city picked it up, and it fit very well into that preexisting vision that the governor was already implementing in other places," Fox said. But, according to him, "It wasn't like it was being driven by the governor. It fit nicely into what was driven by the community." In particular, Fox remembered John Watts visiting his office frequently to make clear that a group of people out there really wanted to see this happen. "At the same time," Fox added, "we also wanted it to happen."[6]

Fox and Sirefman set to work on a memorandum of understanding that would create the Brooklyn Bridge Park Development Corporation, a subsidiary of the Empire State Development Corporation. The memo of understanding also provided that implementation of the park project would be "guided by the Illustrative

Master Plan subject to any refinements thereto arising from the completion of the planning and environmental review processes."

In addition, the memo required that "no less than 80% of the Project will be reserved for open space and will be dedicated as Parkland." Finally, it provided that "consistent with the Illustrative Master Plan, the development of appropriate commercial uses may occur within the Project area, provided that all revenues derived from such uses shall be used exclusively for the maintenance and operation of the Project." The parties to the document pledged to an open and inclusive planning process by which the new subsidiary "shall seek extensive public input, through consultation with an advisory board and/or interested community groups in developing the General Project Plan."[7]

It is hard to imagine a document that more closely served the objectives of the Local Development Corporation and the communities it had worked with over the past four years. The city and the state had now formally endorsed the illustrative master plan, had agreed to revenue-generating uses that fed directly into the park's upkeep, and had required that at least 80 percent of the site be dedicated to parkland. The board of the new subsidiary would be controlled by the state (six members to five for the city), but city and state agreement was required for any major action.

Resolving the issue of control was the most difficult part of the negotiation. Fox remembered "a lot of agonizing over the structure of how many board members there were going to be. Basically, the same issues were going on with Governors Island because we were looking to split control between the city and the state, with this nagging concern that that was going to lead to a dysfunctional future but also that it was necessary to get an actual deal done. If either the city or the state had fought for unfettered control over either project that just wouldn't have happened."

Joanne Witty, John Watts, and David Offensend were appointed to the new subsidiary board, Witty by the mayor and Watts and Offensend by the governor. All three were asked to resign their other park-related positions—Witty as president of the Local Development Corporation and Watts and Offensend as members of the LDC and as chair and vice-chair of the Coalition, respectively. Three other "outside" directors were appointed, one by the city and two by the state. City and state officials filled the other slots.[8]

On Thursday, May 2, 2002, a major public event on Pier 1 celebrated the new accord. Governor Pataki, Mayor Bloomberg, and a host of other officials stood at the waterfront following a heavy rain, with mist still obscuring the tops of Lower Manhattan's skyline. The governor and mayor formally signed the memo of understanding and confirmed the previously agreed-on $150 million in public money for the park—$85 million from the state through the Port Authority and $65 million from the city. "This is a once-in-a-century opportunity here in Brooklyn to reclaim waterfronts that were taken away more than a century ago," Pataki said. "It's time for another new park," Bloomberg said, adding lightly, "We should have them more frequently."[9]

Buoyed by the city-state partnership, Charles A. Gargano, chairman of the new Brooklyn Bridge Park Development Corporation, predicted that construction could start in a year, during which time designs would be prepared and an environmental impact study conducted.[10] Despite his optimism, it would be five years before construction of the park would begin.

There were many reasons for the long delay, some of them due to changes in the state administrations. During Mayor Bloomberg's tenure there were four governors—Pataki, Eliot Spitzer, David Paterson, and Andrew Cuomo. During this unsettled time, intergovernmental agencies like the Brooklyn Bridge Park Development Corporation were often caught between their two sponsors.

The situation was not improved by the first major decision of the new joint venture between the city and the state, the selection of James Moogan as president of the Brooklyn Bridge Park Development Corporation. Moogan's previous engagement with the park had been as the New York State Parks Department official in charge of the New York City region. He had no experience with large construction projects, let alone one as novel and complicated as Brooklyn Bridge Park. But the state, which controlled a majority on the board and a majority of the land, wanted him as president. Since Moogan had worked for Commissioner Castro, perhaps his selection was an effort to get her support for a unified Brooklyn Bridge Park.

To get the park through the process described by Chairman Gargano, the first step should have been to transform the master plan, a planning document that established broad parameters, into a buildable design. Then the buildable design would be incorporated in something called a general project plan. That plan was the legal land-use document that would enable the Empire State Development Corporation to change the zoning on the site. The park site was generally zoned for industrial and manufacturing purposes, and a zoning change to permit a park was required. The plan would define the boundaries of the park and cover all the major elements and uses.

Then the plan would be the subject of the required environmental impact statement, the assessment of the park's impact on air quality, traffic and transportation, noise, soil and water, and energy consumption.[11] Until an environmental review was completed, no property could be transferred to the Brooklyn Bridge Park Development Corporation for construction of the park.

A new body called the Citizens Advisory Council was formed at the end of 2002, consisting of twenty-four public members and seven "resource" members, primarily from park-related government agencies.[12] Their role was to advise the Brooklyn Bridge Park Development Corporation and its professional team as the general project plan was being prepared. The advisory group became the principal avenue for community input. Meetings at this stage were held roughly twice a month and were well attended.

The old planning team, headed by HR&A, was engaged to modify the 2000 illustrative master plan to account for new engineering information as it was developed, regulatory constraints as they were identified, and revenue-generating prospects for the park as costs and revenue sources were analyzed in greater detail. But instead of proceeding with the planning, Moogan reopened contentious issues that the illustrative master plan had apparently resolved. At the same time, little progress was made on marshaling the information needed to figure out how much development would be needed, what kind, and where it would be located. And apparently no meaningful engineering assessment was completed.

Instead, Moogan, at the urging of Chairman Gargano and Commissioner Castro, became distracted with yet another request for proposals for the adaptive reuse of the Empire Stores. The city as well as community representatives on the board resisted this as premature: first because the property would have more value surrounded by new park, and second because it sent the wrong signal to the community that commercial development took precedence over building a park.[13]

In fact, what the park needed was not a narrow focus on a specific project but a comprehensive approach to design. It also needed a technical team of architects and engineers to transform the master plan into a buildable design. It was not possible to create a general project plan without these specialists, and the Empire

State Development Corporation did not have such people on its staff. It would be more than a year before a designer for the park was chosen.

Despite Michael Van Valkenburgh Associates' previous work on the project, the selection of the firm was not a foregone conclusion. Many teams vied for the job. Some of them had experience only with much smaller projects, while others had worked on parks only as adjuncts of commercial projects. Still other teams offered more of a predictable product, which some on the selection committee found appealing. But the majority of the committee believed that the Van Valkenburgh team's appreciation of the site's unique character, its participation in the community process, and its intelligent design approach made it the best choice. A contract was signed in the summer of 2003.

In the meantime, two major events occurred that would have a significant impact on park planning. The first was the city's decision to terminate the Port Authority's lease on Pier 6, which was being used on a month-to-month basis by a company called American Stevedoring that had leases elsewhere in the port. Pier 6 would be added to Brooklyn Bridge Park, which was a significant benefit, as it permitted the design of a real entrance at the foot of Atlantic Avenue, added more than seven acres to the park, and satisfied a longtime request by neighborhoods to the south.[14]

There was also surprising news about the Jehovah's Witnesses, the religious group based in Brooklyn Heights for nearly a century that had acquired extensive real estate holdings there. Among these was the million-square-foot building at 360 Furman Street on the upland of Pier 5, the former flagship of the New York Dock Company. This building, always in private hands, had not been included in the park or thought to be part of the park plan. The announcement that the Witnesses would move their printing operations upstate was coupled with word that the group would give up their lease on a seven-hundred-car parking lot adjacent to their building at 360 Furman Street. Ten weeks later the Witnesses signaled they might actually sell the building itself.

The Witnesses' expected moves carried huge implications for the community and the city, most significantly a return to the tax rolls of properties like 360 Furman that had been exempt because of the organization's religious status, thus making them possible sources of revenue for Brooklyn Bridge Park.

Some in the community wanted the Park Development Corporation to buy the building from the Witnesses or condemn it and tear it down to make room for more park. This was never a realistic goal, since the building was in fact bought for more than $200 million by a private developer, who intended to convert it to condominiums.

While these developments were underway, a new "concept plan" was released, reflecting input from the Citizens Advisory Council. This appearance of forward motion was not informed by engineering or other technical studies. In this plan only minor changes were made: the only new structural elements were at Pier 1, with the existing National Cold Storage Warehouse either converted into a hotel or replaced entirely, and the Purchase Building demolished. The Pier 3 amphitheater was removed after the Brooklyn Heights Association objected to a potentially noisy use at that location and a proposed stairway from the Brooklyn Bridge walkway was eliminated due to its perceived impracticality.[15]

Because of community unhappiness with the earlier-proposed "bio-wall," the question of how to dampen sound from the Brooklyn-Queens Expressway was left unaddressed. The idea of a marsh at the cove in the Empire State Park was eliminated. For the rest, as the *Brooklyn Heights Press* noted in an editorial, "Almost all will be green Park; Piers 2, 3, 4 (and it now appears, Pier 6) will be clear of structures. The upland will have gently sloping knolls and be crossed by pedestrian and bicycle paths (which have now been separated for greater pedestrian safety)."[16] This interim plan did nothing to prepare the public for changing circumstances and tough choices. Instead, it lulled them into a false sense of confidence that creating the park was going to be easy.

On June 26, 2003, the first "scoping session," a legally required step in the preparation of an environmental impact statement, was held at Borough Hall. In this step the project sponsor solicits input from the public on the key issues to be studied in the environmental review. The public was told that annual park expenses were estimated at about $10 million, double the $5 million cited in the 2000 master plan. This figure, as the reporter Dennis Holt noted in the *Brooklyn Heights Press*, became "the target sum for revenue-producing activities within the park."[17] Costs would indeed be higher. But this figure was not the result of adequate analysis—it included nothing for maintenance of marine structures—and the final number would be even higher. Moreover, the public was not warned that the revenue-raising uses indicated on the master plan might not meet the need and would have to be supplemented with additional—and different—sources of revenue.

Perhaps because the revenue issue was not fully explored, the session was generally calm. The Red Hook developer Greg O'Connell did complain that the plan was a "landlubber's park," and he and another maritime-use advocate called for more harbor-related activity. That comment struck a chord with park designers and led to significant changes in the park's design.

It was also noted that further attention would have to be paid to traffic. Thomas Chittenden of the Brooklyn Heights Association urged that monthly meetings of the Citizens Advisory Council continue to keep the public involved in the process.[18]

The environmental review process itself is highly technical and carried out by experts. Fundamental to the process is the existence of a fairly specific plan. However, at the time of the "scoping session" and for a considerable period thereafter, design and planning were not advanced significantly past the general outlines of the master plan.

By the end of 2003 neither the city nor the state was happy with the progress being made and they sought someone with more experience in carrying out a complex intergovernmental real estate project. In early 2004 Jim Moogan left for another state job. A few months later Wendy Leventer, who had been working on a major renovation project at Lincoln Center for the Performing Arts, arrived as Moogan's replacement.

Leventer was no stranger to the Empire State Development Corporation, having served as the president of the Times Square Redevelopment Project, another ESDC subsidiary, and was experienced in public/private real estate ventures. She had the respect of agency staff and the confidence of its chairman Charles Gargano. But she was in for some surprises.

"When I arrived at ESDC," Leventer said, "what I found was different from what I expected, in the sense that Jim had not achieved as much as what was commonly understood. As an example, people had an expectation that much of the work that went into the approvals was further along than it was. There were no files. There were paper files, but there was nothing in them. I was led to believe that the environmental impact statement was complete, when in fact it had not begun."[19]

Leventer knew that an environmental impact statement for a project on the waterfront was much more difficult and time consuming than one anywhere else. That is because the water raises a host of environmental issues that are not confronted by a landlocked project. It was striped bass, after all, that doomed the Westway project that would have made possible a combined highway and park along the Hudson River.[20]

Because the basic information needed to create an environmental impact statement for the park had not been assembled, Leventer was playing catch-up from her first day in office. This problem would dog her throughout her three-year tenure.

TEN
REALITY SETS IN

To give one example of the astonishing detail provided in the
report, we find that to clean and maintain the bathrooms, of
which there will be four, will cost $134,000 each year.

—Dennis Holt in the *Brooklyn Heights Press*

Perhaps it was an omen that when Wendy Leventer (see Figure 10-1) arrived for her
first day of work she found a notice from the Office of the New York State Comptrol-
ler announcing an audit of the organization she had just joined. She was quickly
immersed in accounting for her predecessor's efforts and explaining a project that
would not show results until it was built. In the process, she discovered how much
work was left to be done before those results would be apparent.

In Leventer's recollection, she had been assured before she accepted the job
that the project was virtually shovel-ready. Nothing could have been further from
the truth. The community was operating off what was still a vision plan that had
not been seriously vetted either physically or financially. Her predecessor's work on
the plan was not informed by any professional engineering evaluation of the site's
capacity and its appropriateness for proposed uses. No comprehensive budget or
financial information had been developed.

The public was unaware that the work with Moogan had been largely futile.

In fact, this process contributed to the false sense that decisions were being
made and that the plan was proceeding briskly. It created unrealistic expectations
and assumptions that would only later be challenged with hard facts. This attitude
set the tone for everything to come. Even a decade later, some people were arguing
that it was the 2000 illustrative master plan that should have been built.

The city's transformation of the Main Street lot into a park, a playground, and
a pebble beach as well as improvements in the Empire Fulton Ferry State Park further served to confuse the public about the ex-
tent to which the plan was set and construction of Brooklyn Bridge Park itself was underway.

In addition, there was pressure for interim use of the park site, which helped build a
constituency for the park but also created confusion over its true situation. The Coalition,
after renaming itself the Conservancy, took the
lead in proposing interim uses, which were

Figure 10-1. Wendy Leventer took charge of the
park process and got a stalled project moving.

101

popular in the community and created the sense that the park was moving along. But given the status of the project, many of the ideas were premature, and in any case the presence of commercial tenants on the piers made public access difficult.

Although the approval process for a project on the waterfront was particularly difficult and time-consuming, Leventer put together an ambitious timetable, then supervised a team of specialists to execute it. While parts of the data collection for the environmental statement, on subjects such as historical resources and hazardous materials, could begin on the site, the bulk of the work required a detailed project plan. The focus, therefore, was on moving the plan from the theoretical to the achievable in collaboration with designers, engineers, budget and finance experts, and the community.

When the uses already on the plan and their locations were finally subjected to an engineering review to determine their feasibility, the engineers reached a series of dramatic conclusions. For one thing, they discovered that the existing shed on Pier 5 could not be used for indoor recreation because the closely spaced columns supporting the roof would not permit many of the uses expected in such a facility, such as an indoor soccer field or a skating rink. Building a new structure for this purpose was considered but ultimately rejected because of its considerable cost.

In any case, once engineers found out what was going on below, it soon became clear that substantial new structures could not be built on top of the piers. The Brooklyn piers, like most piers in New York Harbor, were originally built on timber pilings. The waters of New York Harbor were the reason the piers exist, but the water was also their greatest enemy.

It turned out that the worst enemy of the piers was not the chemistry of the water but its biology. Even at their most polluted, the waters of New York Harbor contain a wide variety of marine life. Two of those life-forms, known as shipworms and gribbles, are natural enemies of timber, and together they attack the piles from two directions: the gribbles chew at the wood from the outside and the shipworms create tunnels on the inside. Ironically, as a result of strenuous efforts to attack pollution in the harbor, cleaner water had led to an increase in the population of these marine borers and a corresponding increase in their destructive impact on the pilings.[1]

The Port Authority knew that the piers were vulnerable. The desire to escape the cost of pier maintenance was one reason the agency tried to dispose of them in the first place. To prepare the piers for disposal in the years leading up to the park plan, the Port Authority had spent $40 million on them, in effect a kind of dowry, and most of it was spent on the pilings. The treatment of the piles was complex, but essentially it consisted of encasing the wooden piles in concrete sheaths to strengthen the pier supports and protect them from biological attack. Park planners understood from the Port Authority that the treatment of the piles had brought them to a state of good repair.

When the Local Development Corporation created the master plan, it did not have the funds for the considerable expense of sending engineers into the water to make an independent assessment of the piers' structural integrity. When the Brooklyn Bridge Park Development Corporation's engineers finally entered the water to look at the submerged supports, they discovered that the fix applied by the Port Authority had not achieved its purpose. This discovery had two important consequences: first, that the piers' weight-bearing ability was much less than believed, and second, that the cost of future maintenance to the pier structures would be much greater than anticipated.

The first point, that the piers could not support complex structures, immediately changed the planners' ideas about what the park would look like and what activities it could support. In particular, it became clear that new buildings would be possible only on the uplands, the solid ground at the edge of the water to which the piers were attached. Perhaps more important to the landscape architects who were designing the park, significant dense vegetation such as large trees and shrubs would be possible only on Pier 1, which was built on landfill and not piling. The remaining piers were too fragile to carry the heavy load of significant soil and water that would be required.

Like many other problems that the park overcame, this cloud was not without a silver lining. Faced with deteriorating marine structures, the planners chose to eliminate many of them. News of a rotted bulkhead led to a decision to avoid the cost of rebuilding and maintaining it in favor of a rocky stabilized edge, which brought the park visitor much closer to the water. By removing unstable platforms connecting Piers 2, 3, and 5 to the upland, the designers saved money while simultaneously responding to a community desire for a more water-oriented park and creating a new opportunity for boating. The decrepit condition of marine structures around Pier 5 also led to the creation of a salt marsh. This decision later inspired the addition of a picnic area with outdoor grilling on a constructed peninsula bridging the salt marsh and the canal adjacent to Pier 5, one of the park's most popular features.

The second point, that the park would be more expensive to maintain and operate, led the planners to revise their financial models and conclude that residential rather than modest commercial development would be needed to provide sufficient operating revenue. That conclusion, in turn, would have many consequences in subsequent years. In the long run it reduced the amount of land devoted to revenue-producing uses well below 20 percent and increased the amount of parkland, but it also increased the volume and intensity of local controversy.

As park planners were adjusting to these new facts, they were working to create different aspects of the park experience through design.

For example, to compensate for the park's length, the design team wanted to create at each entrance the opportunity to enjoy a range of activities one would expect from a local park. With only forty-five minutes to spend in the park, a person could visit a playground, spread out on the grass with a book or a sandwich, or sit on a bench and look at the view. More active uses would be found by walking toward the center of the park.

While the designers explored alternatives, they were not working in a vacuum. The community was still a part of the conversation, as the designers and community representative exchanged ideas about what was possible and how the vision for the park could be expressed in a more specific design. Many informal meetings were held with members of different communities to gain their input.

Ideas only touched on by the 2000 illustrative master plan were further developed. The notion of sustainability, for example, was examined from many different points of view. Reusing material from the site, including parts of the shed on Pier 2, became a goal. When the designers discovered longleaf yellow pine in the National Cold Storage Warehouse—the once-plentiful material had become scarce and the trees virtually extinct—all of it was used for park benches and siding. Materials such as granite blocks, rock, and even soil were identified for salvage from other locations in the city that were dismantling bridges or excavating sites.

Establishing a sustainable ecological system was a priority, and this required a combination of water management, native plant selection, and proper placement of plant material. Water from precipitation as well as overflow from the city's storm water was slowed down by plantings and collected for irrigation on the site. Different types of wildlife habitat were identified for inclusion in the park. Finally, close attention was paid to the microclimate conditions on the site, such as strong winds and unshaded sunlight, and efforts were made to lessen their effect.

In some places in the park, noise from the Brooklyn-Queens Expressway was as loud as a jet plane taking off and still needed to be addressed. The general principle to reduce noise was to interrupt the direct line of sight between the noise source and the listener, but the designers concluded that only earth berms or walls would absorb the sound rather than deflect it into surrounding neighborhoods. Wind was an issue that would affect where landforms and planted thickets should be placed. Shelter from the sun was also important.

In late July 2004 Leventer and her team met with the Citizens Advisory Council to review the cost analysis done so far on maintenance and operation of the park. The total was projected at slightly more than $15.1 million a year and was supported with considerable detail. As Dennis Holt reported in the *Brooklyn Heights Press*, "To give one example of the astonishing detail provided in the report, we find that to clean and maintain the bathrooms, of which there will be four, will cost $134,000 each year. Most of this will go to labor costs."[2] The largest annual expense, Holt reported, was $3.6 million to maintain marine structures.[3]

Leventer later explained that the budget was so detailed "because we understood that the amount of effort to maintain the piers was so huge that you had to have the leanest possible operating budget because you were already starting from that maritime base."[4] The community was skeptical about the numbers, Leventer recalled, which engendered heated dialogue. "We had discussions with the community," she said. "OK, we don't have to empty the garbage three times on Saturday in the summer, but we just think it's going to be nasty and gross if we don't."[5]

Even after the budget was better understood, Leventer added, deciding that the principal revenue source should be market-rate housing took a long time. "We didn't default to that position in the first instance," she said. "We rated things according to different criteria; we didn't hide anything from anyone. Those presentations were exhaustive and exhausting. I still believe to this day that housing is the most compatible use with a park."[6]

The choice of housing as the principal revenue source would become highly contentious. Some people thought that the controversy could have been moderated by a slower and better public rollout. Early on, the *Brooklyn Heights Press* reporter Dennis Holt and the paper's editor, Henrik Krogius, met with Leventer for lunch at the Clark Street Diner opposite the Hotel St. George, reminding her that housing would be an explosive issue for many in the neighborhood and urging her to address the issue head-on by presenting a persuasive financial rationale for what everyone would recognize was a major shift in the park plan.

Leventer presented the plan for elected officials and community leaders just before Christmas in 2004 at the Van Valkenburgh firm's new Brooklyn Bridge Park storefront near Union Square in Manhattan. Maps, renderings, and a large model showed a pair of residential buildings on Pier 6, a slender thirty-story tower, and another of fifteen stories (see Figure 10-2). Yet another new residential building was shown at the northern end of the park on John Street. The large existing building at 360 Furman Street that Robert Levine had bought from the Jehovah's Witnesses was also in the park plan, as well as a hotel with connected residential space on the uplands of Pier 1.

At the meeting, participants acknowledged that housing was the only real choice to support the project financially, but they were dubious about the broader community's reaction. Senator Connor echoed the concern that the public had not been adequately prepared for such a big change in the plan.

Leventer was aware of the problem, but she felt pressed by the tight deadline for the environmental review process. The inclusion of 360 Furman Street was a further complication. Robert Levine, owner of 360 Furman Street, had agreed to make a major payment to the park, but only if the review process moved ahead promptly. Since the amount of money involved was significant, postponing the environmental review would be costly. Leventer believed she had no choice but to proceed with a major public presentation.

When the public event took place, in a crowded auditorium at St. Francis College in February 2005, it proved something of a PR disaster. As described in a front-page editorial in the *Brooklyn Heights Press*:

Five speakers, a welcomer and two moderators all contributed to telling people what they mostly already knew from
all the debate that had gone into the 2000 master plan, re-
iterating history and principles and even going into an ir-
relevant slide show of waterfronts around the world. The
session seemed more dedicated to stroking the various
political interests supporting the park than in telling and
showing the audience what it wanted to know: namely,
just what is in this plan and how is it calculated that the
housing component will in fact generate the income needed to maintain the park?[7]

There was actually much to like in the new plan, but perhaps inevitably the
focus was on the housing, which many friends of the park regretted and which its
enemies attacked with relish. The air quickly filled with conspiracy theories. Even
many who were disposed to support the new plan came to share a feeling that the
Brooklyn Bridge Park Development Corporation was trying to put something over
on them, while the plan's opponents argued that since the project was being handled by a "development" agency, not a "park" agency, this must have been the intent all along.

No matter how many budget presentations were made, there was still a res-
idue of disbelief (and worse). Leventer's management of the development corporation was attacked,[8] and she was attacked personally,[9] as were the entire team of
professionals.[10] Anger and suspicion put discussion of facts and even civility well
beyond reach.

The anger resulted in demands that Leventer be fired. Charles Gargano,
chairman of the Empire State Development Corporation and the Brooklyn Bridge
Park Development Corporation, backed her and supported her work. Only after Eliot Spitzer took office as governor did her detractors persuade the new administration to make a change.[11]

Given the length and depth of the subsequent debate over housing, the controversy went beyond Leventer's handling of public relations. For one thing, dealing with the community was always fraught with the possibility of litigation, and
the Brooklyn Heights Association was known to be litigious. Over the course of the
park's construction at least five lawsuits were brought, and more were threatened.
The prospect of litigation shadowed Leventer's relationship with the community.
"You have a conversation," she said, "and because you don't measure your words,

because you think you're having a conversation, they come back at you with a lawsuit. I cannot tell you how many times that has happened to me: 'Well, you said blah, blah, blah.' 'Well, I didn't know I was giving a deposition. I thought I was having a conversation.'"[12]

However, many people would agree that dealing with the public was not Leventer's strong suit. Her prior jobs had focused more on dealing with professionals like architects and builders than courting community constituencies. Josh Sirefman, who witnessed many public projects rise, fall, and rise again, believed that Leventer was not wired for external relations. Nonetheless, he said, "on the substance of advancing a big complicated development and construction project, she did an incredible job of keeping it alive and really advancing it."[13] James Whalen, head of the Downtown Brooklyn Council in the park's early days, agreed. "She could have had better table manners," Whalen said, "but she made the tough decisions."[14]

Looking back on the park's history, it is possible to conclude that Leventer confronted a perfect storm. Long before her tenure, the Local Development Corporation had produced a plan after extended dialogue with the community that raised expectations about both its substance and the sanctity of community participation. But that plan did not deal with what turned out to be the two most difficult issues—the true cost of maintaining the maritime structures and operating the park, which were not known at the time, and the need for more intensive development to cover those costs.

When the true costs were determined the plan had to change, and because of time pressure it did so without the advance public discussion that parts of the community had come to expect. The Brooklyn Bridge Park Development Corporation eventually decided that housing was the only practical source of revenue, but earlier warning might have allowed at least some members of the community to reach that conclusion as well.

This ugly turn of events did not prevent a good plan from being produced. As Michael Van Valkenburgh acknowledged, "You don't design a park without civic engagement."[15] Under Leventer's supervision, Van Valkenburgh and his team produced the 2005 master plan; the general project plan was adopted, and an environmental impact statement was completed.

At the time, many close to the project believed that Leventer was treated unfairly. On her watch a project that had been becalmed and rudderless gained momentum and direction. A plan that might have languished or died was completed, vetted, and approved. Moreover, if it was remarkable that a plan of any kind was completed, the plan itself proved even more remarkable. As the park's designers remembered it, Leventer was a champion of great design, a client who encouraged creativity and insisted on excellence. The park became a widely admired reality, and during a difficult and turbulent period Leventer put her stamp on it.

ELEVEN

HOUSING "IN THE PARK"

The parcels designated for residential/commercial development herein are not parkland, have never been parkland, and were never designated to become parkland.

—New York Supreme Court Justice Lawrence S. Knipel

From its early days the park plan included a self-sustaining financial model, a Grand Bargain between the community and the government that allowed the park to be built in the first place.

The idea of a self-sufficient park had been tested in Battery Park City and Hudson River Park, two other public projects that involved both the city and the state, but with very different results. Battery Park City is really a new town development in which substantial residential and commercial buildings generate revenue to sustain a modest amount of parkland with plenty to spare and return to other public uses. Hudson River Park was intended to be self-sufficient when it was created; however, having found maritime maintenance more expensive and revenues lower than anticipated, it has struggled.

Even for those who lived through the making of Brooklyn Bridge Park, it is hard to remember what the park site looked like before. Rundown piers, rusting pier sheds, chain-link fences, weeds and brush—it was not a pretty sight. Even if some could have tolerated this sad state forever, that was not an option. The site was too costly for the Port Authority to maintain and the real estate too valuable for the Port Authority to ignore. As we know, the agency had a series of plans for commercial and residential development. Some of these plans provided a small amount of parkland, but all of them envisioned a large amount of housing, shopping, and office buildings. When the community resisted, Stephen Berger, the agency's executive director, muttered darkly about building a tannery. That clearly was not in the cards, but one way or another something was going to happen.

Likewise, in the DUMBO section of the site, the real estate developer David Walentas had proposed to use publicly owned waterfront property awash in junk to build a chic hotel, a retail and cinema complex, a private marina, and parking surrounded by a little green space. For a while, at least, the government owners did not seem to rule out such an option.

As part of their effort to make the piers and the DUMBO waterfront a public park and not primarily a private development, the local community and its elected officials agreed to what we have called the Grand Bargain: if the Port Authority, the city, and the state would provide the necessary land and capital to build a park, the maintenance and operating costs of the park would be paid for with dedicated revenues generated from a small part of the site itself. For years, the idea was that 80 percent of the site would become parkland with the remaining 20 percent devoted to revenue-producing private development. The eventual result was actually better than that: 90 percent of the site became a public park, with only 10 percent devoted to other uses.

Over the years a small but vocal group of the park's critics argued that Brooklyn Bridge Park should not contain or be supported by private, profit-making uses. The underlying premise was that private uses are not appropriate in a public park. This argument is not limited to Brooklyn Bridge Park but applies to any park; whenever a private use is suggested for one of the city's major parks, like Central Park in Manhattan, there is an immediate outcry. New York State law supports this sense of the sanctity of parkland; once a property has been officially designated as parkland, it is extremely difficult to use it for any other purpose. Thus the argument against housing "in the park" had considerable precedent in the city.

But those precedents did not apply to the circumstances of Brooklyn Bridge Park. When the plan for the site divided it into parcels for recreation and parcels for revenue production, there was no "park" to divide. In the beginning, the site was 100 percent dedicated to (and zoned for) commercial use; if everything went right, some part of that site might become a park. Ultimately, 10 percent of the total was reserved for continued revenue-generating uses. Moreover, key to the Grand Bargain, the revenues from these uses would forever be dedicated to and support the operating costs of the park. The remaining 90 percent was transformed into a park. The private uses on the development sites replaced commercial development that was already there. The development sites were never "in the park" because they were never park in the first place.

This precise question came before the courts in New York when an organization called the Brooklyn Bridge Park Defense Fund sued to block the plan for housing "in the park." The judge who heard the case, Justice Lawrence S. Knipel, decided that the housing was not "in" the park because, when the housing sites were designated, there was no park for them to be "in" and no expectation they would ever be "in the park."[1]

That was not just the law but also the reality: without housing, there would have been no park. The city and state would hardly have invested $400 million in capital funds to build a new park if they did not believe it would be well maintained, and they knew they could not maintain the parks they already had. At the time, operating funds for parks in the city and state had been inadequate for years. Even Central Park, the crown jewel of the city's park system, was in sad shape in the 1970s, and it probably would have stayed that way if wealthy people living and working along its perimeter had not raised hundreds of millions of dollars in private funds to support the Central Park Conservancy to restore and maintain it. Many parks elsewhere in the city were dirty, defoliated, and unsafe.

Some said it was the public's duty to demand government support for parks. But the lack of funding and its consequences were real and readily observed, as Governor Pataki pointed out in an interview. "I hate the idea that parks have to be stand-alone self-sufficient financially," he said. "I think it is one of the basic missions of the government to provide parks. Having said that and having seen the history of Central Park before the Conservancy was created, Jones Beach, so many of the Hudson River piers, these were a blight. What had been projected as an asset became an enormous blight."[2] When government budgets are tight, and even when they are not, parks never have the highest priority. "If you have the highway collapsing, who's going to put money into maintaining the lawn of a park?" Pataki asked.

From the city perspective, Councilman Ken Fisher reached the same conclusion. "I think most political people believe that parks are an essential service, but they're not a mandated service," he said. "When you have no money to pay for your mandated services, your discretionary essential services get smacked. Then it's about trying to bridge the gaps."[3]

In any case, no one was going to fund the park if its operation was not assured. Robert Lieber, Mayor Bloomberg's deputy mayor with jurisdiction over the park, said the city was "adamant" about a funding source.[4] He was only one in a long line of public officials who felt that way.

Some community residents seemed to believe that providing the development sites and tying them to the park's maintenance was something that had been forced on the community and thus something to be resented and resisted. But while the idea of self-financing operating costs was tied to the idea of government financing construction costs from early on, most of the park's early supporters believed that the Grand Bargain benefited the community as well as the government.

Since the revenues from the development sites would directly fund the park's maintenance, the cost of operating the park would not be subject to the vagaries of government budgets. The community could feel assured that the park would remain clean, safe, and well maintained. The only other parks in New York that were similarly protected were heavily supported by private philanthropy, something unlikely to be available to Brooklyn Bridge Park.

The value of the revenue side of the Grand Bargain to the community is measured by how rare it is. Historically, New York City has resisted dedicating tax and tax-like revenues to a particular purpose. Virtually all revenues go into the general fund, where they are available for any public purpose and subject to annual appropriation by the mayor and the City Council. But as Bloomberg's Deputy Mayor Daniel Doctoroff later explained, "The park itself helped to create the value, so it was a relatively simple argument."[5]

It may have seemed like a no-brainer to Doctoroff, but the city's Office of Management and Budget had a different view. It was one of the jobs of the budget office to protect the city's general revenue so it could be applied to the city's highest priorities, and the agency had never been sympathetic to the idea of earmarking revenue for specific purposes. The fact that the city government was persuaded to accept the Grand Bargain and that it is now enshrined in the legal structure of the park can be seen as a great victory.

The idea of a Grand Bargain dates back at least to the early 1990s. The Thirteen Guiding Principles, adopted in 1992 by all the local elected officials and the Brooklyn Bridge Park Coalition, recognized the need for "so much commercial development in a park-like setting as is necessary to enliven the area, to provide security and to finance ongoing operations." The Thirteen Principles laid out the Grand Bargain, stating, "The revenues from such commercial uses shall be committed to the operation and maintenance of dedicated park and open space areas and contribute to capital development costs."[6]

When it came to the kinds of uses preferred, the principles said, "Specialized commercial uses (e.g., executive conference center/destination resort, restaurants, maritime center) shall be encouraged and residential and office uses shall be discouraged." For many years the planners adhered to these preferences, until it became apparent that they would not satisfy the financial need.

The Thirteen Guiding Principles had become something like gospel. The Local Development Corporation adopted them as the basis of its planning and successfully invoked them to bring the Coalition back into the fold of a comprehensive plan. The memorandum of understanding between Mayor Bloomberg and Governor Pataki referred to them, as did the bylaws of the Brooklyn Bridge Park Development Corporation. By inference, the public knew and accepted them.

But as time went on and the cast of characters changed, some people did not know or care about the history. Some blamed the Port Authority for imposing financial self-sufficiency when it was not even a signatory to the Thirteen Guiding Principles. Some later blamed Mayor Bloomberg, a relative latecomer, whose administration provided an additional $150 million in capital funds to finish as much of the park as possible before he left office. The reality, of course, was that the concept of self-sufficiency as the basis of the park's financial model was a decade old by the time he became mayor.

The Thirteen Guiding Principles, while acknowledging the financial need for revenue-generating sources in the park, also acknowledged another important benefit. Such activities could "enliven" the park and make an isolated site active and safe; in the words of legendary urban activist Jane Jacobs, they would put "eyes on the park." As Michael Van Valkenburgh, the landscape designer, has said, "It wasn't just a financial question, it was obviously a public safety question and it was an urban design question. If you reduced it to a financial question, then it just didn't embrace the complexity of the problem or the needs of the park. The site was a terminal on the edge of a city that turned its back to it." What were needed were "urban junctions" to connect the park to the city; placing the revenue uses at the junctions would help create that connection.[7]

But the revenue-generating sites were primarily about revenue; they had to produce enough revenue to cover the cost. As Dennis Holt noted in the *Brooklyn Heights Press*, the way to figure out how much money had to be raised from revenue-generating sources in the park was to determine the cost of maintaining and operating the park and work backward from there.[8] Jim Moogan knew that the annual budget would be closer to $10 million than the original $5 million estimate, and he knew enough to consider housing as a possible source of revenue. But he did not know the full story.[9]

By 2005 a member of the Van Valkenburgh team[10] had been working for some time on estimating the non-maritime maintenance and operating costs by breaking down the plan into its constituent parts. Based on practices and costs at other similar parks, she compiled an enormous binder of information of each physical item—paving, grass, shrubs, benches, lights—and what it would cost to maintain or replace them and on what schedule. She also considered operational issues, such as how the park would be kept clean and safe, and converted this data into staffing patterns and person hours. All this information was meticulously organized so that it could be easily updated and modified as the plan changed.

The cost of maintaining the piers and the pilings which supported them were harder to determine. The only way to estimate maritime costs accurately is to send divers into the water, something the Local Development Corporation could not afford to do. Now that the Park Development Corporation was doing real engineering, it seemed that every time the divers did go down, the projected maritime costs went up. The divers discovered that the marine borers were more active and plentiful as the water in New York Harbor became cleaner, causing an acceleration of pile deterioration under the piers.

Previous efforts by the Port Authority to encase the piles in concrete had failed to stop the deterioration, even though the agency had spent millions before turning the site over to the park corporation. New information led to a revision in the projected cost of maintaining twelve thousand wood piles, a consequent increase in the park's projected annual expense budget, and a need for more revenue. Spreading the necessary work over a forty-year replacement cycle led to an increase of about $5 million a year.

Moreover, Pier 6 had been added to the park since the original numbers were calculated, and it became the site of well-used and high-maintenance playgrounds. Taking all this into account, total annual operating and maintenance costs were now pegged at $15 million.

Having to raise $15 million a year was much harder than raising the $5 million estimated in the 2000 master plan, and this need drastically changed the revenue-generating options available. A conference center, some restaurants, and a banquet hall would not address the issue, and no one wanted to enlarge the commercial footprint to build more buildings and less park.

When confronted with this new reality, Wendy Leventer began to look at the capacity of different alternatives to generate revenue, the physical footprint of such uses, and their compatibility with a park. Trying to group many small uses together was

Figure 11-1. This map identifies the development sites on the park's periphery, including the maximum allowable height of buildings and the actual height as built or proposed. (Brooklyn Bridge Park Corporation.)

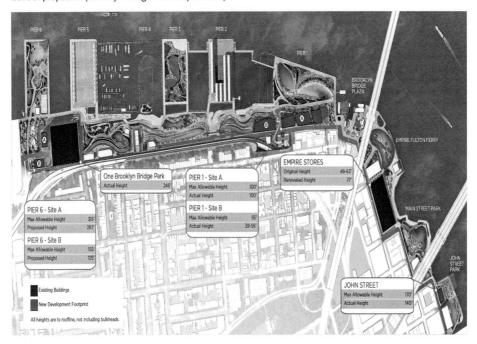

DEVELOPMENT SITES MAP

tricky and would require too much space at the expense of park use. Destination retail uses also required too much space and generated too much traffic. At the time, there was no market for office buildings at the park location, and in any event that use would have competed with Downtown Brooklyn and left the park empty at night. Parking could generate some revenue but in limited quantity, and it had to be carefully placed. Paid recreation and other usage fees would not have provided enough revenue and did not represent the kind of democratic values the park wanted to embody. One by one the alternatives fell away.

Although not favored by the Thirteen Guiding Principles, market-rate residential development produced the most reliable revenue stream, a fact recognized by the Buckhurst, Fish report from the Coalition's earliest days.[11] Moreover, housing produced the most efficient revenue—the most revenue from the smallest footprint—and it was compatible with the goal of enlivening the park and making it safe. If situated at the "urban junctions," the corners of the park that were its entrances, housing could also help connect the park to nearby neighborhoods. Michael Van Valkenburgh supported these design considerations. "People live at the edges of every other great park in New York City," he said. "It just makes sense."[12]

It even made sense to some of the people who already lived at the edge of the park. At a large meeting in Fulton Ferry Landing in 2003, Jim Moogan had discussed a hotel on Pier 1. Someone suggested housing as a better alternative, and a poll was taken; with twenty-five or thirty people in the room, everyone raised a hand for housing.[13]

After looking at all the options, Leventer, the design team, and the Brooklyn Bridge Park Development Corporation board came to the same conclusion: housing was the right choice.

In July 2005 the Brooklyn Bridge Park Development Corporation voted to adopt the general project plan and to certify the adequacy of the draft environmental impact statement, setting the stage for the last required public hearing. Included in the plan were four residential development sites (see Figure 11-1), one in the existing building at 360 Furman Street, a second on the upland of Pier 1 (which would include a hotel and residential condominiums), a third on what was called the John Street (or Con Edison) site at the northern end of the park,[14] and the fourth, consisting of two parcels south of 360 Furman Street on the uplands of Pier 6. Including those housing sites on the park plan unleashed a storm of controversy, which continued for many years.

At first glance, the idea of building housing adjacent to a park would not seem to be especially controversial. Most parks are surrounded by housing; parks are generally located close to where people live.[15] But housing was controversial, and there were many different reasons for that, although the different skeins of the argument were sometimes hard to distinguish amid all the shouting.

Some people insisted that, as a matter of principle, public parks should be purely public and publicly funded. In response to that argument, former commissioner of the New York City Department of Parks and Recreation Gordon Davis, who had struggled with poorly funded parks twenty years earlier, said, "Spare me the philosophy."[16] People who held this view were taking an "all or nothing" gamble, saying, in effect, that having no park at all was better than having one supported with dedicated revenues. Most people preferred a park.

Some old-timers may have opposed housing because that was the Port Authority's original plan. The defeat of that plan had been a signal accomplishment for the community. The very mention of housing seemed to echo that early plan and produced a kind of reflexive opposition. They could not settle for something they had fought so hard against long ago.

For others, the issue was gentrification. Market-rate housing on an attractive site meant housing for rich people, or at least people who seem rich. For people already in the community who were not rich, or did not feel that they were, it was easy to feel affronted by that. Even in neighborhoods that had been gentrified for a long time, well-to-do newcomers might be resented.

A related issue that had saliency was the notion that the housing would "privatize" the park. The idea seemed to be that the residents would become possessive of the park, agitating for rules and practices that would restrict use by the public.

Then there was the fact that market-rate housing represented an opportunity for some developer to make a profit. David Walentas was always a particular bête noire in the community, but few people like developers.

The argument against housing that was easiest to understand was the fact that maximizing the profit from housing—profit to the park, not just the developer—meant maximizing the size of the buildings. To minimize the amount of land used for development, it was necessary to build up, not out. Brooklyn Heights, Cobble Hill, and other nearby communities are historic districts whose character and charm are defined by small-scale structures and defended by zealous and effective community organizations. Large new buildings would affect the character of the neighborhoods, and tall ones especially would make their presence felt. Many residents of the brownstone communities had moved there because they seemed an exception to the general rule in New York that everything was always changing, and the direction of change was always bigger and taller. The buildings at Pier 6 were slated to be quite tall indeed, and undoubtedly many people opposed them for that reason alone.

The proposal to include the existing building at 360 Furman Street in the general project plan was the first concrete consequence of the decision to focus on housing. The Jehovah's Witnesses had sold the building at 360 Furman Street to the developer Robert Levine, reportedly for more than $200 million. Levine wanted to convert the structure to residential condominiums, but that required a zoning change. Ordinarily the request would require him to go through the Uniform Land Use Review Procedure, the city's long and complicated rezoning process.

The park had no part in Levine's transaction with the Witnesses, but the Park Development Corporation's parent, Empire State Development Corporation, had the unusual legal power to override local zoning by conducting an environmental review. Since the Park Development Corporation was embarking on its own environmental review for the park, there was an opportunity to include 360 Furman Street, which would both achieve Levine's objective and benefit the park. In exchange for participating in the park's review process, Levine would provide revenue for the park, something the park could not otherwise require him to do. Levine agreed to make a lump-sum payment to the park, and the city agreed to allow the park to collect and keep the property tax–like payments from the condominium owners.[17]

This arrangement was attractive to the park not only because it received revenue from Levine that was not otherwise available but also because some of the money would come quickly. This provided the resources to maintain the park in the early stages.

The building at 360 Furman provoked the least controversy. It is a massive structure, but it already existed and would remain no matter what. Still, it was the first test of the public's reaction to housing as a revenue source for the park, and some members of the public were critical.

The second development, the 1 Hotel and Pierhouse residential project on Pier 1, caused more problems. The heights of the building were somewhat limited by various restrictions, and their bulk was not completely out of scale with buildings previously on the site, but the project would obstruct views from Brooklyn Heights north of the Promenade[18] and from Fulton Ferry Landing.[19] It had always been understood that there would be development on Pier 1 and Pier 6 outside the protection of the view plane, but the reality was disconcerting. When construction of the buildings on Pier 1 reached the point where their bulk and height were apparent, the uproar was considerable, as we shall see.[20]

The John Street site was also allowed a taller structure, but it occupied a less conspicuous location at the very northern end of the park; perhaps because the building was remote from the brownstone communities and fit its context better, its construction proceeded largely without comment.

The housing sites that produced the loudest uproar were on Pier 6, near the southern entrance to the park and visible from the landmarked communities of Brooklyn Heights and Cobble Hill. They were slated for two buildings, one fifteen stories tall and another thirty stories. That these buildings would block the view from some parts of 360 Furman Street did not help. And it did not seem to matter that this problem had been fully disclosed in the prospectus given to every condominium buyer for 360 Furman.

These development sites would present different problems and be subject to their own disputes. But once the idea of housing was included in the park plan, the public did not wait for specific cases to react.

Many people believed that the underlying cost estimates for park maintenance and operation were made up. Speaking of Wendy Leventer, Councilman Ken Fisher said, "I could be wrong about this, but I don't think I am. I think she rigged the numbers."[21] Tony Manheim and Roy Sloane insisted that the basic maintenance costs, which they viewed as primarily policing the site and mowing the grass, would not exceed $5 million annually. Regardless of how much documentation was presented about the budget and how many experts discussed it, there was a tremendous upwelling of distrust. As it turned out, when the park neared completion the actual annual maintenance costs seemed likely to exceed $15 million.[22]

Sloane, a graphic artist, also engaged in a battle of renderings. Challenging the blocky, sketchy official drawings of how the proposed new buildings at Pier 6 would look from Atlantic Avenue near Hicks Street, Sloane pictured a building somewhat more slender and more articulated but taller than the park designers' version (see Figure 11-2).[23] Along with other residents of Cobble Hill, Sloane had long feared that Brooklyn Heights would receive the lion's share of benefits from the park. As long as he saw the benefits distributed more evenly among the local neighborhoods he had remained a champion of the park planning process, but he never supported housing. The fact that two substantial buildings were proposed at Cobble Hill's park entrance was clearly too much for him, even if there would also be housing opposite the North Heights and in DUMBO.

Conspiracy theories abounded. The Empire State Development Corporation was a development agency and always intended to build as much housing as it could; the developer Robert Levine was a friend of the governor and got some special deal. Some people claimed the rules had changed, that pier repairs were capital maintenance and the Thirteen Guiding Principles never intended to include pier repair in the self-sufficiency concept. Councilman David Yassky, in particular, thought the government should pay for that, and Tony Manheim thought the park should issue bonds for it. But government funding was unavailable, and bonds could not be issued unless there was a source of revenue for their repayment. As always, it was easy to suggest alternative plans or solutions if you did not have to prove or guarantee their feasibility.

Figure 11-2. Roy Sloane, a graphic artist living in Cobble Hill, produced a drawing showing the residential tower at Pier 6 dwarfing 360 Furman Street; the Brooklyn Bridge Park Development Corporation supplied its corrective, shown in the lines drawn over Sloane's rendering. (Roy Sloane and Brooklyn Bridge Park Corporation / *Brooklyn Heights Press*.)

Many community meetings later and after much study of the model and renderings and listening to Michael Van Valkenburgh and his partner Matthew Urbanski explain the new plan, most of the major groups came to the conclusion that there was so much to like, they could swallow any misgivings they had about the housing. A few came to think it was actually a good idea. The Brooklyn Heights Association somewhat cautiously came on board, though its president, then Nancy Bowe, warned that "this is still not a final plan," and raised objection to the thirty-story height of one of the buildings at Pier 6. The Fulton Ferry Landing Association supported the plan, as did other groups, and the *New York Times* gave its editorial endorsement.[24]

The recently renamed Conservancy, with the veteran planner Claude Shostal as its new codirector, both supported the plan and publicly rebutted criticisms of it.[25] Borough President Golden, State Senator Connor, and State Assemblywoman Millman also endorsed the plan.

The Cobble Hill Association was not reconciled. Murray Adams, its president, called the park proposal "a planned unit real estate development." Roy Sloane had come to support the Brooklyn Bridge Park Defense Fund, now led by Judi Francis of Willowtown.

The Brooklyn Bridge Park Defense Fund sued to block the park plan, contending that the government was in violation of the public trust doctrine by permitting luxury housing to be built in a park.[26] However, on November 27, 2006, New York Supreme Court Justice Lawrence S. Knipel rejected that argument by rejecting its very premise: the housing, he found, was not *in* the park. In his decision he wrote, "The parcels designated for residential/commercial development herein are not parkland, have never been parkland, and were never designated to become parkland. As such, they fall entirely outside the scope of our public trust doctrine."[27] The Appellate Division affirmed this decision on April 22, 2008.[28]

Thus, despite challenges, the Grand Bargain remained intact, and eventually many in the community accepted and even welcomed it. "The majority of the people in the neighborhood, and the majority of our members, have long ago understood that we need to have housing on the edges of the park, and that the area where the housing is will not be mapped parkland," Judy Stanton, the longtime executive director of the Brooklyn Heights Association, said in an interview.[29] The majority, perhaps, but not all. The park continued to move forward, but the controversy over housing would continue.[30]

TWELVE

AT LONG LAST, SHOVELS

Guys, we have to start building it!
—Regina Myer, third president of the Brooklyn Bridge Park
Development Corporation

Upon the certification of the final environmental impact statement, construction was legally authorized to begin. But a number of practical steps had to be taken before work could happen. The first task was acquiring control of the site from the Port Authority. While the agency was only too willing, its tenants were not. By then, all tenants were on month-to-month leases in anticipation of the coming park, and they had plenty of notice that they would have to leave. Strober Brothers, the lumber company occupying Pier 3, promised repeatedly an imminent departure but refused to go, costing the park corporation thousands of dollars in liability insurance. Several other firms, including a paper storage company and a U.S. Marshals tow pound, promised to leave when Strober did. American Stevedoring on Pier 6 made it clear they were not going anywhere.

After negotiations failed, Wendy Leventer was advised by counsel to serve the tenants with eviction notices. Strober Brothers fought the eviction, arguing that it could not find a comparable site and, as a local business, should be given deference over Brooklyn Bridge Park. The housing court judge who heard the case, Alice Fisher Rubin, who happened to be Ken Fisher's sister, agreed with Strober Brothers and gave them more time to relocate.[1] Political pressure on Strober Brothers eventually produced a settlement and the company's departure.

Meanwhile, American Stevedoring avoided being served with an eviction notice until a process server staked out the place at five in the morning. Nevertheless, the tenant refused to budge and made clear to Leventer she would be sorry if she continued to pressure them to go. Leventer—who had been threatened by a demolition contractor while in charge of 42nd Street Development Project (another subsidiary of the Empire State Development Corporation that had played a significant role in the revitalization of the area around Times Square), was undeterred; nonetheless, she was unable to dislodge the company during her tenure.

After the election of former attorney general Eliot Spitzer as governor in November 2006, as the days of the Pataki administration ticked down, Chairman Gargano decided it was more appropriate to allow the incoming governor to break ground on Brooklyn Bridge Park. Spitzer's arrival was awaited with great anticipation. He was well aware of the park through his friend and supporter Hank Gutman,[2] whom he had appointed to the Brooklyn Bridge Park Development Corporation board. Joanne Witty was assured by her friends on the Spitzer transition team that the Empire State Development Corporation's new downstate chairman, Patrick Foye,[3] had been fully briefed and was aware that the park was ready to go. Departing Chairman Gargano gave his final approval to the park plan before he left office.

Then nothing happened. Leventer, who had reported directly to the Empire State Development Corporation chairman, had almost no access to Foye, who, despite being the chairman of the Brooklyn Bridge Park Development Corporation, did not attend a single meeting of the board. Instead, a city official, Robert Lieber, who had replaced Dan Doctoroff as deputy mayor for economic development and consequently as the vice-chair of the Park Development Corporation, chaired the park board meetings, which continued to be held at the ESDC's midtown offices. No one could figure out who was in charge at ESDC. Avi Schick, a principal deputy to Spitzer at the attorney general's office, was named president of ESDC and quickly formed a competing center of power at the agency. From the outside it looked as if he and Foye were fighting over several significant projects, of which Brooklyn Bridge Park was only one.[4]

The gridlock at the Empire State Development Corporation was a source of frustration at City Hall, where the mayor's team was ready to go. They had already collaborated with Leventer to capture revenue from the 360 Furman Street conversion, which would allow construction of parkland before any new development would be needed. It was also known by then, at least among the government sponsors, that the park construction costs would far exceed original estimates; the city was ready to supply more capital when needed, but the state was silent.[5]

As city officials came to understand that they would ultimately bear the greatest burden of funding the park, they concluded that they had to be in charge as well, and City Hall began insisting on control of the project as a condition of further funding. As an interim measure, a new study of the future park governance structure was commissioned, and the city received two additional seats on the park board.

Wendy Leventer left the Brooklyn Bridge Park Development Corporation in March 2008 amid charges by park foes of "monumental waste" in the project, contending that she spent "more than $16 million in the last five years—more than it cost to build the Brooklyn Bridge in the 1880s,"[6] not adding that the cost of the bridge represented nineteenth-century dollars. Outrage was also expressed that so much money had gone into the planning team headed by Van Valkenburgh with no park to show for it. In fact, the fees were well under the guidelines for projects of this scale, and the park was actually ready for construction to begin.

During the summer of 2007, with the park still leaderless, an interim use proved a reminder of how welcome the park would be if only it could be built. The philanthropist and parks advocate Ann Buttenwieser had converted a barge into a floating pool reminiscent of wooden versions that had been seen in the city in the late 1800s, and she offered to moor it at what was to be Brooklyn Bridge Park.

A promising idea in theory, it was rejected by the state's Department of Environmental Conservation, which refused a permit on the ground that the barge would cast illegal shadows on the water and the fish beneath. Following complicated negotiations, a consent decree was signed. The "Floating Pool Lady," as the project was called, then moored at Pier 5 and a temporary "beach" was created next to it (see Figure 12-1).

Managed by the Conservancy, the pool immediately became a popular attraction despite the desolate surroundings. The Local Development Corporation, which was still in business, ran a free jitney service to the pool from Borough Hall to help bring in people from various parts of Brooklyn. By the terms of the consent decree, the pool could stay only for two months. At a cost of $1 million for staff, beach creation, fines, mooring preparation, and legal fees—all paid for by the park corporation—it offered an expensive but memorable experience. Many people for whom the pool represented their first use of Brooklyn Bridge Park went home as park advocates.[7]

At the same time, a transportation study of park access, with funds secured by Congresswoman Nydia Velázquez,[8] was proceeding with significant public input. The Local Development Corporation hired a team of traffic engineers to examine many of the transportation and access ideas that had raised concern earlier but had not been fully studied. After looking at pedestrian improvements, bicycle access, waterborne possibilities, bus routes, and vertical connections from Brooklyn Heights, the study concluded that there were significant opportunities to improve public access to the park. Moreover, the recommendations were relatively easy to implement without the expenditure of large capital sums. The study also proposed a possible vertical connection from the foot of Remsen Street just south of the Promenade instead of a Montague Street connection. Generally well received, many of the study's suggestions were ultimately adopted.[9]

Finally, after the project floundered for six months without a leader, Hank Gutman called some people he knew in the governor's office to help move along the appointment of the park's new boss, Regina Myer (see Figure 12-2). At the time Myer was the second in command at the city's Hudson Yards project. Previously she had been head of the City Planning Department's Brooklyn office, where she had overseen the rezoning of Downtown Brooklyn, and she was familiar with the strains among local communities and politicians regarding development. She also brought strong managerial skills coupled with a calm and unpretentious manner.

Although Myer was supported by the city, the Empire State Development Corporation subsidiary was still running the project, and Myer became a state employee. But the continuing morass at the ESDC stymied her initially, and she would have to wait for another change in state administration to achieve any traction. This came unexpectedly soon when Governor Spitzer resigned on March 12, 2008, and was replaced by his lieutenant governor, David Paterson, who eventually surrendered the project to city control.

Myer found an important ally in Carol Ash, the new state parks commissioner, who would stay on after Spitzer left.[10] As soon as she saw that Myer and the city were actually going to build the park, Commissioner Ash supported

Figure 12-2. Regina Myer decided to start park construction before all the financing was in place, and to focus first on the more accessible ends of the park, which established the place as a popular destination. (Eugene Keilin.)

the integration of Empire Fulton Ferry State Park into Brooklyn Bridge Park, a goal that had proved elusive under her predecessor, Bernadette Castro. In any case, Ash was not interested in hanging onto this small parcel; she had no money for it, and many other state parks called for attention. When the time came, Ash facilitated the transfer of the state property to the new entity that would eventually build and manage the park, the not-for-profit Brooklyn Bridge Park Corporation.[11]

Early in her tenure, Myer made two decisions that had a profound impact on the park's development. Rather than wait for full funding for the complete park, she chose to start building with the funds she had and to proceed in phases. The decision to build the park in phases may seem obvious in retrospect, but many did not expect construction to begin without funding commitments to build all or most of it. By then, the city was well aware that the park would cost much more than $150 million, and it committed another $75 million, with no strings attached, to get started.

At the same time that Myer was pushing ahead to build the park, she overruled her own consultants and put the brakes on the process of offering development sites to potential bidders. Because she already had revenues coming in from 360 Furman Street, the large Jehovah's Witnesses building that had been converted to condominiums and brought into the park plan, she could start building the park, knowing that she would have a flow of funds to pay for its operation when she needed them. The disposition of other development sites could wait until park development was further along and the market was stronger.

This approach made financial sense. As the park grew, its tangible existence would increase the value of the development parcels and thus increase the revenues they would produce to support the park. In practice, this approach also postponed the bidding process until real estate values recovered after the Great Recession of 2007–2009.[12]

In the meantime, Myer quietly told her team to put down their pencils and pick up their shovels. "Guys, we have to start building it!" she said. She decided that enough public groundbreaking ceremonies had been held without visible progress on the park. While much of the initial work, such as laying utilities and

Figure 12-3. Large underground tubes were part of the park's water retention system to collect and recycle water. (Brooklyn Bridge Park Corporation.)

storm water drainage systems (see Figure 12-3) and repairing marine structures, was invisible to the public, soon enough the shed on Pier 1 would be demolished (see Figure 12-4), and so would the Purchase Building.

To underscore the reality that the park was beginning to take shape, Myer announced a timetable for construction through the spring of 2011 that anticipated the opening of a significant park section at Pier 1 and a series of imaginative playgrounds at Pier 6, both developments at key park gateways. The decision to start at the gateways in Phase 1 was designed to show evenhandedness to two strong constituencies and to create an easily accessible and pleasing park experience to attract new visitors. The decision to build substantial portions of the park before beginning work on any of the new commercial developments was also meant to underscore the fact that the undertaking was a park, not a development project. Brooklyn Bridge Park was finally under way.

Figure 12-4. The clearing of Pier 1 in 2008 revealed an expanse of more than eleven acres of landfill on which the park designers could raise a hill and create a variety of park experiences.

THIRTEEN

THE POLITICS OF HOUSING

If the funding halts on this, it's going to be on your watch, so think about tumbleweeds and chain-link fences around Brooklyn Bridge Park.

—Robert Lieber, New York City deputy mayor,
to his counterparts in state government

Though the appeals in litigation challenging housing in the park had, for the time being, been exhausted, the opponents saw new hope for their cause as the sub-prime mortgage crisis exploded in 2008 and the real estate market was buffeted. The Cobble Hill Association, the Atlantic Avenue Betterment Association, and other groups renewed their attack on housing. But to prove they were not just anti-park, they looked for alternatives to generate revenue to cover park maintenance. Like many new political groups, they chose a name for themselves that claimed the high ground: "Campaign for Brooklyn Bridge Park."[1]

For help they turned to Fred Kent, founder of Project for Public Spaces and a critic of Brooklyn Bridge Park's design. He advocated a much more commercialized destination environment with lots of activities and food, similar to South Street Seaport or Chelsea Piers in Manhattan or Granville Island in Vancouver, all of which the community had examined during the planning process and rejected for not being enough like a park.[2]

With no acceptable alternatives to offer, the opponents tried their hand at politics as a way to influence the process. They focused on Marty Connor, their longtime state senator who had been so instrumental in obtaining state funding for the park and who supported housing as the principal revenue generator for its maintenance. In his previous election, Connor had faced a primary from a candidate backed by the Working Families Party. Although Connor won, the challenge revealed his vulnerability.

Unfortunately for Connor, Dorothy Siegel, a Cobble Hill resident, chair of the local Working Families Party club, and the party's treasurer, was a passionate member of the Campaign for Brooklyn Bridge Park. This time around, she convinced party leaders to make opposition to housing "in the park"[3] a litmus test for Working Families support. Connor would not agree to it, but another candidate, a protégé of Senator Charles Schumer named Daniel Squadron, did agree and subsequently won the Working Families Party endorsement. Squadron also ran for the Democratic Party's nomination. In the Democratic primary held in September 2008 Connor lost the election to Squadron, and the Campaign for Brooklyn Bridge Park took credit for his victory. Although there were many other explanations for the election's outcome,[4] it no longer seemed safe for a local politician to support housing in or near Brooklyn Bridge Park.

Meanwhile, at the state level, Eliot Spitzer had resigned as governor and was replaced in March 2008 by Lieutenant Governor David Paterson. Six months later, in September, Lehman Brothers, the nation's fourth-largest investment bank, filed for bankruptcy. Weeks later, on October 3, the Troubled Asset Relief Program was signed into law by President George W. Bush and the federal government began taking significant action to stabilize the country's financial system. The Dow Jones Industrial Average Index declined about 20 percent from October 2007 to June 2008; the country was officially in the grip of the Great Recession.

Long before the recession, the economy in upstate New York had been in decline, and the state budget, always adopted late, had become an annual embarrassment. Unlike New York City, which routinely issues bonds for capital spending, New York State is severely restricted in the issuance of bonds[5] and often funds capital projects out of scarce tax revenues. Even when Governor Pataki made the initial financial commitment for the park, he did so not from the state budget but from the Port Authority. Once that money was spent, it was hard for the state to come up with more.

In contrast, the city's economy held up fairly well, as the financial sector survived and was soon paying hefty bonuses again amid much public anger. The city had been well and conservatively managed by Mayor Bloomberg and had a solid credit rating for its bonds. As Brooklyn Bridge Park required more capital to keep construction moving, the city had committed much more than its original $65 million. It continued to push the state to contribute more or to give up control of the park, but it was tough to find anyone on the state side with the desire and authority to negotiate.

With the arrival of Governor David Paterson, Deputy Mayor Robert Lieber saw an opportunity and proposed a strategy: "Why don't we offer to step up and pay the funding, make the commitments to the funding, but we'll do so only if we can have control?" Lieber also painted the picture of what would happen if the state did not agree: "If the funding halts on this, it's going to be on your watch, so think about tumbleweeds and chain-link fences around Brooklyn Bridge Park."[6]

It took the help of New York Assembly Speaker Sheldon Silver and Secretary to the Governor Larry Schwartz—who saw the sense of off-loading joint projects that the state had neither the interest nor the money to complete—to push things along. According to Peter Davidson, executive director of the Empire State Development Corporation under Paterson, and, as it happened, a resident of Brooklyn Heights, "We just hit a perfect convergence of events that allowed it to happen," by which he meant that "nobody had their back up against the wall."[7]

With all egos at least temporarily in check, Davidson recalled thinking, "Look, let's make it work for the park and let's make it work for everybody if the state can get comfortable with giving up control of the process, which I thought was the right thing to do as a citizen, not necessarily as a state employee."[8] Lieber, his negotiating counterpart, credited Davidson with bringing a stabilizing influence to the Empire State Development Corporation, which Lieber described as a "can't-do, rather than a can-do, organization."[9]

As part of a larger arrangement between the city and the state, the city would agree to take over Brooklyn Bridge Park and Governors Island while the state would remain responsible for the Convention Center Development Corporation.[10] This deal was also a tacit acknowledgment that the governance problems associated with multi-government ventures should not be underestimated.[11]

As the city-state negotiations unfolded, Senator Squadron injected his concern about housing as the financing mechanism for the park. As long as a subsidiary of the state's Empire State Development Corporation was building the park, each development deal had to be approved by the state's Public Authorities Control Board. The board was created to provide oversight of the state's public authorities, one of which was ESDC. The board had five members appointed by the governor: one representing the governor, and one each representing the majority and minority in the Assembly and the Senate. As a Democratic state senator, Squadron could influence several of those votes. Once the park switched to city control, however, different rules might apply. Squadron had a big stake in preserving his influence and demonstrating to his new constituents his ability to follow through on promises.

While the city and state were negotiating, Lieber was also meeting with Squadron. Lieber said of their sessions, "I thought Daniel was smart enough to understand the math, so we sat down with him and opened up the kimono and said, 'Here's how we look at this.'" Referring to Seth Pinsky, then president of the city's Economic Development Corporation, Lieber continued, "Having Seth at the helm of EDC, with his experience and his knowledge and his math skills, was huge because he helped develop the model for the capital and the operating plan for Brooklyn Bridge Park and sat with me to go through it with Squadron."[12]

Lieber's sense was that Squadron understood the reality of the numbers but "wasn't going to march out there and take the bullets himself." At the same time, Lieber said, "It was important enough for the Bloomberg administration to make sure we continued and were able to deliver on these park plans."[13] A deal was struck that let Squadron record a win and the city gain control of the park.

On March 10, 2010, the city issued a press release with the headline, "Mayor Bloomberg, Governor Paterson, Senator Squadron, and Assembly Member Millman Announce Agreement on Development, Funding, and Governance of Brooklyn Bridge Park." The announcement reflected two separate "agreements" dated March 8, 2010, one a "term sheet" between the city, the state, and Empire State Development Corporation containing the terms of restructuring Brooklyn Bridge Park, and the other a memorandum of understanding among the city, Squadron, and Millman, the provisions of which were conditioned on approval by the Public Authorities Control Board and completion of the restructuring outlined in the term sheet.

The restructuring document contemplated the creation of a new city-controlled not-for-profit corporation to continue planning, constructing, maintaining, and operating Brooklyn Bridge Park. In addition, through leases and subleases, the city entity would control all of the property within the general project plan and be assigned by the old Empire State Development Corporation subsidiary all the revenues from development parcels.

The board of the not-for-profit would comprise seventeen members: the mayor would choose nine, the governor four (at least two of whom had to be community members), and the Brooklyn borough president, a City Council member designated by the Council speaker, the state senator for the 25th District, and the State Assembly member for the 52nd District one each.[14] Among those named to the new board were seven local residents—Joanne Witty, Hank Gutman, and David Offensend (all veterans from the previous LDC and park development board); Peter Aschkenasy (also from the park development board); Marty Connor (appointed by

Borough President Marty Markowitz); and Steven Cohen and Stephen Merkel (appointed by the governor). In the wake of Connor's recent loss to Squadron, Markowitz's appointment of Connor signaled his strong support for the park and its financial model. The city confirmed its previous financial commitment to the park of $139 million, agreed to fund an additional $55 million, and committed to complete the park.

The memorandum of understanding signed by Squadron and Millman was more complicated. First, it promised yet another study of park financing alternatives. A board committee, called the Committee on Alternative to Housing, was created. The mayor had three representatives on the committee, the governor had one, and the state senator and the Assembly member had one each.

Limitations were imposed on what could be considered an alternative source of revenue. It could not displace revenue to which the city would otherwise be entitled, and the timing and level of risk of the alternative revenue had to be consistent with the revenue projected from the development sites. The memorandum laid out a specific process for the timing and number of public meetings as well as the presentation, revision, and adoption of the study recommendations.

Finally, the agreement gave the state senator and the Assembly member a veto over any development on the John Street[15] and the Pier 6 development sites. The memorandum protected the city from having to fund above the $139 million level if the revenue from those development sites was compromised by a veto.

This might have seemed a high price to pay to prevent Senator Squadron and Assemblywoman Millman from opposing the transfer of Brooklyn Bridge Park to city control, especially since it had the potential to sabotage the park by undercutting its financial basis. But in Lieber's view, the study of alternative revenue sources was not likely to turn up any significant new funding streams, so it was really political cover he was willing to provide. Little did he know that neither the study nor subsequent agreements with the city would satisfy Squadron for long. Fighting City Hall over housing in the park, for Squadron, became the political gift that kept on giving.

While Squadron and Millman sought to limit maintenance funds available to the park, they also had a list of park projects they insisted the city pursue: a bubble over Pier 5's soccer fields, a skating rink, a bridge at Squibb Park, tennis courts and community space at a maintenance and operation building, and a floating pool that would have cost at least $10 million to create. Some of these were planned anyway; some could not be done, but the two officials got credit for the effort.[16]

The officials also insisted on the creation of a new "Community" (instead of "Citizens") Advisory Council to the new Brooklyn Bridge Park Corporation, and they heavily influenced its membership. State Senator Squadron in particular had been supported by many people who were unhappy with some of the park's fundamental decisions and some who were opposed to the park itself. His victory seemed to vindicate those views. Not surprisingly, some of these people were named to the new Community Advisory Council and used their new role to advance their views. Relations between the Community Advisory Council and the park corporation, difficult from the beginning, did not improve with age.

In accordance with the agreement, the new Brooklyn Bridge Park Corporation put out a request for proposals and subsequently hired a California firm, Bay Area Economics, to take a fresh look at alternatives to housing. The study stretched over six months and involved three public hearings in which testimony was taken, plus many smaller listening sessions, solicitation of written comments, a draft report, and a final report.

After identifying thirty-six ideas, the consultants helped the Committee on Alternatives to Housing hone the list to those with the greatest revenue potential. Nine alternative revenue sources were studied in detail, of which only four were found to have revenue-generating capacity that met the necessary criteria, and all of those combined had the potential to provide less than $1 million annually.

The most controversy surrounded the idea of capitalizing on the expected disposition of Jehovah's Witness properties. Because these sales would transfer the properties from ownership by a religious body—where they were tax-exempt—to private, profit-making, and ultimately tax-paying hands, they were seen by many as a potential source of substantial revenue for the park and, thus, as the silver bullet to kill the planned Pier 6 project.

The Bay Area Economics study did not mollify Squadron or his supporters who had believed that the way to avoid housing lay in the Watchtower properties, but the majority of the Committee on Alternatives to Housing found that premise too speculative to meet the park's needs.

The most serious problem with the Squadron proposal was that the Watchtower was an independent entity, and no one knew if any rezoning transaction would be required by a buyer of its property to facilitate the capture of revenue for the park. The park, on the other hand, was under construction and would need revenue for maintenance as each new section was completed. How to reconcile these different interests? A compromise, of course, one of great value to both the city and the senator.

A new memorandum of understanding was negotiated and signed on August 1, 2011. In it, the city agreed to accept as valid $750,000 worth of alternative revenues identified by the BAE study; to permit a formula trade-off between the height of buildings on Pier 6 and any Watchtower buildings that were rezoned for residential use prior to December 31, 2013; to reduce the size of the development on John Street by four stories; and to reaffirm its commitment to continue building the park, including pursuing the possibility of a list of park amenities contained in the previous agreement.

In exchange, the senator and Assembly member gave up their veto authority over any residential development on John Street and Pier 6. This arrangement seemed to work for the time being, and Squadron had delivered something to most of his supporters.[17] At the same time, the city was free to proceed with development on the Pier 1 and the John Street sites and had a binding time frame for Pier 6.

However, that would not be the last time the politics of housing would have an impact on the park.

FOURTEEN
THE PARK BEGINS TO MATERIALIZE

We were like kids in a divorce.

—Regina Myer, president of the Brooklyn Bridge Park Corporation

By the autumn of 2009 hills and winding paths were rising on Pier 1. Bulldozers, backhoes, and cranes were busy everywhere. In addition to the contoured landscape appearing on Pier 1 (see Figures 14-1 and 14-2), an unusual spiral pool flume was under construction at the base of Pier 2 (see Figure 14-3), and work was rapidly proceeding on a series of playgrounds on Pier 6 with names like Swing Valley and Water Lab.[1] The work, which also included sand volleyball courts on Pier 6 and a playground on Pier 1, was aimed to draw visitors to either end of the stretch of piers as soon as possible, with the area in between left for the next stage when more money would become available.

During the same time, State Parks Commissioner Carol Ash worked closely with Myer to negotiate the donation to the park of a historic carousel owned by David and Jane Walentas. Ash warned against taking on donations that came with operating expenses. This advice proved important to Myer, and she was able to secure from Jane and David Walentas a commitment for the long-term operating costs of the carousel and a substantial sum to upgrade the surrounding park.[2]

Exactly where in the park the carousel would be situated became yet another issue. David Walentas wanted it in DUMBO, where he owned much of the adjacent property and where the couple could see it from their apartment at One Main Street. Some members of the community wanted it on Pier 6, at the other end of the park. Van Valkenburgh, the park's designer, resolved the dispute, making the carousel the focal point of new parkland around the historic warehouses in DUMBO and drawing visitors to the northern part of the park.[3]

Once the city and the state became embroiled in negotiating the transfer of the park to the city, Myer and her team were trying to do many things at once—oversee construction, manage operations, develop con-

Figure 14-1. A bulldozer pushes dirt in October 2009 as the major hill on Pier 1 takes shape.

nections with groups to partner in programming the park—all the while shuttling back and forth between meetings with the two governments that would determine their fate. "We were like kids in a divorce," Myer remembered.[4] She meant that her project was the subject of discussion but she and her team were not always invited to participate. Nonetheless things worked out. "When we did raise the concern about what was best for the park to the city," said David Lowin, director of real estate for the park, "they were responsive."[5]

The transfer to city control was finally accomplished by creating a new not-for-profit corporation called Brooklyn Bridge Park Corporation, with the mayor appointing a majority of the directors. The decision to create a freestanding park corporation was a matter of substance as well as style: the park might have been folded into the city's Department of Parks and Recreation, either during construction or once it was operating. If it had, the design would surely have been different, as would the programming and operation, and maintaining the dedicated revenue stream that was designed to distinguish the park from other city parks would have been impossible. In the end, the choice seemed to reflect the Bloomberg administration's confidence in nontraditional models and confidence in Myer and her staff.

By then Myer had developed a good relationship with Borough President Marty Markowitz, who promptly gave the park $5 million in a public show of support. Myer also spent time engaging others in the city government who could help. City Hall ran interference on projects that required interagency coordination. For example, she got help in making the park entrance at the foot of Old Fulton Street more generous and welcoming by negotiating reduced parking for the River Café (a venerable establishment on a barge moored just south of the Brooklyn Bridge) and realigning Water Street and making the foot of Old Fulton Street more pedestrian friendly, actions that required coordination among the city's departments of parks, transportation, and others.[6]

Myer and her small staff donned their hard hats and gave countless public tours of the construction site. Most people had never visited the site or had done so when the sheds were still up and it was impossible to feel the full impact of

Figure 14-2. The platform on Pier 1 was removed to reveal the piles that would form one border of a salt marsh. The balance of Pier 1 is seen well under construction. (Alex MacLean.)

the connection with the water. The tours kept people engaged and eager to see what was coming next. They opened up a completely new sense of what was to come.

Finally, on March 22, 2010, Pier 1 opened.[7] Mayor Bloomberg stood with Governor Paterson, Borough President Markowitz, and other dignitaries as the Fort Hamilton High School Band paraded before them. "Thirteen months ago," Regina Myer said to warm applause, "this was an abandoned parking lot, the remains of an active port."[8] Bill de Blasio, the newly elected public advocate, called the park "New York's front yard," and Markowitz, never to be outdone for Brooklyn superlatives, called it "Eden on the East River."[9] David Lowin, the park's director of real estate, recalled, "The weirdest part about opening it was not closing the gates when we left because the park was actually open."[10]

The Pier 6 playgrounds opened on a sparkling June 5, thronged by children and their parents. With the help of funds from the Port Authority and former City Council member Bill de Blasio, a dock at Pier 6 for free weekend ferry service to Governors Island was added, thereby getting people on the water and creating synergy between the two parks (see Figure 14-4). That summer the Conservancy relocated the movies to Pier 1, and the old Empire Fulton Ferry State Park closed for renovations and the construction of the carousel pavilion. Finally, the park worked closely with the Department of Transportation and its own construction team to create a temporary greenway, a task that was difficult and expensive but another big boost to the project. For the first time, bikers and walkers could move directly between greenway sections north and south of the park.

With the opening of the park, money was needed for operations. As Myer had anticipated, that funding came from 360 Furman Street, which was already in place and making payments to the park. "The fact that we were able to get operations underway with no government money was pretty incredible," Myer remem-

Figure 14-4. From the air, the playgrounds on Pier 6—Swing Valley, Sandbox Village, and Slide Mountain—can be seen adjacent to the Governors Island Ferry. (Alex MacLean.)

bered with pride.[11] And Lowin said, "You don't build development first and then park for all sorts of reasons." But, he added, "If you're going to have park first, you need to have revenue to support it. Having a couple of years of 360 Furman–generated revenues before we even had any park to spend it on gave us this cushion that allowed us to have a financial model that worked."[12]

It proved of long-term benefit to the park that both the park and the organization that would run it were being built at the same time. The new city organization, the Brooklyn Bridge Park Corporation, was still planning and building the park, and it was now managing it as well. The phasing of construction allowed everyone to learn as things went along, to see how spaces in the park were being used and adjust their thinking about what was needed. It was not like constructing a building and simply turning it over to the client.

The fact that the same organization was both building and managing the project encouraged an even stronger effort to ensure that the park would be well designed. "We all were working both from our hearts and brains. Of course, we wanted to get the engineering right, and stay on budget, but we were also passionate about what it would look like and how it would feel and how it would be used," Myer said. "We didn't just want a park that people would like; we wanted a park they would love."[13]

Meanwhile, work had begun to turn Pier 5 into a two-hundred-thousand-square-foot active recreation space that, in different configurations, could hold several fields for soccer, lacrosse, rugby, flag football, and Ultimate Frisbee. The playing surface would be an innovative artificial turf with an underlying shock pad made of sand and coconut fibers. Sail-like triangles on poles were devised to shade spectators from what could be brutal sunlight, and lights on the poles made night games possible. In addition to a thirty-foot-wide promenade around the perimeter of the pier, fishing off the end would be encouraged by the placement of large sinks to clean whatever was caught, although signs would warn that the catch might not be safe to eat.

Work was also proceeding on the inland side of Pier 5, where the platform connecting the pier to land had been removed, leaving only bridge-like attachments at the pier's north and south ends. Having discovered that most of the material holding up the platform had eroded, the designers decided to create a freestanding peninsula and walkway with water flowing under it. The "Picnic Peninsula" was to have benches, umbrellas, and charcoal grills, providing a practical, unusual, and quickly popular spot for families.

Without trees a park is hardly a park. A temporary nursery on the Pier 3 upland had been transferred to the pier platform itself when work on the upland began. Pier 1 was well forested by 2011, but many other sections remained to be planted. Michael Van Valkenburgh had toured the East River to see which kinds of trees flourished, and his selection for Brooklyn Bridge Park included Kentucky coffees, honey locusts, catalpas, magnolias, lindens, sweet gums, serviceberries, London planes, and various species of oak. Many of these would grow to be "massive," he predicted, doing more than any other feature to transform the look and character of this once-commercial waterfront.[14]

In September 2011 the old Empire Fulton Ferry Landing State Park was reopened, along with Jane's Carousel. It was not long before *Time Out New York Kids* named the carousel one of the city's fifty best family attractions.[15] In prior years the carousel had been housed in a ground floor space in DUMBO where passersby could look at it but not ride on it. To see it in the custom-designed Jean Nouvel enclosure near the water offered a new perspective; to ride on it, while harbor and park and bridges and the Manhattan skyline seemed to whirl around you, was an exhilarating experience. Although critics of its placement continued to snipe, young users were delighted, and even some of the opponents could be seen enjoying the carousel with children, grandchildren, or friends.

By now the second agreement with Senator Squadron had been signed, and a request for proposals was issued for housing and a hotel on Pier 1. This would be the first real test of the real estate market's appetite for Brooklyn Bridge Park. It proved voracious. Two packed-house briefing sessions for bidders were held at Bargemusic, the converted barge used for chamber music concerts that was moored at Fulton Ferry Landing. A joint venture of Toll Brothers and Starwood Hotels was ultimately selected to build an integrated hotel and pair of residential buildings along the uplands of Piers 1 and 2. The financial package, calling for $27 million up front, annual payments of $3.3 million, and provision of public restrooms, and an acre of parkland, altogether had a value of almost $120 million. This was a gratifying result in itself and a powerful sign that the other sites would also meet the park corporation's expectation and needs. The park had passed an important milestone.[16]

For a brief moment in the spring of 2012 it looked as though the lost indoor recreation center might have a new lease on life in the park. A wealthy bicycle-racing enthusiast, Joshua P. Rechnitz, offered to build a $40 million facility housing a velodrome (a bicycle racing venue) that could also be used for other indoor recreation. The facility would have replaced an existing building on the site just south of Montague Street. Operating funds for ten years would be part of the package. The plan was supported by Senator Squadron and Community Advisory Council member Roy Sloane, but there were many who were skeptical or even opposed to the project including many Brooklyn Heights residents. After the high floodwaters of Superstorm Sandy, the tricky design challenge of fitting in all the activities people desired and keeping the building height under the view plane proved complicated and expensive, and the donor withdrew to look elsewhere for a more accommodating site.

In the meantime, Myer sought to bring to life available parts of the park while construction continued apace. She began a partnership with a group called Celebrate Brooklyn! that brought music and dancing to Pier 1. Jazzmobile held performances, and the City Parks Foundation brought the Metropolitan Opera to the harbor lawn on Pier 1. One summer, Brooklyn Flea, a hip Brooklyn flea market, set up shop under the Brooklyn Bridge, drawing yet another audience.

The Brooklyn Bridge Park Conservancy, with Nancy Webster as its executive director, presented a program of public activities that included free movies in the summer as well as readings, classes in yoga and Pilates, public tours, and educational programs for both children and adults. Unfinished though it might be, the park was very much in use.

FIFTEEN
DEEP DIFFERENCES OVER A NINETEENTH-CENTURY RELIC

Within the next ten years, if it wasn't taken care of, that baby was coming down.

—Samara Daly, on the need to preserve the Tobacco Warehouse

Over the three decades of the park's gestation, many issues arose that dominated the saga for a time, then were resolved and laid to rest, becoming a part of its history. One such issue was the controversy over the Tobacco Warehouse.

The Tobacco Warehouse was built in the 1870s and used for the collection of tax revenue on tobacco brought into New York for processing. Made of brick and timber, it stood with many other post–Civil War structures along the East River waterfront in Brooklyn. Originally a five-story rectangular warehouse, it was later reduced to a trapezoid when the Brooklyn Bridge was built and New Dock Street was created just to the south (see Figure 15-1). Later still, it suffered the loss of three stories. Nevertheless, in 1974 the Tobacco Warehouse was placed on the National Register of Historic Places.

Through the efforts of local residents and preservationists and over the objections of Con Edison, by then the owner of the Tobacco Warehouse, Empire Stores, and surrounding property, in 1977 the New York City Landmarks Commission created the Fulton Ferry Historic District. Within two years the New York State Legislature appropriated funds to acquire the Con Edison property and create Empire Fulton Ferry State Park. Whether the Tobacco Warehouse and Empire Stores were actually thought to be parkland is unknown, but a chain-link fence was erected to keep out the public.

Years of neglect followed, and by the time the Local Development Corporation was about to begin planning for Brooklyn Bridge Park in 1999 the Tobacco Warehouse roof had caved in, and trees and weeds were growing inside the structure. After some bricks fell to the adjoining sidewalk, the regional state parks commissioner at that time, James Moogan, fearing that the building was in danger of

142

collapse, contacted the New York City Department of Buildings to inquire about condemnation. This triggered a chain of events that led to protests by local advocates and preservationists. State Senator Martin Connor eventually obtained the funds to provide scaffolding and to stabilize the building.

Once stabilized, the building was secured with new iron window gates and remained closed to the public for several years. Access to the building was not safe, and using it was not legal.

During the park planning process there was much discussion of how the Tobacco Warehouse—which by then consisted of a walled rectangular space and a smaller triangle, all roofless, with an uneven concrete floor—might be used. The overwhelming sentiment was for a walled garden within stabilized walls and a complementary use such as a small café. That concept was embodied in the 2000 illustrative master plan. The 2005 concept plan, based on further public input, expanded the potential use somewhat, suggesting that "the restored shell of the former tobacco warehouse may house a walled garden, café, or space for community and arts groups." The final environmental impact statement also suggested that

"the restored exterior shell of the former Tobacco Warehouse, which may require other improvements, could house a walled garden, café or space for arts groups."[1]

As planning progressed, State Parks Commissioner Bernadette Castro was willing to consider interim use of the Tobacco Warehouse. The Local Development Corporation commissioned a study of possible cultural uses for the building, which concluded that a covered space was necessary.[2] The architect, preservationist, and former Brooklyn Heights Association president Fred Bland produced drawings of a possi-

Figure 15-1. A rare photograph shows the Tobacco Warehouse with its original five stories. Behind it, the Purchase Building is shown under construction. (Berenice Abbott / Museum of City of New York.)

ble permanent tent structure that would sit inside the walls without compromising the historic structure. When that idea proved too expensive, a commercially available tent was investigated, and funds were secured in 2002 from the City Council and Borough President Markowitz to pay for it. Open-air events held little potential for revenue because of the risk of weather, but with a tent private events and ticketed events became possible.[3]

At first it seemed that the Conservancy and the not-for-profit theater company St. Ann's Warehouse would team up to present programming in the tent.[4] But the Conservancy decided to go it alone. Marianna Koval, executive director of the Conservancy, and Susan Feldman, founder and artistic director of St. Ann's, both remember the decision as contentious and emotional.[5] The breakup left the two parties at odds with each other, and the bad feelings would reverberate into the future.

The Conservancy presented a proposal to Commissioner Castro whereby the Conservancy alone would manage both public and private (revenue-generating) events. The proceeds would be split, with the state's share going into maintaining Empire Fulton Ferry State Park and the Conservancy's share into the direct costs of public programming.[6] The venue proved attractive for corporate events and other private parties, and the revenue represented a welcome windfall for cash-strapped state parks.

But there were others with programming ideas for the Tobacco Warehouse. St. Ann's Warehouse, renewing its interest, and the Brooklyn Academy of Music wanted to use the location for a summer residence. The two would be funded by the Independence Community Foundation, a respected funder affiliated with Brooklyn's Independence Savings Bank. The Conservancy and the Brooklyn Heights Association immediately opposed this proposal as a "commercial" and "private" use of the space, although both of the potential users were not-for-profit arts organizations and the Conservancy had been renting the space for commercial events. The two cultural groups and their funder beat a hasty retreat.

Some groups thought there was too much private use of the Tobacco Warehouse already. In 2007, local community groups and potential users of the space wrote to the new state parks commissioner, Carol Ash, complaining of too much emphasis on private, money-making events under the Conservancy's administration and not enough access for other nonprofit users.[7] Conservancy Executive Director Koval thought the instigator of the letter had been David Walentas, the Coalition's old nemesis.[8]

Ultimately, Commissioner Ash revoked the Conservancy's agreement, cut back on private events, and provided access to a wider range of users,[9] earning the enmity of Koval. St. Ann's Warehouse did produce a summertime performance of a Polish-language *Macbeth* in 2009.

The tent was not a permanent solution—it fell apart a few years later—but its existence and use had established the value of a protected venue. It had sheltered everything from local exhibiters at Brooklyn Designs to music and dance programs for children to private events that produced revenue for the Conservancy and the state park. The idea of putting a roof on the Tobacco Warehouse and using it for a performance space had been introduced. The next logical step was to work out the physical and financial requirements of doing something lasting.

The physical requirements were daunting. The tent had proved the wisdom of covering the space for all-weather use, but it also demonstrated the need to improve the drainage when the weather turned bad. As Samara Daly, who worked for the Conservancy and later for the speaker of the City Council, observed, "Even the most magnificent tent wasn't going to support something long-term." Moreover, the building itself required serious work. "Within the next ten years," Daly said, "if it wasn't taken care of, that baby was coming down."[10]

It took less than ten years to solve the problem. In 2010, long-term use of the Tobacco Warehouse received fresh scrutiny. By then, the city had taken control of the Brooklyn Bridge Park project. The city administration had evidenced its commitment to public art and culture and was eager to move forward with such programs in the park.

In particular, the city urged park president Regina Myer to request proposals for the adaptive reuse of the Tobacco Warehouse to "create a year-round facility to house cultural, educational, and/or civic and community uses with a focus on performing arts." Since there was no money in the park's budget to renovate the empty shell or maintain it, a further objective of the request was to identify an organization capable of doing that.[11]

Several meetings were held at Borough Hall with representatives of the Brooklyn Heights Association and other community groups to discuss the future of the Tobacco Warehouse. These meetings were heated and reflected disagreement within the community about how the space should be used and what physical changes to it should be permitted. A variety of opinions were expressed, but there was a broad division between those who wanted to preserve the Tobacco Warehouse as a roofless ruin and those who supported a permanent enclosure.

In the end there was a compromise of sorts. A request for proposals was published that contemplated a closed structure but required users to allow some elements to remain uncovered, to stay within the existing walls, and to guarantee good care for the historic building. The request for proposals also cited the desirability of both free public programming that would serve different users and public access to the building.

Only two bidders vied to be the prime tenant. St. Ann's Warehouse again renewed its interest, and a second proposal came from Lava Love, a local not-for-profit dance company. After extensive interviews, the Brooklyn Bridge Park Corporation signed a conditional letter of designation with St. Ann's Warehouse, which undertook to raise all of the project's funding. The conditional agreement contained timelines for reaching the fund-raising goals,[12] completing an architectural design, and meeting the requirements for historic preservation.

A month later the Brooklyn Heights Association, the Fulton Ferry Landing Association, and the New York Landmarks Conservancy filed a lawsuit in federal court accusing the National Park Service and the Brooklyn Bridge Park Development Corporation of conspiring to remove the Tobacco Warehouse from protection as parkland in violation of federal law.[13] Simultaneously, the Brooklyn Heights Association and the Fulton Ferry Landing Association filed a lawsuit in state court alleging that officials of the New York State Office of Parks, Recreation, and Historic Preservation had surreptitiously conspired with officials of the Brooklyn Bridge Park Corporation to "de-park" the Tobacco Warehouse under state law.[14]

There had been no advance discussion of the issues raised by the plaintiffs, and the litigation came as a surprise to the defendants. Many in the community were also surprised, not only by the fact that the Brooklyn Heights Association led the litigation but also by the tone of the action. Lawsuits always have an edge to them, but the papers in this case seemed to go out of their way to include allegations of willful and nefarious behavior. Public agencies and officials were accused repeatedly of acting secretly and improperly, of lying and of engaging in what amounted to a conspiracy among St. Ann's, developer David Walentas, the park corporation, and other government agencies. The New York State Parks Department was accused of "pursuing a secret agenda" on behalf of "private, commercial interests," having "knowingly made material misstatements of fact" and shuttering the Tobacco Warehouse "as part of a secret ploy to privatize it." Regina Myer and Carol Ash, the state parks commissioner, were alleged to have had "improper communications" with an unnamed private developer (apparently David Walentas) who was said to control St. Ann's.

The legal issues in the lawsuit concerned the permitted uses of public property, but the papers transformed the case into an argument about ethics and morality. The allegations sounded personal, and the defendants took them personally.

Park corporation board members Joanne Witty, Hank Gutman, and David Offensend immediately resigned from the BHA, but they were not alone in their reaction to the litigation.[15] Why had not the BHA tried talking before it went to court? And why was the language so inflammatory? Many could not understand how things could have gone so far off track so suddenly.

As it turned out, it was not so sudden after all. The seeds of the litigation had been sown years before, and the reasons to support it varied.

Some people were attached to the romance of the Tobacco Warehouse as a ruin.[16] They had lost that fight in the discussions at Borough Hall, but they had not given up on it.

Others believed that proper process had been violated. The complaint argued that because a map had been submitted in connection with an application for certain state and federal funds, the buildings had become protected parkland. The map indicated that an entire block adjacent to the state park was included in the park, encompassing the Tobacco Warehouse. If the property had become protected parkland, there was a procedure for changing its status; however, the plaintiffs said the proper procedure had not been followed and, indeed, that government bureaucrats had contrived to make the change with suspicious secrecy.

In response, state officials claimed that the federal money had not been used on the Tobacco Warehouse and, in any event, that the property should never have been included on the map. They pointed out that the same map and the same argument also encompassed the Empire Stores (always scheduled for private development) and two other buildings that were already privately owned at the time and could not possibly have been included in the park. In essence, they said, they were correcting an obvious error in paperwork.[17]

For some people, though, the motivation to oppose the plan was the widespread belief that David Walentas would somehow benefit from St. Ann's securing a home in the Tobacco Warehouse and that his influence must have played a role in the selection. Community opposition to Walentas was nothing new, but it was heightened at this time because of opposition to his plan for a large building close the Brooklyn Bridge. The Dock Street Building, as it was called, was eventually modified to move its tallest section back from the bridge and to incorporate a middle school, but the Brooklyn Heights Association vigorously opposed the building and was disappointed that it would be built at all.

By this time, Marianna Koval had left her position as executive director of the Brooklyn Bridge Park Conservancy, but she was still very interested in the Tobacco Warehouse, perhaps as a continuation of the Conservancy's multiyear struggle with St. Ann's over control of the property. In an interview, she recalled that she had played a role in finding the documents that were the basis of the lawsuit, and she suggested, "People didn't like David Walentas and believed that there were quiet deals being made with Walentas for a whole series of things."[18] The Conservancy and Koval had had a well-known running feud with Walentas, too.

The Brooklyn Heights Association had always associated St. Ann's Warehouse with Walentas because he was a member of its board of directors and had provided free space to the theater in one of his warehouses when it was forced to leave its original home in the Church of St. Ann's. That warehouse would have to be demolished to make way for the new Dock Street Building, thereby dispossessing St. Ann's, so a connection was drawn among St. Ann's, Walentas, and the Tobacco Warehouse. The Brooklyn Heights Association also assumed, incorrectly, that Walentas was providing the bulk of funds required to carry out St. Ann's plans for its new home.[19]

The plaintiffs' lawyer, James Walden, had made a name for himself representing citizen groups opposing government actions. He had already worked with Boerum Hill residents fighting the city's reopening of the Downtown Brooklyn House of Detention. Subsequently he represented local residents opposing bike lanes on Prospect Park West and the closing of Long Island College Hospital in Cobble Hill.

The lawsuit had some technical merit, though it had a strategic flaw. As Hank Gutman, a successful litigator as well as a Brooklyn Bridge Park Corporation board member, remarked, "You shouldn't start a lawsuit unless you know how you want to end it and have a plan for getting there. You don't just launch the thing and figure, 'OK, I'm going to beat them up.' Then what?"[20] What the plaintiffs in this case really wanted was to exercise control over what would happen in the Tobacco

Warehouse, but that objective could not be achieved through the lawsuit. The plaintiffs won initial victories in the federal and state courts, which temporarily stopped the St. Ann's project, but, because their victory essentially left the property in limbo, nothing else could happen on the site either.

Moreover, the lawsuit clouded the future of the Empire Stores as well as the Tobacco Warehouse. Although the plaintiffs directed their attacks against the Tobacco Warehouse, the courts' decisions applied equally to both structures, encumbering them with use restrictions. The Empire Stores, slated for revenue-generating activities to support park maintenance, could no longer be used for that purpose, and the Tobacco Warehouse could not be leased to St. Ann's Warehouse or anyone else. The plaintiffs had won, but, with no source of funds to maintain these historic buildings, they would deteriorate further. Superstorm Sandy proved how much at risk they really were.[21]

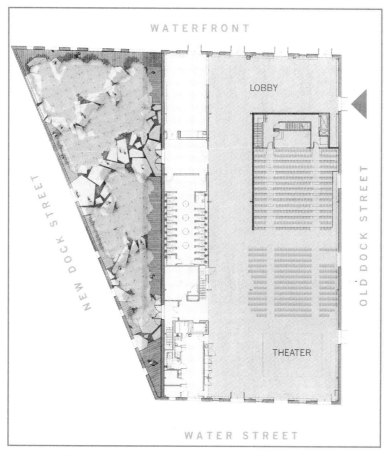

Figure 15-2. The plan presented for the Tobacco Warehouse in late 2010 proposed that the rectangular section be roofed over to create flexible theater space and the triangular section remain open to the sky as a public garden. (Rogers Marvel Architects.)

Despite losses at the trial level, the government parties involved were still committed to adaptive reuse of both the Tobacco Warehouse and the Empire Stores. The courts had not found that the plans for these structures were forbidden, only that the proper process had not been followed. The government participants made clear that they were willing to go through that process—obtaining state legislation to clarify the fact that the Tobacco Warehouse and Empire Stores were not "parkland" and obtaining permission from the National Park Service to provide the park property of equivalent value to the Tobacco Warehouse and Empire Stores in order to release the restrictions on their use. With no good alternative for the plaintiffs, negotiations became possible over a plan that would actually increase the size of the park by about an acre. It took six months, but eventually enough consensus was achieved to move forward and the litigation was settled.[22]

What the National Park Service called the conversion process was difficult, with the BHA submitting competing appraisals of the properties to be swapped, but the park gained the last piece of property along the DUMBO waterfront that made the entire stretch of park contiguous, a result that had been sought for years.

Figure 15-3. The walled garden as it looked in its first winter before it was open to the public and in bloom. (Eugene Keilin.)

As a bonus, the city paid to renovate a former water meter facility on the new property so it could be used for environmental education and other park purposes.[23]

In the end, community participation in the design made important contributions. The Marvel Architects design of the Tobacco Warehouse restoration kept the new work within the old walls, as was widely desired; it permitted views of the bridge from inside the building and created a large community studio and a large, flexible, and adaptable space that could be used for anything from performances to graduations (see Figure 15-2). The triangular part of the structure remained open to the air, containing a walled garden of intimate, contemplative spaces (see Figure 15-3) reminiscent of the original concept in the 2000 master plan. A roof was applied to a shallow clearstory of glass brick that left the building's profile and aspect largely intact (see Figure 15-4).

The Brooklyn Heights Association president Jane McGroaty and executive director Judy Stanton were hard to convince, but they ultimately agreed to the final settlement. Marianna Koval remained unreconciled to the fate of the Tobacco Warehouse. "I believed then and I believe now that it is a terrible precedent and was a great misuse of a public facility," she said. "I go by now and look at it, and I think it's a great tragedy."[24]

Cooler heads prevailed and a solution was found. Many observers believe an excellent result was achieved, and the project has received a number of awards for the preservation and adaptive reuse of the historic structure.[25] When the Tobacco Warehouse and Empire Stores were completed and open, park visitors would find them as they found the rest of the park—comfortable in their setting and seemingly timeless—blissfully unaware of the litigation and hard feelings that almost produced a very different result.

Figure 15-4. The restored Tobacco Warehouse was transformed into a venue for St. Ann's Warehouse theater productions and other cultural and community uses; the glass bricks above the original roofline seem to disappear.

SIXTEEN
A HURRICANE HAS UNEXPECTED CONSEQUENCES

New York is a town of developers and preservationists. Everyone who is not a developer is a preservationist.

—A Brooklyn Heights resident commenting on the controversy over the height of commercial development on Pier 1

By the fall of 2012 about 25 percent of Brooklyn Bridge Park was open to the public, with quite a bit more under construction. Sustainability, whether ecological, structural, or economic, had been ingrained in its design and character. Still, no one guessed that the decisions related to the park's sustainability would be tested so soon and so thoroughly.

On October 29, 2012, Superstorm Sandy, the conjunction of a slowing hurricane with a powerful nor'easter, hit New York. The surf in New York Harbor reached a record level of thirty-two-foot waves, more than six feet higher than the previous record set by Hurricane Irene in 2011. The surge level at the foot of Manhattan in Battery Park topped 13.88 feet at 9:24 p.m., surpassing the old record of 10.02 feet set by Hurricane Donna in 1960.[1]

Along with nearly everything else in New York City, the park was closed and battened down as much as possible before the storm hit. The newly laid artificial turf on the Pier 5 soccer fields (due to open in the next few months) was weighted down with bricks. All playgrounds and equipment were secured. But there was no holding back Mother Nature, and the piers were inundated with saltwater for up to four hours (see Figure 16-1). For park planners watching from the Promenade as portions of their creation disappeared beneath the waves, it was hard not to feel a sense of dread.

The next day, the visible damage to the park was assessed. Electrical transformers had been harmed, knocking out all lights and most of the park's irrigation system. Electricity would not be fully restored until February, and until then the park would close at dusk. Artificial surfaces in two playgrounds had been destroyed and would have to be replaced. Three young trees had been knocked over, debris brought in by the waves had been scattered all over the park, and even structures as heavy as shipping containers had floated to new locations. Miraculously, nothing of the park itself had washed out to sea.[2]

The water reached the level of the platform on which Jane's Carousel stood, damaging the mechanical equipment below, but Jean Nouvel's glass structure enclosing it held up without damage and the restored antique carousel was unharmed. The Walentases subsequently paid for and installed state-of-the-art flood protection for the structure.[3]

Despite the damage that did occur, Brooklyn Bridge Park fared better than many other waterfront parks and won praise from Mayor Bloomberg for its resiliency.[4] It was not good luck that saved the park but good planning. Scientific predictions of rising water and surge levels due to climate change had been taken into account in the park's design. On what would otherwise have been a flat site at low elevation, engineered topography changes created barriers to the storm's surge. The maximum elevation on Pier 1 reaches thirty feet and on the upland berms as much as thirty-seven feet.[5]

The decision to replace constructed edges at the waterfront, which can break up in the face of powerful wave action, with natural and stabilized edges wherever possible, proved prescient. Much of the park's shoreline is made up of sloped sections covered with large stones and boulders, called riprap, which are more effective in preventing soil erosion and providing protection from violent wave action (see Figure 16-2). Another example of resilient shoreline treatment was the nature-based salt marsh at Pier 1, of which there would be more in the park's north end (see Figure 16-3), designed to absorb and filter storm water.[6]

The strategy of using durable, salvaged material and appropriate plantings also paid off. Huge granite boulders recovered from local bridge demolition and longleaf yellow pine, used in the past for boat construction, all helped stabilize the

Figure 16-1. On the night of October 29, 2012, the Pier 2 platform lay under water, and most of the park's upland was flooded as well. (Julius Erdei.)

landscape. The soil chosen, which was 70 to 90 percent sand, allowed rapid drainage of salty water. The plantings themselves were all selected for their tolerance to salt and placed carefully, with all tree root balls at a minimum elevation of eight feet above the flood plain. The park's extensive drainage system allowed the saltwater surge to recede quickly, and staff immediately began flushing the plantings with clean water.[7]

Sandy tested the park's sustainability, and it passed the test in spectacular fashion. That was the good news. But Sandy was also responsible, if only indirectly, for another sort of storm in Brooklyn Heights. As usual, the controversy involved a development site—in particular the height of buildings on Pier 1, as we shall see below.

Prior to Sandy a request for proposals for the Empire Stores had been released, and, as it happened, a walk-through of the site for bidders had been scheduled for the week after the storm. Even with a further week's delay, staff and volunteers in hip boots were still picking up debris and sweeping water out the doors when undeterred developers tromped through the buildings, which were lit by power from very long extension cords connected to the nearest working source of electricity.

While developer enthusiasm for the new sites remained high, the rules governing construction as it related to flooding would change. The devastation wrought by Sandy confirmed the Federal Emergency Management Agency's growing concern that its Flood Insurance Rate Maps did not accurately assess the risks of coastal zone flooding. The agency promptly issued new guidance that raised the level of the flood plain in the New York area.[8] In response, Mayor Bloomberg and the City Council adopted significant changes to the city's Building Code designed to

Figure 16-2. The soft edge of riprap in the foreground and background meets a hard bulkhead securing Plymouth Street, all of which encircles a beach in DUMBO. This treatment was designed to handle a difference of almost five feet from low to high tide to resist wind and water damage. (Eugene Keilin.)

mitigate future flood damage. The new rules included a requirement that buildings be constructed from a higher base above the new flood plain established by FEMA, and that mechanicals and electricity be housed well above the flood plain instead of in the basements of buildings, as had been the practice.[9]

These new rules were applied to all of the park's development projects. Two of the new projects in the works involved historic structures, which complicated what was possible to achieve.

In the case of the Empire Stores, it was decided that the ground floor would be dug out and a new concrete slab poured to distribute the load and improve stability. Drains and pumps would be installed, along with an aqua fence designed to make the building watertight in case of a storm. Mechanicals were tucked out of sight in a mezzanine alcove above loading docks.

The Tobacco Warehouse, by contrast, was designed to meet the standards of what the new rules described as "wet" flood proofing, which relies on "the use of flood-damage-resistant materials and construction techniques."[10] This option assumed that water would penetrate the building but that it would leave only minor damage after it drained.

Changes were made to other development sites. The residential site at John Street was elevated to take account of the higher flood plain measurement. This placed the building at a different, and higher, elevation than the surrounding park and street, requiring modification to the building design to incorporate an access ramp compliant with the Americans with Disabilities Act along with other adjustments to reduce the impact of the grade change.

In all three of these cases, notice of the changed rules was given in time to plan accordingly. However, in the case of the Pier 1 project, the Toll Brothers' Pierhouse, and Starwood's 1 Hotel, a lease and other contracts had been signed, and construction drawings were already well along.

Figure 16-3. This salt marsh, marked by scattered iron footings from a long-demolished sugar refinery and refreshed by tidal waters from the estuary flowing under the bridge in the background, helps protect water quality and reduce flooding. (Eugene Keilin.)

Before a building permit could be granted, extensive redesign of the project, with its two-hundred-room hotel and approximately one hundred residential units, would be necessary. The southern building had to be raised 3½ feet. To mitigate the visual effect, the architect, Jonathan Marvel, added steps, ramps, benches, and planters. Because the building was within the scenic view plane protecting the Promenade view, raising the base of the building meant that its height had to be reduced by one full story. According to Marvel, "The result was the building got a lot nicer."[11]

The northern building, which combined residential units and a hotel, was also raised 3½ feet. This building was outside the view plane and was always intended to be taller than the southern building. In principle this was not an issue because the new buildings were replacing older buildings (collectively called the National Cold Storage Warehouse) that were about the same height and had been demolished to make way for the park.

The cold storage buildings had been gone since 2011—a short period but long enough for people to become accustomed to their absence. In particular, demolishing the buildings improved views of the Brooklyn Bridge as seen from the Promenade and of the Lower Manhattan skyline as seen from Columbia Heights between Orange and Middagh Streets. The temptation was to assume these improvements were permanent.

That the replacement of the cold storage buildings had been planned since well before their demolition did not register widely, especially among those new to Brooklyn Heights. Nor was it generally understood that the northern section of the Pierhouse/1 Hotel complex lay outside the view plane. The hotel and the northern residential building were designed to be one hundred feet tall to the roofline, about the height of the roofline of the tallest cold storage building. On top of the roof were bulkheads that housed stairwells, elevators, and mechanical equipment including generators. When the bulkheads on the roof of the new building proved more numerous and taller than those that had topped the cold storage buildings, protests began.

The taller bulkheads had come about primarily because, after Sandy, mechanical equipment that would earlier have been housed in the basement was moved to the roof. The bulkheads rose about thirty feet higher than the roofline. Generators to be used in case of power emergency were also placed there.[12]

These additional roof structures were "permitted obstructions" under the New York City Zoning Resolution. According to park president Regina Myer, the Empire State Development Corporation, the arbiter in the matter, had advised the park corporation to defer to the local zoning code in the absence of specific guidelines adopted in the general project plan. The result of applying the local zoning code to Pierhouse and 1 Hotel was a basic height not to exceed one hundred feet, but the designers were allowed to put bulkheads on top.[13] And because of Sandy, those bulkheads were tall.

Years earlier, Otis Pearsall, the Brooklyn Heights preservationist, had wanted to make sure he had a visual record of the height of the cold storage buildings. In 2005 he asked Henrik Krogius to photograph the view north from roughly the midpoint of the Promenade (see Figure 16-4). At that time the cold storage buildings obscured a section of the bridge's roadway but left the cables in clear view. Having been involved in the establishment of the scenic view plane, Pearsall was well aware that a triangle of land at either end of the view plane was not subject to the regulation. The Port Authority had from the very start of discussions about the waterfront proposed taller buildings for those triangles, as, later, did the park's planners. (The cold storage buildings had been located in the northern triangle with parts actually within the protected plane but they had been exempted from regulation as long as they stood.)

Therefore, Pearsall initiated a discussion with park planners on the issue of height and views. Foreseeing the replacement of the cold storage buildings, Pearsall hoped to persuade the designers that new structures there should actually be lower than those they replaced in order to give an unimpeded view of the Brooklyn Bridge roadway from the Promenade. He was trying, as he acknowledged, not only to preserve a bridge view but also to improve it.[14]

When the northern Pierhouse building topped out, Pearsall observed that large bulkheads rising atop the hotel roof actually blocked the view of the Brooklyn Bridge roadway (see Figure 16-5); instead of improving the view, the bulkheads had made it worse. He angrily accused the park corporation of reneging on an agreement he said he had made with the previous leader, Wendy Leventer, about the height of those buildings and their bulkheads. As he described it, the height was supposed to be limited to one hundred feet, *including* bulkheads.[15]

Regina Myer and the members of her board were startled by the claim of an earlier agreement with Pearsall. Myer began looking into the matter.

It turned out that Pearsall, along with some of the park's designers, had in

Figure 16-4. A photograph taken in September 2005, from the midpoint of the Promenade, shows the then-existing National Cold Storage Warehouse obscuring part of the Brooklyn Bridge roadway, but leaving a view of the bridge's cables and distant Manhattan buildings behind them.

fact discussed how to improve the then-existing view through a one-hundred-foot height limitation, which would include any roof structures. Pearsall said that empirical observation demonstrated this would allow an "unobstructed view of eastbound vehicles along the full arc of the bridge from as far north on the Promenade at a point between Pierrepont and Clark Street."

E-mails about the issue were circulated among Leventer, Pearsall, Brooklyn Heights Association governors, and a member of the Van Valkenburgh staff, which Pearsall felt constituted an agreement on the matter.[16] The only reflection of these discussions in the formally adopted general project plan was a requirement that the buildings not exceed one hundred feet, without specifying at what point they should be measured and without specifying that the height limit included bulkheads for elevators and other equipment. Other documents from the period provided some support for Pearsall's position but ultimately did not persuade the judge who considered the matter.[17] Had the text of the plan mentioned the goal of an unobstructed view of the Brooklyn Bridge roadway, it might have raised a useful red flag later.[18]

Many things happened between Pearsall's discussions and the issuance of requests for proposals for the Pier 1 development. To recap, Eliot Spitzer replaced George Pataki as governor, bringing an entirely new cast of characters to the Empire State Development Corporation; Leventer left and, after a six-month hiatus, Regina Myer arrived without the benefit of an orderly transition. Then Spitzer resigned and was replaced by Lieutenant Governor David Paterson, the third governor in two years. His administration negotiated a transfer of control to the city, leading to an entirely new entity to design and build the park. Although the park had finally found its true institutional home, it had lost some of its institutional memory along the way. Myer was unaware of the prior discussions.

When it came time to think about a request for proposals for Pier 1, Myer conferred with all the interested parties, including the Brooklyn Heights Association, the Brooklyn Bridge Park Conservancy, and the Community Advisory Council. Some people in these organizations had been privy to the earlier Pearsall discussions, but that institutional memory also failed; no one mentioned them to Myer.

Figure 16-5. A photograph from approximately the same point in November 2015 shows the Pierhouse and 1 Hotel structure, draped in construction shrouds, narrower than the cold storage buildings but, because of taller bulkheads, blocking a larger portion of the cables.

At three meetings of the Community Advisory Council between November 2011 and September 2013, representatives of Marvel Architects presented the evolving plans, saying they were consolidating the mechanical equipment and moving it as far north as possible (to reduce the angle at which it interfered with the bridge view). While the Community Advisory Council was not happy about the bulkheads, some of the council's members acknowledged that the Marvel efforts had at least been sensitive to their concern. Construction proceeded on that basis. Pearsall himself was not involved in these new discussions.

Clearly the ball had been dropped at several points along the way, although the rules, as best understood, were followed. While Jonathan Marvel appreciated the problem of scale posed by what he was commissioned to design and did what he could to soften the visual impact, many who considered the issue during the design phase were not design professionals and did not fully share his ability to visualize the future structures. Plans, renderings, and even models do not fully convey a sense of an actual structure in the ground or how it will appear from different vantage points.

As the size of what was being built became evident, an uproar ensued. Early in 2015 a meeting at the Brooklyn Heights Synagogue called by a new group, "Save the View Now," drew about seventy people, and an online petition garnered an impressive four thousand names. Steven Guterman, whose Columbia Heights residence faced Pierhouse, contended that the unfinished hotel had reached a height of 130 feet and might rise to 144 feet. He added, "Brooklyn Bridge Park Corporation, the Empire State Development Corporation, and Toll Brothers[19] are stealing an American view from the millions that visit every year."[20]

Guterman's focus was not exactly the same as Pearsall's. Whereas Pearsall was looking north from the Promenade to the Brooklyn Bridge, Guterman lived on Columbia Heights facing west toward the Lower Manhattan skyline. The cold storage buildings had blocked that view, but the new buildings were situated somewhat differently, were somewhat different in shape,[21] and were in fact more obtrusive from Guterman's perspective.

When Guterman entered the argument, the southern building was still a hole

Figure 16-6. An aerial view shows the relationship between the extensive landscape on Pier 1 and the Pierhouse/hotel combination. Tall white buildings in the background were owned by the Watchtower and are not part of the park. (Alex MacLean.)

in the ground. Though that building fell within the view plane, Guterman discovered that the official plans filed for it exceeded the view plane's height limitation. Making a similar discovery, the park corporation asked the buildings department to halt construction until the plans were revised.

In the heat of battle, hyperbole sometimes replaced precision. The website for Save the View was topped with the headline "Help Save the Iconic View from the Brooklyn Promenade." The headline was superimposed over a dramatic photo of the view looking west to Manhattan from the Promenade—the view that tourists come to see but one fully protected by the view plane and not threatened by Pierhouse or any other structure. The park corporation requested that the photo be removed, and it was replaced with a new image showing the bulk of Pierhouse affecting the view to the north.

In any event, construction of the northern buildings had gone too far to make scaling them back a likely prospect. Such an outcome at that point would have been costly to the developer, the park, or both. Nonetheless, Susan Rifkin, a member of the Brooklyn Heights Association's park committee, said, "It's safe to say that we are exploring any and all options."[22] On April 22, 2015, Save the View Now went to state court seeking an injunction limiting the height of both the northern and southern buildings.

The lawsuit was heard by Justice Knipel, who granted a temporary restraining order to halt construction on the southern building until a full hearing could be conducted. After hearing the arguments, however, he found for the defendants in all important respects. He decided that the general project plan, which contained no limitation on the bulkheads, was the governing document, that no binding agreement to the contrary existed, that the community had ample notice that bulkheads were intended and would add to height, and that the buildings as constructed complied with the plan.[23]

The judge indicated sympathy for the plaintiffs' perspective, saying, "The casual passerby walking along Brooklyn's majestic Promenade is struck with an indelible impression that these buildings, now nearing completion, are simply too large. No matter that the Cold Storage Warehouse which they replaced may have been, in at least some dimension, larger." But he also recognized that those buildings reflected "a compromise without which the Brooklyn Bridge Park might not have been created." "In hindsight," he said, "this court cannot now say, and it is not within the provenance of this court to say, that the compromise was erroneous as a matter of law."[24]

Regardless of the outcome in the litigation, the reputation and credibility of the park board and management had been damaged by the events surrounding the Pier 1 development. This was especially unfortunate because, with the passage of time, as the black construction shrouds came down and the vegetation grew, and as people simply got used to the presence of the buildings, the buildings might well recede into the background (see Figures 16-6 and 16-7). But for the moment general unhappiness reigned.

In any case, new buildings and controversy invariably go hand in hand. As one Brooklyn Heights resident observed, "New York is a town of developers and preservationists. Everyone who is not a developer is a preservationist." Another remarked, "Every building built in New York blocks someone's view." Large as the buildings on Pier 1 proved to be, they were lower than those slated for Pier 6, the source of the next big controversy over structures intended for the park's financial support. And bad feelings generated by the Pier 1 controversy would carry over and infect with distrust the conversation about Pier 6.

Yet, for many people, this controversy came with the territory. Connie Fishman, former president of Hudson River Park and a resident of the Eagle Warehouse apartments near the park's Fulton Landing entrance, recalled how the view from her window had changed: "I used to see the Woolworth Building," a Gothic temple of commerce and the world's tallest building when it completed in 1913. "I now see the Frank Gehry building," strikingly modern, with shiny undulating skin, built in 2010. "In a couple of years, the people at the Seaport are going to put something in front of the Gehry building, and I will see that."[25]

Figure 16-7. The construction shrouding gone, the architecture styles of Pierhouse and 1 Hotel were revealed to be different from, yet complementary to, each other. (Mary Frost / *Brooklyn Daily Eagle*.)

SEVENTEEN
THE GROWING EXPERIENCE

Building a permanent link between Pier 1 and Pier 6 has been
an overriding goal of this community for over a generation.

—Regina Myer, on opening a greenway linking
the piers from north to south

Despite all the political and legal wrangling, the park was growing and, in the process, drawing a crowd. By 2013 Brooklyn Bridge Park was about one-third complete and thriving, although still very much a construction site. The Pier 5 soccer fields and adjacent picnic peninsula had opened, but because of upland construction, visitors had to traverse a narrow path along Furman Street to get from Pier 1 to the southern portion of the park.

Over the course of the year, however, much was completed and even more was begun. Work began on the Tobacco Warehouse, and an earthen barrier to reduce noise from the Brooklyn-Queens Expressway arose on the uplands of Piers 2, 3, and 4. A pedestrian bridge from Squibb Park in northern Brooklyn Heights into the park opened, as well as a new beach at Pier 4. Perhaps most emblematic of the progress, the upland between Piers 2 and 5 was opened to the public, which meant that the full length of the park was now in use. The park was more than a series of pieces; a unified park had become a reality.

Following the resolution of the legal impasse over development of the Tobacco Warehouse and the Empire Stores, plans for the reuse of both properties surged ahead in 2013. A new group of developers was selected to create new uses for the Empire Stores, a row of seven adjoining brick warehouses built between 1869 and 1885. Midtown Equities, after beating out nine other bidders, signed a ninety-six-year lease and entered into partnership with Rockwood Capital and the HK Organization for their development. Almost 80 percent of the total space was planned for offices (the West Elm furniture chain came on as the anchor tenant), while 3,200 square feet were designated for educational use. The Brooklyn Historical Society signed a sublease and would be working closely with both the park and the developer to display graphic presentations of the site's history. There would be shops and restaurants, plus a landscaped open space of about 7,000 square feet along the roofs.

Figure 17-1. A two-story addition to the Empire Stores, moved back to be less visible from the water's edge, is seen nearing completion in November 2015. The Tobacco Warehouse is in the foreground.

"It's a milestone, and this gives us firm financial footing so the park can continue to be self-sustaining," Regina Myer said.[1] The additional parcel received by the park in the legal settlement would be given new lawn treatment and park features as part of the Empire Stores conversion. "We were not expecting the Empire Stores to be torn down and turned into parkland," a philosophical Tony Manheim said. "The redevelopment doesn't seem terribly offensive to me as long as it aids park uses."[2]

But as so often is the case with development schemes, the devil was in the details. Studio V Architecture, commissioned to design the Empire Stores' adaptive use, added a glassed-in, two-story party structure on the roof, and the land-use committee of Community Board 2 approved the addition. Although the final decision rested with the state's historic preservation office, the plan was also brought before the city's Landmarks Preservation Commission for advice. "The massive addition will alter the building forever without making it better," said Doreen Gallo, a member of the DUMBO Neighborhood Association and the Community Advisory Council.[3] "I am troubled by its generic quality," added Landmarks Commissioner Michael Goldblum. And Robert Tierney, chairman of the commission, told Jack Cayre, a principal in Midtown Equities, "Take to heart the good-faith advice we are tendering."[4]

In the end the architect was replaced, the party venue was eliminated, the size of the glassed-in structure was reduced and relocated to reduce its noise, and the amount of public space on the roof was significantly increased (see Figure 17-1).

In the meantime, the conversion of the Tobacco Warehouse had moved on to a groundbreaking. Mayor Bloomberg and Borough President Markowitz, both celebrants of development, bantered like a comedy duo at a ceremony held on October 31 within the multi-arched enclosure (see Figure 17-2). Joining them on the stand were a host of officials, community leaders, and cultural figures who had been involved in the project, including Susan Feldman, St. Ann's founder and artistic director.

Figure 17-2 (below). Mayor Michael Bloomberg (left) broke up Borough President Marty Markowitz (right) at the groundbreaking ceremony for St. Ann's Warehouse in the Tobacco Warehouse on November 31, 2013. The two had become something of a comedy duo as they attended Brooklyn construction milestone events. State Senator Daniel Squadron is behind Bloomberg; St. Ann's Warehouse founder and artistic director Susan Feldman is at center, and Board Chairman Joseph Steinberg is at upper right.

Dramatic readings from *Henry V* by the all-female cast of St. Ann's upcoming production of Shakespeare's *Julius Caesar* reflected the venturesome nature of the St. Ann's theatrical enterprise. "I feel like we're starting out new again," Feldman later said of this, the fourth home of her theater.[5]

Still other controversies continued. Even so universally desired an element as an additional entryway into the hard-to-reach piers section did not escape criticism. When the construction cost for a pedestrian bridge from Squibb Park playground jumped from $4.9 million to $6.3 million, Roy Sloane of Cobble Hill complained that the bridge was mainly an amenity for the hotel planned at Pier 1. "Why

can't the hotel build its own bridge?" he was quoted as asking. "This is the kind of cost inflation the park has incurred all along, only to suit a massive real estate development."[6]

When the bridge opened March 21, 2013, with the hotel only in the earliest stages of excavation, the number of people taking advantage of the bouncy new walkway into the park at Pier 1 quickly

demonstrated its popular appeal. The time saved by not having to go down and around by way of Old Fulton Street was of less consequence than the fact that the springy, 450-foot "trail bridge," its planks of locust wood held together by steel cables, proved an adventure in itself. "I'm amused by the bounce; I trust the engineering," one early visitor said. "The views are tremendous," said another, adding, "I love the way it meanders. It's not just a straight pathway—it's really nicely designed."[7] In the days and weeks that followed, the bridge would be busily used well into the evenings, its wire mesh railings illuminated for safe passage.

Only a year later, the bridge would be closed for repairs after the park's staff noticed "unusual movement of the bridge from side to side"[8] (see Figure 17-3). Questions were raised about who should be held responsible for the structural prob-

Figure 17-3. Tension cables still crisscrossed the Squibb Park pedestrian bridge sixteen months after the bridge became unstable and was closed to the public. The designer was finally fired, and a new engineering firm was brought in to correct the problem.

lems, which may have led to the prolonged closure, much to the chagrin of many of the bridges' admirers. After working with the bridge designer, MacArthur "genius" fellow Theodore Zoli of HNTB, for sixteen months without resolution of the structure's instability, the park corporation replaced his firm and filed a lawsuit against them alleging a defective design. A new engineering firm was brought in to fix and reopen the bridge.[9]

Another important but troublesome entryway to the park got at least a superficial improvement. The underpass of the Brooklyn-Queens Expressway where Atlantic Avenue leads into the park was decorated with a mural of people both going to the park and enjoying it. Josef Szende, executive director of the Atlantic Avenue Improvement District, which sponsored the project, said he hoped the work would "create buzz." Teenage artists, funded by a $75,000 grant from the city, painted the mural. While a series of expressway ramps and street crossings still complicated pedestrian access, a dreary underpass on the way was brightened by this work.[10]

Other welcome events of the year were the opening of a Conservancy-run floating dock for kayaking at Pier 2 and the return for the second year of the "pop-up" pool near that pier (see Figure 17-4). Free instruction by park volunteers and free use of kayaks were offered. The dock, reached by a gangplank from the pier, could by its buoyancy float above rising storm waters. Another temporary attraction returning for the second year was "The Fence at Photoville," an international photographic exhibit of large images of varied subject matter imprinted on mesh banners stretched along walkways and construction fences in the park. This was complemented for ten days in September by photos exhibited in fifty freight containers near Pier 5.

But the most transforming experience for the park took place on November 15, 2013, when the greenway and most of the upland between Piers 2 and 5 was open to the

Figure 17-4. A "pop-up" pool with adjacent beach, near Pier 2, was a popular but temporary attraction pending further construction of the park. It is seen here in August 2012; its last season would be the summer of 2016.

Figure 17-5. A sound-damping berm runs along much of the park's central section to reduce noise from the BQE. It is seen here in May 2015 with greenery just beginning to cover most of its east side.

public. Previously, demolition and then construction of this area had been seen only from the Promenade. Pier sheds were stripped and rocks, gravel, and piles of earth scattered about amid construction equipment, to be replaced eventually with ball courts on Pier 2. Earth spread and pressed by rollers created a firm, high berm from Montague Street to Clark Street (now planted) to protect the outer portions of the emerging park against the noise of the Brooklyn-Queens Expressway (see Figure 17-5). There were also outcroppings of trees from rocks and riprap that bordered the main walk and its subsidiary paths around three lawns as, for the first time, the general public could stroll along there, experiencing the harbor and the skyline across the way.

At the opening ceremony, Mayor Bloomberg was praised in absentia by his latest parks commissioner, Veronica White, who was joined by local officials, including Congresswoman Nydia Velázquez. "Building a permanent link between Pier 1 and Pier 6 has been an overriding goal of this community for over a generation," Regina Myer said happily, "and we are thrilled to welcome everyone here today."[11]

Next came two additions to the park's periphery designed to pay for the park's maintenance. Myer had been setting the stage for such development by readying as much park for public use and enjoyment as money allowed before new private elements kicked in. If the public character of the park could be clearly established, the private elements presumably could do little to detract from that.

One such element was the combined residential and hotel complex on Pier 1 that would contribute $3.2 million annually to the park's maintenance budget.[12] The other was a housing development at John Street on the DUMBO waterfront, the very northern end of the park. A joint proposal by Alloy Development and Monadnock Development was chosen for building a forty-seven-unit residence, whose ground floor would be occupied by an annex of the Brooklyn Children's Museum. This project, which would occupy part of the former Con Edison site, would be fronted by a thirteen-thousand-square-foot lawn and pedestrian bridges crossing a salt marsh.

At the other end of the park, Regina Myer introduced an unusual new proposal for an outer portion of Pier 6. The up-and-coming Danish architect Bjarke Ingels designed a gently inclined, triangular platform from whose apex, seventeen feet above the level of the pier, spectators would have extraordinary views in all directions. The *New York Times* architecture critic Michael Kimmelman enthusiastically compared the structure to the prow of a ship. "The architect calls this the work's 'Titanic' moment—he means the movie, not the wreck—the point to which one or two people could climb and stand at the railing, gazing out over the city," Kimmelman wrote. "In essence, the architecture invites us all to come to a spot where we can feel alone." The platform would in part also form a roof under which people could find shade at café tables. As envisioned the project would not come cheap; even if it received all the necessary approvals, its $8 million cost would have to be funded by private money.[13]

One more idea surfaced, or rather resurfaced, before 2013 was out. The previously discarded marina plan was restored on the north side of Pier 5, off the Picnic Peninsula, where an earlier plan had also placed it. Requests went out for proposals to build a 186-slip marina there as well as a roller-skating rink on Pier 2.[14] The bid for the marina was won by the Singapore-based SUTL Group in partnership with Edgewater Resources. Because part of the marina was above a subway line, the usual anchoring was ruled out. Instead, 160 concrete blocks weighing ten tons each were lowered into the harbor to help anchor the slips (see Figure 17-6).

Although still a work in progress, the park was popular. On a summer weekend 120,000 people could be expected to pass through, and 25,000 on an average summer weekday. The Brooklyn Bridge Park Conservancy reported that attendance at its programs had reached 160,000 people, the most in its five years of programming seasons.

One popular attraction was Smorgasburg, a sprawling outdoor fair of local artisanal food under scores of brightly colored tents, held seasonally on

Figure 17-6. One of 160 concrete blocks weighing ten tons each is sunk into the harbor floor, where it will provide an anchor for the marina dock. The blocks were selected over drilling piles into the waterbed because of the risk to a subway line running underneath.

Sundays. Smorgasburg, which originated in Williamsburg, moved from spot to spot in the park depending on what space was not under construction at the time. It invariably drew crowds, which some local residents did not much like, along with a certain amount of litter on adjoining streets, which engendered complaints even though the park management sent in its own cleaning crews to tidy up.

The new basketball and handball courts were busy, too. But when local children left their gear unattended, despite the presence of lockers, and found it gone when they returned, local parents complained about security. Legitimate fears were raised when a gun was fired on a handball court (no one was hurt), and police presence was increased.

The park was on its way. But now another new mayor was entering the scene. Despite his history as a Brooklyn councilman, it was not certain that Bill de Blasio would be as friendly to Brooklyn Bridge Park as Michael Bloomberg had been. We will take this up in Chapter 19, but first, before the discussion of further controversy, we will pause to consider the park itself.

EIGHTEEN
LEARNING FROM THE SITE

They think those hills were there, the glaciers left them.

—Hank Gutman, board member of the
Brooklyn Bridge Park Corporation

Backhoes were busily scrambling rocks before daybreak as the year 2014 arrived. Almost before anyone knew it, their random-seeming work had produced the park's true form, including such unexpected details as a small island, ringed by a wall of stone, behind the barely surviving railhead at Pier 4, hardly separating it from a small beach that had appeared in equally mysterious fashion. The reality was very much like the master plan of 2000 and at the same time very different. Some of the differences reflected the conditions on the ground—the need to shift heavy loads off the piers, the unsuitability of the pier sheds for indoor recreation—but most of the changes were refinements and elaborations that reflected the skill and imagination of the park's designers.

Meanwhile, on the upland of Pier 1, the "ka-chunk" of pile drivers was heard as columns were sunk for 1 Hotel and Pierhouse, and the hotel's skeleton began to rise. Skanska, the giant Swedish company, had been the construction manager when the park began being built, and it had posted its name in large letters on the shed of Pier 2. But the name had now been replaced by New York–based Turner Construction, another giant in the field, which had won the bid for the next phase of construction.

During interviews with the design principals at their new Downtown Brooklyn offices later in 2014, Michael Van Valkenburgh (see Figure 18-1), wearing a navy zippered jacket, leaned casually back against a wall, his hair a red-blond jumble. His two fellow principals, Matthew Urbanski and Gullivar Shepard, sat upright, attired in business suits. The designers spoke of learning from the site.

"We had an attitude that this was more like a found object," Urbanski said, "and we're going to collaborate with the site. Paraphrasing Louis Kahn, I asked the site what it wanted to be." The answer: "'I'd like a post-industrial landscape,' is what it said to us. In other words, we were not going to try to convert the site into something else than a public space, but the image of that was going to come out of the materiality of the site."[1]

Figure 18-1. Michael Van Valkenburgh explains a park model to schoolchildren. (Michael Van Valkenburgh Associates.)

The materiality of the site: long and narrow, bounded by water on one side and a heavily used highway along most of the other; flat and treeless; punctuated by dominant bridges and featureless piers; hard to reach on foot or by public transportation; exposed to wind and tide and noise and pollution. Thinking of the site as a park at all had been a great feat of imagination thirty years earlier; thinking of it as the park it became was a triumph of planning and design.

In a 2013 *Harvard Magazine* cover story, Van Valkenburgh was described as taking delight in people's use of the park. "To see how his design serves people," the article noted, "consider the care that went into planning the lighting. Rather than line the shore path with lights down by the water's edge, Van Valkenburgh has erected tall wooden poles some yards back [see Figure 18-2] and topped them with fixtures that cast an even glow, like the moon, bright enough to provide safety but dim enough to leave the water and far objects like the Manhattan Bridge visible. 'I was trying to give a little dignity to looking at the views at night,' he says."[2]

Different as they are, Brooklyn Bridge Park and its contemporary, Manhattan's High Line, share a quality of being very much *in* the city even as they offer refuge from it. "If Central Park's main concern was to be an escape from the city," Robert Hammond, one of the High Line's two founders, told the *New York Times*, "what makes the High Line special is that it is not an escape from the city. It is part of the city."[3]

Both the High Line and Brooklyn Bridge Park make significant use of recycled urban features and industrial elements. The High Line reclaimed nearly all of an entire elevated railway structure. In a similar way, Van Valkenburgh recycled the piers and used abandoned or discarded

Figure 18-2. A stone-paved walk reinforced a sense of boundless landscape along the water's edge between Piers 2 and 1.

material that he obtained in or near the park. His team discovered and recycled vast amounts of longleaf yellow pine from the National Cold Storage Warehouse slated for demolition and used it throughout the park. The team used granite from a demolished nearby bridge for a viewing terrace and fill from a nearby railway tunnel to build up the terrain.

Where they could, they kept the framework of the pier sheds and repurposed it for recreation. They left in place a railroad float bridge that lay half submerged between Piers 3 and 5 as well as pilings exposed by the removal of decking from Pier 1 that roughly outlined the subway tunnel beneath.

Still, if Van Valkenburgh was attracted to industrial artifacts, he was by training, inclination, and employment a landscape architect, fascinated by nature in all its profusion. According to *Harvard Magazine*, he spent his early professional years working for a landscape architect who had him visiting tree farms to select specimens for planting, an activity that gave him great knowledge of vegetation. Van Valkenburgh was quoted as boasting, "I can name every plant in the Northeast from a car traveling at 30 miles an hour."[4]

Many of those plants, at least the hardy and durable ones, found their way to this unpromising site and became part of its transformation. Anne Raver, who writes about gardens and the environment for the *New York Times*, admired the granite terrace but was charmed by the "shady trails through a series of freshwater marshes created by collected rain, where you can see dragonflies hovering over the water or a mother duck leading her babies through the reeds. Butterflies and bees, flies and little wasps sip nectar from the pink flower puffs of joe-pye weed, the tiny purple blossoms of ironweed, the bright yellow daisies of silphium, or cup plant, whose big leaves are held together like hands to catch the rain"[5] (see Figure 18-3).

Figure 18-3 (above). The nature writer Ann Raver remarked on the "shady trails" on Pier 1 that led past a freshwater marsh and provided sights of dragonflies, bees, and a wide variety of flowers.

A park of the city, yes, but, as Raver wrote, "Nature *in* the city. There are thousands of trees and plants here—sycamores and maritime oaks, sumac and paulownia trees so tough they grow out of sidewalks and vacant lots. They can take the salt and wind, the beating sun, drought and driving rain. They hang on when a storm like Sandy blows up over the riprap, which buffers the shoreline from the pounding waves" (see Figure 18-3).[6]

Nature in the city. Consider the Squibb Park bridge as Raver described it, a plank-and-cable bridge that zigzags down to the park from the bluff that gives the Heights its name: "The airy walkway, made of heavy black locust, so naturally resistant to rot and insects that it needs no chemical treatment, bounces a bit—alarming grown-ups, delighting children—as you cross, like a hiker over some canyon in Yosemite. Only this is Furman Street, not a river you look down on, with the roar of the expressway, not a waterfall, at your back."[7]

The master plan for the park had left room for these details, but they were supplied over the considerable time it took to arrange the financing, governance, and approvals, and it was time the designers used to impress their own skill and creativity on the plan. In Raver's article, Van Valkenburgh recalled walking down to the end of the piers early in the process and saying, "I'd think, all we have to do is just not mess this up." And he added, "There are 8 million people in New York City, and none of them knows that this incredible view is going to be theirs."[8]

Although tours of the piers had been held in the early days, most people knew the site only by looking down on it from the Promenade. "Who designs a park that a whole other park looks down on?" Van Valkenburgh said in an interview. That perspective, he thought, had given many people a false sense of knowledge: "The funny thing is they know something about the park site from looking on it in this kind of imperial view. Meanwhile, they know nothing about the felt experience of the site, the sense of walking around the piers and seeing the vastness of the water and all that."[9]

In the park Van Valkenburgh designed, visitors did get a chance to experience the vastness of the harbor; however, in coves and pools and along the riprap that lines the water's edge they also got an intimate view. Then, stepping back, he allowed people to climb sixteen feet up the sound attenuation berms where they could see the same thing they saw from the Promenade, but, as Van Valkenburgh said, from an entirely different vantage point (see Figure 18-4).[10]

And that is only half the park—the splendid views, the close encounters with the river, the profusion of plant life and, if you look as closely as Anne Raver did,

Figure 18-4. The berm looks very different from within the park than it does from the Promenade. Covered with a profusion of vegetation, it looks like a natural hill.

animal life, too. The other half of the park invites a more active experience, and draws a crowd to experience it. Basketball, beach volleyball, and bocce (an Italian street game); soccer and shuffleboard; handball and hockey (the kind played on roller skates).

There is room for large-scale entertainment: movies, concerts, and a theater in the Tobacco Warehouse. There are smaller, imaginative, popular spaces for children at either end of the park: Jane's Carousel, the Water Lab, Swing Valley, Sand Box Village, and the Picnic Peninsula on Pier 5.

The park has proved hugely popular. It is thronged at peak periods and well used year-round. In February 2015, one of the coldest on record in New York, there was sledding on Pier 1 and basketball on Pier 2. Some of the park's original supporters were not reconciled to its popularity, but the response of the broader public appeared to be delight.

Designing such a large and complex park was a collaborative exercise. "A big idea requires 1,000 IQ," said Matthew Urbanski, one of the principal designers. "It comes from more than one person."[11] Van Valkenburgh agreed. In an interview, he described the design process as resembling "five or six people sitting around and all simultaneously knitting a sweater together," adding, "Although we didn't know anything about the sweater, we all had a shared sense, a collective sense, a commonality about what it was going to become." Switching metaphors, he said that "if we were cooking food, we had some shared sense of what delicious is and all the ways that you get to delicious."[12]

"One of the beauties of this project is that it happened over such a long period of time," he continued. Regina Myer, he said, "got to watch, and we got to watch how people used the early pieces, how plants perform—so many things. Then, as we built it in phases, we were able to come back. To call some of the changes 'refinements' is almost to completely reinvent some pieces."[13]

In talking about the park, the designers consistently remarked on the way liabilities became opportunities, how lemons became lemonade. As Matthew Urbanski said, "One of the so-called liabilities we embraced was that the site should be made as continuous as possible, but the site should not become a slave to some expression like a continuous expression." By "continuous expression" Urbanski meant that consistency should not preclude different sections of the park expressing their own distinct qualities. As the firm's fellow principal Gullivar Shepard was quoted as saying in the *Harvard Magazine* article, "The need for one rigorous visual order is compelling in architecture, but landscape architecture is inspired by nature's diversity and complexity."[14]

The diversity and complexity of the park was not inevitable. In his office Van Valkenburgh had a model of the Tuileries Gardens, a classic French design characterized by order and geometry. He might have been seduced by the repeating rectangular piers to impose geometric order on Brooklyn Bridge Park, but he thought that such an approach was wholly unsuitable. The order of the Tuileries, he said, "has to do with the royal order of the French court. It's so beautiful except you remember that it's all about having a king."

He explained his own very different approach to design in highly personal terms: "You don't even know the puzzle of your life is being assembled, and one piece shows up and it attaches to another. Then suddenly it's you; it's not a puzzle at all, it's a mirror: you're looking at yourself."[15] The design for the park came together in that way. First, the site dictated one piece, then another piece called for in the master plan became attached to it, then another and another, until you were not looking at pieces anymore but at the park.

"We have some continuous elements," Urbanski said, "some of which are very low key: like the pavement, for instance; the lighting, which is also intentionally very low-key, the benches, which are low-key also, really, and the railings. Those are continuous, but the idea that we should somehow make the park have a sameness, it seemed to us impossible, first of all. Second of all, not desirable—that it was 1.3 miles on the short distance on the road side, 2.4 miles on the shore side—and it would be boring. You wanted to allow the inherent variety of the geography to . . . form all the different parts."[16]

In designing the hotel and condominiums that would replace the National Cold Storage Warehouse, the architect Jonathan Marvel, of Marvel Architects, sought ways to make the structures less obtrusive. Saying he had been given "a perfect 1,000-by-100-square-foot" rectangle to build on, he and the members of the firm looked for ways to reduce the apparent scale of the buildings to make them as friendly as possible to the park. "Bending makes them smaller," he said, demonstrating with small plastic foam pieces various configurations that had been tried. He also said he thought of the condominium units in townhouse terms because "empty nesters buying the units love the townhouse connection" (see Figure 18-5). Thus nearly all the units would be duplexes, all with terraces facing the park and separated from each other by vertical limestone fins.[17]

Since, walking along the park, "people will see the buildings slantwise, the fins will be conspicuous," he said, further serving to break up the buildings' length and reduce the sense of overall mass. Having "wanted the hotel to be different," the architects conceived of it as a more nearly cubical, ten-story glass structure, connected to a residential structure of similar height, from which, in turn, a lower four-story section would be separated by the Squibb Park footbridge leading into the park.

"I felt we were never going to win," Marvel said of the competition, "but we could offer more money to the park than any other design." He said his firm achieved that through reducing corridor space by having corridors on every other floor rather than every floor, giving their client, Toll Brothers, the chance to outbid the competition. It also meant the creation of duplexes, giving every unit harborside views. On the rear, the units would have small, double-glazed windows against noise from the Brooklyn-Queens Expressway. And the walls

would be made of anodized aluminum. Those next to Squibb Park bridge would be limestone, a material Marvel called "neutral, abundant, not expensive," and having a "luminosity" to pick up light from the water. "Limestone adapts to colors of light," he said.[18]

One of the most delightful things about the park is its unpredictability. The park changes around every bend. Although everything reflects the landscape designers' imagination, their fingerprints are not obvious—the park seems to grow organically, like the city. As in the city, you can be lost in it, anonymous, or you can revel in the splendid panoramic views, the sheer size of the site, the harbor, and the whole of New York seemingly spread out before you. "Urbanistic, deliberately diverse," *Harvard Magazine* described it.[19]

Told that someone had objected to the hill on Pier 1, which blocks ground-level views from its landward side, Van Valkenburgh said, "You want to know why we put the hill on Pier 1? Because we could. I mean that, because it's the only pier that isn't on structure, and therefore you can pile up something heavy, and it's not going to break the bank, which was a huge issue for this project all along." This was a frugal way of creating landscape interest, he added, noting that the budget for Manhattan's High Line was "ten times the square foot cost in Brooklyn Bridge Park." Well, maybe not ten times, he acknowledged, but every dollar spent on Brooklyn Bridge Park was hard-won and carefully considered.[20]

On whether the hill was something the community had wanted, he said, "The community doesn't know how to say, 'You should make a hill here.' And they shouldn't. That's our job." And in contrast to an architect commissioned to design a building, he said, "We don't say, 'We're going to make a hill on Pier 1.' We would say, 'What would happen if we put a hill on Pier 1?' In other words, the design ideas are all questions."[21]

Matt Urbanski took that thought a step further:

> The water's edge is a really dynamic place—you have amazing and expansive views of the Brooklyn Bridge, of New York Harbor and the Manhattan skyline. But the middle of the site was a boring place—a completely flat stretch of concrete. So that defined the challenge—how to draw people into the middle, how to make it a dynamic place without competing with what's happening at the edges.
>
> That was our answer: a thirty-foot hill! We constructed the hill from rock that was being excavated for the construction of a Long Island Railroad tunnel under Manhattan. We got it cheap, for only the cost of trucking. And with that one design move we created eight different places, all different in character, and all emphasizing or celebrating the elements that make this space unique—the

water, the sky, the bridge, the skyline. So the hill creates a huge inviting lawn and its various slopes offer different perspectives, engaging the fantastic context of the site. Then we carved and shaped and pulled the hill to make smaller spaces and experiences, and to catch storm water and create microenvironments that would support diverse ecosystems.[22]

Drawing people away from the obvious and seductive charm of the view, creating variety and novelty in the middle of the pier, not because the community wanted a hill, but because a hill would give the community what it wanted.

Shepard, who came to the job from architecture rather than landscape architecture, described the firm's work on the site another way. "It took a lot of time just being educated by the site," he said. "I think how we approach projects now," he said, "comes out of sort of a faith that the site is more interesting than this traditional, formal conception of parks, and that you guys are sending us out on expeditions to explore the site." He recalled the "famous day" he and an associate went into the demolition-slated cold storage building at Pier 1 "with helmet lights, and we looked at all the wood, going, 'Oh, wow!' We were like, 'Wait a minute, there's miles of wood in there.'" One thought was, "Look at all those light poles!"[23] The recycled wood was used for park benches and park buildings as well.

Those light poles were novel, even provocative. Most parks in New York—indeed, most parks everywhere—use modern copies of nineteenth-century cast-iron standards topped by gas-era, lantern-style fittings. In Brooklyn Bridge Park, the tall poles surmounted by subdued spotlights suggest the site's industrial past without re-creating the industrial glare. Lining the shore, they barely light the water, which is not treated as a boundary of the park but as a part of it, a natural extension.[24] In the *New York Times* Anne Raver described Van Valkenburgh pausing at a "sandy beach that now meets the river, where most of a rotting Pier 4 was carried off in a storm years ago. Mr. Van Valkenburgh beamed at the children wading and wriggling their bare toes in the

Figure 18-6. Warning signs cannot keep this little one from dipping her toes in the water.

sand (see Figure 18-6). A little sign poking out of the beach grass says, 'No swimming or wading.' Nobody pays attention."[25]

Sometimes the designers' art involved knowing what to leave alone. On the south side of Pier 1, a small forest of wooden piles lies low in the water, the remains of a former pier structure. The platform had to be removed during the park's construction, and the piling could have been reused or removed, but it was allowed to remain as a fossil of the park's history. A visitor can come right up to the water's edge, where piles mark the way to a classic view of the Manhattan skyline. The view is intimate and vast at the same time. At sunrise and sunset and after dark it is among the most photographed views of the park.

More than most parks, Brooklyn Bridge Park is lively at all hours, but like all parks it throbs with life during the day. As park corporation board member Hank Gutman described the space:

> This isn't the fancy park for the rich white people in Brooklyn Heights. You sit down there on a nice sunny day and you will see people walk by representing the full diversity of this borough and this city and from all over the world, carrying guidebooks that send them to Brooklyn Bridge Park. Speaking more languages than you can count, and all loving it, just loving it [see Figure 18-7]. Probably thinking it's been there forever, not having a clue that three years ago there was a flat, abandoned pier. They think those hills were there, the glaciers left them.[26]

Figure 18-7. On Pier 2 the restrooms are identified in the twelve most commonly spoken languages in Brooklyn: English, Spanish, Chinese, Russian, Yiddish, French Creole, Italian, Hebrew, Polish, French, Arabic, and Urdu. (Sean Shapiro.)

The Water Lab at Pier 6 welcomed delighted families when it opened on June 5, 2010.

Crowds spread out on the Pier 1 lawn to enjoy a Metropolitan Opera concert in July 2012. (Courtesy of Alexa Hoyer.)

The Picnic Peninsula was busy on July 4, 2015.

A diverse group enjoyed the park on a sunny weekend: soccer players on Pier 5, foodies at Smorgasburg, barbecuers on the Picnic Peninsula.

Soccer players on Pier 5 were ready for any attack on their goal.

There was always plenty of action under the basket on Pier 2.

Recycled granite provided a seat for a young girl in front of piles that formerly supported part of Pier 1.

Traditional outdoor activities could be seen on Pier 1, including old-fashioned hula-hooping. (Courtesy of Elizabeth Felicella.)

Henrik Krogius saw himself reflected in artist Jeppe Hein's *Mirror Labyrinth*, an example of the park's public art program.

A sculpture in DUMBO by Deborah Kass said "OY" or "YO" depending on your vantage point. (Courtesy of Eugene Keilin.)

Beyond a support for the Squibb Park pedestrian bridge, a runner passed by a salt marsh and Pier 1 on the north–south greenway in the park.

Mallow was blooming by a freshwater marsh on Pier 1.

South of the Manhattan Bridge in DUMBO, park features included an expansive lawn, a nautical playground, a pebble beach, an environmental center, a dog park, and a bouldering wall. (Courtesy of Alex McLean.)

After dark, Jane's Carousel was still aglow and entertaining children in January 2016. (Courtesy of Eugene Keilin.)

The Squibb Park pedestrian bridge was a popular entrance to the park in 2013, before it closed for repairs.

By the time marina construction began in late 2015, the Pier 4 railhead had collapsed and was left as a remnant of the park's history.

NINETEEN
THE POLITICS OF HOUSING, CONTINUED

It felt very Nimby, like, "We don't want poor people in the backyard."

—Nina Collins, a resident of 360 Furman Street, about opposition to housing on Pier 6

Despite the park's popularity, or perhaps because of it, controversy continued to bubble.

From early on, when Brooklyn Bridge Park was no more than a community dream, most of its proponents accepted the idea embedded in the Thirteen Guiding Principles that it would have to be financially self-sustaining. But some people never accepted this, while others thought it could be achieved with modest commercial activities short of housing. After the Bloomberg administration asserted its leading role in the park's development and promoted a self-sustaining model for other parks as well, a perception grew that Brooklyn Bridge Park and the idea of self-sufficiency was a Bloomberg creation.

Some Bloomberg administration officials contributed to this impression. In an interview former deputy mayor Daniel Doctoroff said that the community had played some role in creating the park but that "government runs the process and it's not something that the actual community wants to hear." He felt the same way about the local officials, who, he said, "had zero to do at the end of the day with the achievement of Brooklyn Bridge Park," and about the state, which he thought did not have a strategic view of the park.[1]

To be sure, the Bloomberg administration was known for big initiatives and attention to quality. Many people believed that Brooklyn Bridge Park was yet another example of this. Doctoroff echoed that view.[2] It is certainly true that the Bloomberg Administration put more emphasis on high standards than low cost when it came to the park.

It is undeniable that had the city not been committed to both starting and finishing the park, it would not exist today. Doctoroff's belief that city investment in the park would pay off in many ways made him a dedicated supporter of the project. And after he left government, Deputy Mayor Patricia Harris made sure the money continued to flow and supported public art and cultural initiatives that helped make the park a special place.

Still, when the Bloomberg administration left office, the park was not yet finished. Funds were provided in the budget to complete the balance of the project, but no one knew whether the incoming mayor, Bill de Blasio, would spend them for that purpose. He had run on a platform of equity in services for all New Yorkers, and there was much talk about inequities in the citywide park system. Providing funds to complete Brooklyn Bridge Park would mean that money was not available to fund parks in poor neighborhoods. Marianna Koval, former head of the Brooklyn Bridge Park Conservancy and a candidate for parks commissioner in the de Blasio administration, predicted that completing the capital funding for Brooklyn Bridge Park would not be a priority. "It wouldn't be my first priority sitting in his seat, even now, for me," she said in an interview. "For all my history of Brooklyn Bridge Park, it wouldn't be my first priority."[3]

The other unfinished business when Bloomberg left office was the park's final development site, for which a request for proposals could not be issued until the memorandum of understanding with Senator Squadron and Assemblywoman Millman expired on December 31, 2013. Money generated by 360 Furman Street had allowed early park construction to push ahead. Subsequently, development and park creation were timed to have revenue available as new sections of the park came on line. The money expected from the Pier 6 development would be needed to complete the park's financial plan, providing enough money for operations and maintenance, especially of the maritime structures.[4]

Park management was ready to prepare a request for proposals for Pier 6 but did not know how the new team at City Hall would receive it. Alicia Glen, the new deputy mayor for housing and economic development, soon made known the city's intention to complete Brooklyn Bridge Park and proceed with soliciting proposals for Pier 6. This move was not a given, and it may have surprised some of the mayor's supporters. As a candidate, de Blasio had strongly criticized Mayor Bloomberg; as mayor, he abandoned many of Bloomberg's policies. Therefore, it was also surprising that Adrian Benepe, Mayor Bloomberg's parks commissioner, said of de Blasio, "It took political courage and independence for de Blasio to say: 'Hey, the development is part of this. It doesn't happen without development.'"[5]

But de Blasio's support for the housing on Pier 6 was not unconditional. As

Deputy Mayor Glen made clear, the development destined for Pier 6 would be an early example of the mayor's intention to create more affordable housing. This meant that housing on Pier 6 would have to include a component of what is called "workforce housing": 30 percent of the units would be designed for residents who met certain income limits; for a four-person household that meant an annual income of between $67,100 and $138,440.[6]

Requiring developers to include affordable housing was not new in New York, but it was new to Brooklyn Bridge Park and it would change the economics for the developers and the park. Until then, all solicitations for the park's residential sites had called for only market-rate housing because the park's financial plan had been based on maximizing revenue per square foot to minimize the development footprint. The introduction of workforce housing, which would affect the developer's ability to profit from the development, would also affect the revenue the park could expect. Thus a new variable clouded the old argument over how much height, if any, could come off the taller of the Pier 6 buildings without compromising the park's finances.[7]

A presentation on the proposed request for proposals was made to the park's Community Advisory Council on April 1, 2014. By April 7 a group of local officials consisting of State Senator Daniel Squadron, State Assemblywoman Joan Millman, Representative Nydia Velázquez, and City Councilmen Stephen Levin and Brad Lander had written to Mayor de Blasio, protesting "the breakneck speed at which the Bloomberg administration's project appears to be moving forward without significant modification or community input, especially since other viable options have not been revisited under your leadership."[8]

Senator Squadron's 2011 agreement with Bloomberg regarding the Watchtower properties had expired without producing any reduction of Pier 6 housing. A new mayor might give him another bite at the apple. His latest idea was to link the park's revenue to a potential housing conversion of the nearby Long Island College Hospital complex; this project was likely to go forward, but it was tied up in litigation. Yet, if nothing else, further delaying the Pier 6 project would keep the options open for those who wanted to reduce or eliminate the housing.

Mayor de Blasio, for his part, did not bite; he was publicly supportive of the park without being defensive about the housing. He told a press conference that the park would have a "transcendent impact on peoples' lives, and be a really wonderful contribution to New York City." But, he added, "it's a costly endeavor by definition, and it has to be maintained. And we know, in an atmosphere of fiscal discipline, that we have to make sure that these parks are self-sustaining whenever possible. So here's a chance to do that." Affordable housing, he continued, "allows us to make sure that the neighborhood has economic diversity, which is something I value across the board in this city."[9]

Nonetheless, the decades-old controversy over housing, fanned in part by newer elected officials, flared again with new intensity. "I don't care if it's luxury or affordable," said Judi Francis, president of the Brooklyn Bridge Park Defense Fund and a plaintiff in the unsuccessful litigation to prevent the park from using residential development as a source of revenue. "Housing corrodes the soul of the park." Her new spouse, former LDC board member Roy Sloane, added, "Parks are for people, not high rises."[10]

In the latest installment of the Pier 6 battle, the traditional opponents of housing were joined by a new group of supporters who came from a surprising quarter and whose opposition was surprisingly virulent. They were, by and large, people of means who had purchased condominiums in what was now called One Brooklyn Bridge Park, the building at 360 Furman Street adjacent to Pier 6 that was the first of the park's development sites. They had apparently gotten used to not having neighbors, even though the prospect of the Pier 6 buildings was fully disclosed in the offering prospectus for their apartments. New housing on Pier 6 might block some of their southward views, increase the crowds in the park, and create more competition for local services. Moreover, this group had not participated in the original community planning process and had not signed onto any of the compromises necessary to achieve consensus.

Opposition to the Pier 6 housing blossomed on the internal online bulletin boards at 360 Furman and quickly became public. The news that the mayor would require affordable housing in the development only intensified the opposition.

The clamor from 360 Furman was loud and ugly enough for the *New York Times* to take notice. In the first paragraph of an article bearing the heading "The Battle of Brooklyn Bridge Park," the *Times* reporter Liz Robbins wrote, "The internal message board of the One Brooklyn Bridge Park luxury condominium is generally used to remind residents to pick up their dry cleaning. Last spring, it was used to air their dirty laundry."[11]

Not everyone at No. 360 agreed with the complainers. To one resident, Nina Collins, as the *Times* reported, "It felt very Nimby, like 'We don't want poor people in the backyard.'" Eventually she sent an e-mail to her neighbors saying, "You are making me ashamed to be your neighbor; please stop."[12]

But her request did not stop the complaints; the critics simply shifted to arguments recast to sound more legitimate. How could the park justify workforce housing (which would necessarily mean lower revenues per square foot for the park) when it had promised to build the least possible development to cover park maintenance, critics asked. They argued that conditions had changed since housing was first included in the plan, some for the better (housing values were much higher) and some for the worse (congested traffic, crowded schools). Maybe the money from a new development project was not really needed; maybe it was time for a new environmental assessment.

Other newcomers joined the opposition. Martin Hale, who had recently bought a house on Willow Place, two blocks east of the Pier 6 site, reportedly paying $7.6 million,[13] became a major player. Critics organized a "Save Pier 6" campaign, plastering posters around the Heights urging people to sign an online petition aimed at stopping the "tower" in the park. The posters described the park as a place "for kids to play in," not one for condo owners. Of course, kids were already playing in the park, and condo owners were already making payments to maintain it, without which the park could not have been built in the first place. Hale had no children and had not been involved in the park's history; however, like some residents of nearby Willowtown, he did have a personal interest in the outcome and seemed to have the financial resources to advance that interest.

Hale created a new organization called People for Green Space Foundation, which, together with Lori Schomp and their neighbor, a well-known local architect named Joseph Merz, filed a lawsuit seeking to prevent Pier 6 development from proceeding. As Liz Robbins pointed out in her article in the *Times*, "They make an odd couple of litigants—Ms. Schomp, who wants her view of the water on her frequent runs preserved, Mr. Merz, who lectures softly on social theory, insisting on separating parkland from development."[14]

Adrian Benepe, parks commissioner from 2002 to 2012, was more direct in his criticism of the group's stance: "The grouch remarks, 'Whatever it is, I'm against it.' Anything you can think of to try to deny affordable housing, so that they can stop this from happening, is the ultimate sort of chutzpah and political machination and sort of unbelievable."[15]

The lawsuit resulted in a temporary injunction that allowed the park to receive and evaluate responses to its Pier 6 request for proposals but not to sign a

Figure 19-1. Rendering of the two residential buildings slated for Pier 6 sited just south of One Brooklyn Bridge Park. (ODA-RAL Development Services / *Brooklyn Heights Press*.)

lease with any developer, pending the outcome of further hearings.[16] Subsequently, a settlement was reached in which the plaintiffs withdrew their lawsuit in exchange for a promise that the park corporation would seek an amendment to its general project plan.

In the meantime, park management had been negotiating with a short list of final bidders for the Pier 6 development to achieve some of the objectives it thought the community and its representatives sought. Developers were urged to satisfy as many as possible without compromising the amount of revenue the park needed to receive from the project. A deal was reached for a three-story height reduction for each building, the inclusion of workforce housing units, a prekindergarten, and construction by unionized labor (see Figure 19-1).[17] The announcement of this conditional agreement was intended to provide a concrete plan for the public to consider in the context of the pending request for modification of the park's general project plan. Nevertheless, it was met with outrage from the local officials as well as the Brooklyn Heights Association and every other neighborhood group, all of which had expected the modification process to open, not close, options.[18]

In all of this the twenty-six-member Community Advisory Council had become a negative force. One member, Peter Flemming, who had opposed the Tobacco Warehouse conversion but supported housing, commented on the difficulty of bringing more varied opinions to the CAC because the membership committee rejected qualified stakeholders who did not agree with their views.[19] By this time the CAC contained an active core of people opposed to the park's financing plan. The elected officials, who had proudly opposed housing, made at-large appointments of their like-minded supporters. The CAC replaced one of its co-chairs, Nancy Webster, because she was thought to have a conflict of interest by virtue of her position as president of the Brooklyn Bridge Park Conservancy. Her successor was an antidevelopment activist.

Thus it was not surprising when the Community Advisory Council adopted a resolution on May 27 requesting that the Brooklyn Bridge Park Corporation conduct a review, with extensive public participation, of the general project plan as it related to Pier 6. On July 22 a second resolution was forwarded that urged a full-scale public review of the existing plan "to include financing parameters and environmental considerations that have evolved since 2004."[20] If carried out, these resolutions would have resulted in a substantial delay in the Pier 6 project, and perhaps its significant modification or even abandonment.[21]

Both resolutions were taken up at the August meeting of the park board. The meeting was long and contentious, with housing opponents often shouting down speakers whose views differed from their own. Whereas fear of privatizing the park had been an earlier argument against housing, overcrowding the already-popular park was now the objection.

To many supporters of the Pier 6 plan, the new opponents seemed to be looking for any argument that might resonate and stick. Many speakers pursued the tack taken in the lawsuit: the park's environmental impact statement had not accurately predicted the future. It had greatly underestimated impacts, they said, and, anyway, Brooklyn had changed all around it. Therefore, before proceeding with Pier 6 development, a fresh look was required. "In no way do the plans as they were generated account for this new population," Brooklyn Heights resident Andrew Kern maintained, while board member John Raskin, representing State Senator Squadron, said, "It was 10 years ago that we looked at this. And the world has changed." Superstorm Sandy was also mentioned as a reason to reconsider housing on Pier 6.[22]

Park management explained that the legal requirement for environmental review did not demand that predictions of impact be correct, only reasonable. Supplemental review would be required only if the project itself changed or experienced significant delays in construction. In accordance with environmental statutes, a less-extensive technical review had been done to examine whether the proposed Pier 6 project would have a "material" impact in any of the categories required to be studied. It was determined that the project was well below the materiality standard set forth in the statute.

The park board voted ten to three against the Community Advisory Council resolutions to reopen the general project plan and redo the environmental impact statement.[23]

By the time the park board met again in November, the opponents' arguments had shifted emphasis again, with public speakers, three of whom owned penthouses at

360 Furman, complaining that the park's financial model was a sham. Henry Richmond, also associated with People for Green Space, handed out a financial analysis challenging the park's model as grossly underestimating existing park revenues and claiming that it proved construction of Pier 6 housing was unnecessary.[24]

Park management prepared a critique of that analysis, challenging its assumptions as reckless and inconsistent with good stewardship of the park.[25] Regina Myer had earlier said that the sites already under development (360 Furman; Pierhouse and 1 Hotel; Empire Stores; John Street) would cover 92 percent of the park's operating expenses but only 39 percent of what was needed for pier maintenance.[26] The idea of "pier maintenance" did not have much sex appeal,[27] but failure to maintain the piers was an existential threat for the park; after all, it had been the high costs of pier maintenance that had driven the Port Authority to dispose of the piers in the first place.

The park corporation commissioned a study of its financial plan by an outside consultant, the economist Barbara Denham.[28] Denham, who was a specialist in real estate economics, concluded that the management numbers were, if anything, too optimistic. But the opponents renewed their attacks, disparaging Denham, her credentials, her analysis, and her impartiality.[29] The park corporation publicly rebutted these claims in December.[30]

Some of the opponents' arguments resonated with the public. After all, no one was really happy about a thirty-story apartment tower. The Brooklyn Heights Association was an advocate of self-financing for the park but it had always been concerned about the height of new buildings, and the recent appearance of Pierhouse had made everyone more sensitive to the height issue and more suspicious of the park management and the city. Brooklyn had become more popular, the park was very popular, and traffic did seem worse. There was a need for a new school. To alleviate crowding, the Department of Education had made changes in the catchment areas for two local schools but it was not clear whether this would satisfy everyone. Maybe the park did have enough revenue, after all; maybe a new environmental assessment was in order. In any event, why not make the buildings lower?

Opponents were not always consistent. Frank Carone, the lawyer representing People for Green Space in the litigation, told the *New York Times*, "The intent is to have a supplemental environmental impact study. I've told my clients that we are not bringing litigation to stop development but to do it more carefully."[31] This statement was contradicted by his client, Lori Schomp, in an interview with Michael Randazzo posted on the *Brooklyn Heights Blog*: "After digging through the park's financial model, our position at this point is that there should be no housing on Pier 6."[32] The goals of housing opponents had gone from reducing the taller building by a few stories, if workforce housing could be beaten back, to complete elimination.

Expressing his opinion about the issues that had been raised, Bloomberg parks commissioner Adrian Benepe said, "They are legitimate issues for the BHA and others to take up, but I think it's sort of immaterial to what's happening in the park because the park deal came along first." As to the claim that Pier 6 development was no longer needed, "That's not true," Benepe stated. "People can say many things; they are entitled to their own opinions, but not their own facts. They need the buildings and that's part of the deal. You can't change the deal midstream."[33]

Two other park experts, well known for having revitalized large New York parks, were also frustrated with those who seemed not to appreciate the importance of adequate funds for park maintenance. Elizabeth Barlow Rogers, former administrator of Central Park in Manhattan, and Tupper Thomas, former administrator of Prospect Park in Brooklyn, had recent and hard-won experience with park maintenance.

Both stressed in interviews the importance of finding money from sources other than the Parks Department budget to keep parks in good repair. Both had inherited rundown gems that had received neither the public funding nor skilled management they deserved. Both spoke admiringly of Brooklyn Bridge Park's design as well as its independent stature, which gave it the capacity to be funded and managed to a high standard.

Thomas said she saw the value of Brooklyn Bridge Park's financial model from the beginning: "If Olmsted and Vaux had only done for Prospect Park what was done for Brooklyn Bridge Park, where they set aside an area around the park for residential development that could have paid for the park, I wouldn't have to have spent all those years fund-raising." She pointed to Riverside, an Olmsted project outside Chicago, undertaken after he realized that cities would not adequately fund their parks. "He actually had the parks built right into the infrastructure of the taxing base so that they were always maintained. That's a very interesting concept, and I think we have to look for new ways to fund these things because the city government has been incapable of properly funding their parks."[34]

On a more mundane level, Thomas said, people rarely consider the need to frequently empty trash containers (an empty container encourages people to drop waste into it; a full can invites littering) or the need to have adequate security officers to make sure that the park is kept safe as well as clean.

In the case of Central Park, Rogers explained, "We got every dollar we could get from the capital budget and married those up with private dollars."[35] With the wealthiest residents of New York City living across the street from the park, Rogers was able to convince many of them to support what she called her "missionary" work to slowly improve the staffing and managing of the park. Rogers built the Central Park Conservancy into an organization that brought cachet to contributors, such as hedge fund manager John Paulson, who later made a gift of $100 million.

Over time, opponents of Pier 6 housing came up with another argument designed to avoid building it. They proposed that the park borrow to cover pier maintenance, which they characterized as capital maintenance. Capital or not, it was not at all clear that the park had authority to borrow; the city's budget office said it would not permit it.[36] Regardless, park management demonstrated that, without the revenues from Pier 6, it would not have the funds to cover its debt service on borrowing. Moreover, who would buy the park's debt in such a case? Opponents, undeterred, pressed on to generate support for the idea.

Housing opponents, now including the Brooklyn Heights Association,[37] hired their own consultants to challenge the park's analysis of maritime maintenance needs and costs as well as the park's entire financial model. The marine consultant said that maintenance costs could be spread out over time; the financial consultant said the park's revenues would be higher (because properties near the park were more valuable) and come sooner than projected.

The park corporation responded in turn, pointing out that the marine consultant was an expert in submarine propulsion, not subsurface piling, and that the financial calculations assumed the city's finance department would change its basic methodology. One observer pointed out that changing the tax calculation meant the opponents of Pier 6 would increase their own taxes as well as those of every condominium owner in the city. And so it went.

Stepping back from the specifics, the parties were arguing about projections that extended forty or fifty years into the future. Like most projections—and all long-term estimates—the outcome depends on the assumptions.

In the simplest terms, the park corporation believed that it was cheaper and safer to fix the marine structures before they wore out, and it made the conventional assumption that property values would rise and fall at historical rates. The opponents of housing were making much different and distinctly more optimistic assumptions: that costs would be lower and come later and that revenues would be higher and come sooner.

The opponents of housing said it was too early to tell if additional revenues would be required, that the housing on Pier 6, once built, would be permanent, and that the park could always borrow money if it encountered a shortfall.

The park corporation answered that overestimating revenues and underestimating expenses was a classic recipe for trouble, and that giving up present revenue was a permanent loss, while relying on future revenue was speculative. They believed the same was true of maintenance, remembering that the collapse and loss of Pier 4 in 2008 showed the folly of waiting too long to fix the piling.

Moreover, the park corporation felt that it had no fallback if optimistic projections proved to be wrong, since going into debt was unwise in any case and likely to be impossible if the park were forced to depend on it. Though not often said, many members of the park corporation board felt that they were stewards of a $400 million public investment and that their opponents, many of whom had personal reasons for objecting to the new buildings, would not be around to pick up the pieces if they were wrong.

Meanwhile, members of the Community Advisory Council were in open rebellion against the park. Community Board 2, whose representative served as its cochair pursuant to the CAC bylaws, finally withdrew, describing the reason as the body's "dysfunctional dynamic."[38] District manager of the community board, Robert Perris, observed that the CAC had become "increasingly adversarial towards the park administration."[39] Even Tony Manheim quit the CAC.

This turmoil in the community was not lost on the governor, whose Empire State Development Corporation had been asked to approve a modification of the park's general project plan for Pier 6. After a public hearing was held in July 2015, the city administration expected the state to act on the narrow issues of permitting some affordable housing and a prekindergarten in the proposed buildings and increasing parkland by closing a road. But time passed and nothing happened.

Eventually the state agency let it be known that it was prepared to give the city more time to reach a consensus with the community on Pier 6.[40] By then, however, it was hard to see how a consensus could be reached. The opponents may not have been a majority of the community but they were loud, well organized, and appeared determined to block any housing, not just reduce its height and bulk.

In effect, the state agency that had been a party to the Grand Bargain at its birth was about to abandon it, but this was not entirely an argument on the merits. It was also about politics. The governor and the mayor had been at odds for some time. An adversarial relationship between mayor and governor seems to be built into New York's DNA, but the animosity at this time was as sharp and unforgiving as anyone could remember. Most arguments between city and state are carried on quietly, even surreptitiously, but this fight was public, persistent, and personal. The possibility that the governor did not want to help resolve what could be viewed as the mayor's problem could not be dismissed. If that were the case, the park would once again be caught in political currents beyond its control, the very thing park supporters had been trying to avoid for years.

In truth, the mayor's desire to provide affordable housing did not fundamentally change anything. Some would argue that it was expensive and wasteful to build affordable housing on such valuable real estate, but the city's insistence on adding affordable housing on Pier 6 only affected how tall the buildings would be. Reasonable people could disagree about which was more important—the height of the buildings or the availability of affordable housing—but this was ultimately a public policy question that would be decided by public officials like the mayor. If the public did not agree with the decision, those public officials would come up for election soon enough.

TWENTY
WATERFRONT, PARKS, AND COMMUNITY PLANNING

I'd like to see more color. Grass, flowers, paint—just more color.
—A Queens resident at a ceremony announcing the refurbishing
of Bowne Playground in Flushing

Brooklyn Bridge Park was not created in a vacuum. New York City has more than five hundred miles of shoreline, and every mile presents its own challenge and its own opportunity. The same is true of urban waterfronts throughout the country and the world. The designers of the park in Brooklyn drew on their experience with other parks and on the experience of other people, while the solutions they devised in Brooklyn have had a profound effect on other parks and other cities.

As we have seen, the evolution of New York City's waterfront has been halting, haphazard, and scarcely half completed. When manufacturing and commerce receded, competition among various possible uses and users made coherent planning and decision making frequently problematic. This problem was not new or unique to New York. As early as 1972, a federal statute called the Coastal Zone Management Act provided the framework and the funding for states and localities to "maximize the benefits of economic development, environmental conservation, and public use of the waterfront while minimizing the conflicts among these objectives."[1]

Mayor Dinkins and his planning department took steps to revise and enhance the city's waterfront revitalization program in the 1990s. Through a public process they created a document called the "New York City Comprehensive Waterfront Plan, Reclaiming the City's Edge." The plan considered four principal functions of the waterfront: the natural waterfront (the water and related ecosystems), the public waterfront (parks, esplanades, and view corridors), the working waterfront (water-dependent, maritime, industrial, transportation, and municipal uses), and the redeveloping waterfront (where land uses had recently changed, or where vacant or underused property offered opportunity), and suggested strategies to guide planning and public investment. Like most such ambitious plans it had little impact, a victim of tight budgets, economic uncertainty, competing interests, and changing administrations.

Twenty years later Mayor Bloomberg and *his* planning department initiated a new community planning effort for the city's waterfront and waterways called "Vision 2020." Using the same organizational framework as the Dinkins plan, he added a fifth waterfront, the network of waterborne transportation. The effort included a three-year waterfront action agenda with identified goals and "specific, high-priority projects that demonstrated the city's commitment to investing in the transformation of the waterfront."[2]

To prove the seriousness of his intent, the city created a Waterfront Management Advisory Board to help track the progress of the 130 projects identified and publish the results. As a consequence, Bloomberg left a waterfront legacy that goes well beyond Brooklyn Bridge Park, although the fate of his long-term plans would still rest with future mayors.

During the Bloomberg years, the City Council also created a new Waterfront Committee, originally chaired by Councilman David Yassky from Brooklyn Heights, which gave new attention and occasionally resources to waterfront issues.

About a year into Mayor Bill de Blasio's term he announced his own planning vision for the city, known as "One New York." His plan did not deal with the waterfront per se, but changed the framework to four categories encompassing growth, equity, sustainability, and resiliency. Goals for water quality as well as parks and natural resources were discussed in the sustainability section, while coastal defenses were covered in the section on resiliency.

As for parks, Mayor de Blasio followed through on his demand for equity by announcing his Community Parks Initiative, a $130 million plan to improve thirty-five less-well-tended parks in poorer neighborhoods. City Parks Commissioner Mitchell Silver described this plan as "a down payment" on a longer effort to invest in smaller neighborhood parks. He said his department would take a look at other needy parks in the following year. At Bowne Playground in Flushing, Queens, where the mayor made his announcement, a local resident commented, "I'd like to see more color. Grass, flowers, paint—just more color."[3] Meanwhile, a group of nineteen city agencies, together with the state and federal government and about a dozen community groups, joined in a project called "100 Days to Progress" to work on numerous projects in Brooklyn's long-neglected Brownsville neighborhood. One of these was an extensive "Imagination Playground" to serve public housing residents in Brownsville.[4]

Mayor de Blasio also announced an agreement with eight of the largest conservancies to provide expertise and other in-kind services to needy parks.[5] The Central Park Conservancy would send a horticultural team and other staff to two dozen parks and train local crews in park maintenance. "For some, this is the first opportunity for formal training," said Jamey Hewitt, the Parks Department's deputy chief of operations for Brooklyn.[6] The Prospect Park Alliance undertook to redesign Stroud Playground in Crown Heights, one of the original Community Parks Initiative sites.

The eight participating conservancies ranged significantly in financial capacity. For example, the Central Park Conservancy raises $40 million a year and the Prospect Park Alliance $4 million. As Councilman Mark D. Levine, chairman of the City Council's parks committee, said of their contribution, "I really think the conservancies are sharing their most valuable resource, which is their expertise in how to run a heavily used urban park."[7]

Williamsburg and Greenpoint, two neighborhoods up the East River from the Brooklyn Bridge, had been diligently planning and forcefully advocating for significant public space on their waterfront for some time. But despite strenuous community efforts, they were stymied. There had been rezoning and residential development but so far insubstantial public investments in promised parkland. Perhaps the communities did not have the same political influence as Brooklyn Heights, and perhaps the time for a bold new public park had passed. But to Luis Garden Acosta, founder of a community group called El Puente, the city needed to live up to its promise. "This is not just a promise. This is a moral responsibility and a human right," he was quoted as saying. "We need this. It is not just a luxury."[8]

In contrast, if you had access to private funds, you could do a lot. The movie mogul Barry Diller and his wife, the designer Diane von Furstenberg, offered to pay $130 million (the same as de Blasio's outlay for thirty-five neglected parks) for a 2.7-acre landscaped park on stilts to rise out of the Hudson River in place of downtown Pier 55. The Dillers would also pay to maintain the park for twenty years. Of the elaborate design by the British artist-architect Thomas Heatherwick, James S. Russell wrote in the *New York Times*, "A 62-foot hillock tops a grassy bowl that opens to vistas of the city. Fissures in the landscape frame river views from intimate passageways, one of which can host spontaneous performances. A 700-seat amphitheater replaces Pier 54's scaffolded stage."[9] The Hudson River Park Trust was happy to accept the project, although there were mutterings that this was a "billionaire's park" aimed principally at the well to do.[10]

Apart from the waterfront, there was a movement to reclaim other kinds of spaces for parks. Queens wanted a High Line of its own, with a proposal to turn the Long Island Rail Road's abandoned Rockaway Beach Branch line into a 3.5-mile park to be called QueensWay. The project, twice the length of Manhattan's High Line, and with a price tag estimated at $122 million, was promoted by the Trust for Public Land and would require a combination of public and private money. Writing in the *New York Times*, Lisa W. Foderaro noted that the project would require less structural work than the High Line, given that much of the route runs on top of earthen berms or through gullies, which would require nothing more than the clearing of tracks, the removal of some trees, and the pouring of asphalt.[11]

The ultimate recycled park was growing in Staten Island as the old Fresh Kills landfill was slowly being turned into a 2,200-acre park nearly three times the size of Central Park. For decades, much of the city's garbage had been dumped onto this large expanse on the west side of Staten Island, but in 2001 the landfill was closed and the city's garbage shipped elsewhere. A temporary reopening took place after the terrorist attacks of September 11, 2001, so that part of the area could be used to sort through debris from the World Trade Center site in search of remains of the victims. In 2008, construction of a park on the site began under the leadership of the Freshkills Park administrator Eloise Hirsh, pursuant to an agreement between the city's Department of Parks and Recreation and Department of Sanitation. As a thirty-year project to be carried out in phases, Freshkills Park found it hard to compete for capital funds. But if completed, the park would represent a model of reclamation and ecological restoration for the country and a spectacular resource for the city.

How does Brooklyn Bridge Park fit into the broader context of waterfront-park planning elsewhere? This is a critically important question. While others across the country have closely watched the progress of Brooklyn Bridge Park, the circumstances in other places are typically very different—geographically, politically, and financially.

Many waterfront projects are on riverfronts, not oceanfronts, and may serve a different need than Brooklyn Bridge Park. In Louisville, Kentucky, for example, and other cities of its size along rivers, riverfront park projects are often motivated by concerns about economic development. Louisville Waterfront Park is operated by a nonprofit organization, the Waterfront Development Corporation, created in 1986 by an agreement between the city, the county, and the state "to oversee redevelopment of Louisville's waterfront from a blighted and underutilized area into a vibrant area."[12] A master plan was adopted in 1991 to guide development for the park and the surrounding waterfront neighborhood. In an inverse of the model for Brooklyn Bridge Park, the corporation relies on both public and private dollars to fund construction of Waterfront Park but only on government funds to cover maintenance and operations. Park construction is considered a civic enterprise to which local businesses, foundations, families, and individuals contribute.

Seattle offers an interesting comparison to Louisville. The city is also engaged in a grand project promoted by the local government and civic leadership. More than economic development, the vision there was to reconnect the city to its shoreline and the natural marine environment at its western edge by tearing down the elevated highway that ran along it, burying the highway underground, rebuilding the adjoining seawall, and building a new waterfront park on top. If this sounds familiar, it is because it resembles New York's scuttled Westway project, the plan to cover an expressway buried in landfill with a park, which was the predecessor plan to Hudson River Park.

In contrast to Louisville's project, Seattle's waterfront plan is actually an enormous infrastructure project costing more than $1 billion in local, state, and federal dollars and requiring the coordination of multiple jurisdictions and authorities. The park portion of seventy to eighty acres was designed by James Corner, the British landscape architect who designed the High Line, and its realization is led by the city's Office of the Waterfront with an advisory body of civic leaders. The expected capital cost of the park alone is about $700 million. About 30 percent of the money will come from the state and about 10 percent from the city. About 14 percent is expected from private philanthropy, but 16 percent, or $115 million, will come from a real estate excise tax and a local improvement district, a device frequently used to fund public projects in Washington State.[13]

While Business Improvement Districts, known as BIDs, are widely used in New York City, where local business owners agree to tax themselves primarily to fund supplemental sanitation and security services, local improvement districts are not. A BID is voluntary and applies only to commercial property owners, where-as the government imposes the local improvement district.[14]

The downtown Chicago waterfront represents another example worth examining. The city has a long-standing commitment to parks and planning. More than a century ago, Daniel Burnham and Edward H. Bennett developed a comprehensive plan for the Chicago metropolitan region that encompassed a public park and waterfront on Lake Michigan. Burnham crossed paths with Frederick Law Olmsted during the course of his career, collaborated with him on the World's Columbian Exhibition in Chicago, and had a similar approach to planning. Burnham's dreams for a large public lakefront have been largely realized and the city named a 598-acre park in his honor.[15]

Since Burnham's death in 1912, Chicago has continued to build an extensive complex of parks along its waterfront. The 24.5-acre Millennium Park, part of the much larger Grant Park, was built over the Illinois Central rail yards and was conceived by the city as a civic amenity for which it could raise substantial private funds. Cindy Pritzker, whose family is a major philanthropic force in Chicago, attracted Frank Gehry by offering a $15 million gift for a proposed band shell. Soon $90 million in additional contributions matched that. The project would grow to include the Jay Pritzker Pavilion, the Crown Fountain, the Lurie Garden, the Harris Theater, the Nichols Bridgeway, the McCormick Tribune Plaza and Ice Rink, the Chase Promenade, the AT&T Plaza, Wrigley Square, the Exelon Pavilion, the McDonald's Cycle Center, the Boeing Galleries, and the BP Pedestrian Bridge.[16]

The long list of private givers shows that in certain places, for projects that offer naming opportunities, and given the right economic environment, it is possible to raise enormous amounts of private and corporate capital (having multiple cutting-edge architects helps). But this sort of thing is the exception, not the rule, and it brings its own costs. Private donors want control and recognition, while it is difficult for members of the public to feel they are in a democratic park when everything around them is branded.

Yet another approach is to be found in Washington, D.C., where it is hoped that the 11th Street Bridge Park will breach the physical, economic, and cultural divide that for decades separated communities on either side of the Anacostia River. The project, which involves the world-class designers OMA + OLIN, calls for reusing an abandoned highway bridge that connects gentrifying Capitol Hill with Old Anacostia, a historic African American neighborhood. The city government in Washington and a local not-for-profit group called Building Bridges across the River have a big vision for a small space: they are not just building a park but seeking to improve public health, connect communities, and reengage residents with the river itself. Many of these ideas came from a public planning process.[17]

Bridge Park is expected to cost about $45 million, of which the city has allocated $14.5 over three years. The Kresge Foundation recently committed $1.2 million, but substantial sums remain to be raised.[18]

The charismatic leader of Bridge Park, Scott Kratz from Building Bridges across the River, has been tenacious and persuasive. In his vision, the park serves much more than a conventional purpose. He speaks about community, equity, and equality. He has plans for community gardens, farmers' markets, cleaning up the river, and bringing in clams and mussels to help reduce pollution. He has created an entity called the Equitable Development Task Force to plan for and mitigate the negative aspects of the economic changes Bridge Park may produce.[19] There is also talk of devising strategies to provide more affordable housing, promote local businesses, and provide more jobs. If it all seems a lot to ask of a plan for an abandoned bridge, the ambitions illustrate the texture of devising, designing, marketing, and funding public projects in the twenty-first century.

TWENTY-ONE
REFLECTIONS ON BROOKLYN BRIDGE PARK

It has been said that democracy is the worst form of government except for all the others that have been tried.

—Winston Churchill

The creation of Brooklyn Bridge Park marked four departures from the norm of American park development: in the park's physical character, its method of financing, its origin in popular protest, and its public planning.

A park of lawns, trees, rocks and flowers, yes, but Brooklyn Bridge Park also incorporated the remains of the waterfront's commercial history. Pier platforms and parts of their sheds were preserved and turned to use for park activities. Old warehouses on the park's edge were preserved and converted for modern use. An expanse of piling left sticking out of the water was preserved as a reminder of the past. Old lumber was discovered and turned into park benches. There was a precedent in Europe for this sort of thing, with parks created around industrial relics with almost no green.[1] But for many in the local communities who initially pressed for the park, the emerging reality proved very different from the sylvan refuge they had envisioned.

The park also represented something different in the way its maintenance would be financed. As we have seen, the possibility that there would be a park at all rested on its paying for its own upkeep, as it could not count on already-overstretched city and state park budgets, especially at a time when the general mood was for cutting taxes. Elements in the park (restaurants, concessions, a conference center and hotel) were to generate sufficient revenue to pay for the park's maintenance and operations. But overly optimistic estimates came up against the hard truth that the maintenance costs would be far higher. The consequent turn to private housing to cover costs in the smallest footprint possible set off an acrimonious debate over whether this amounted to "privatizing" the park—a debate (replete with lawsuits) that would resurface well after the matter appeared to have been settled.

The very idea of housing was what had gotten the park idea started in the first place. To recover lost income from piers that had become obsolete the Port

Authority of New York and New Jersey had proposed housing on the piers and all along their upland. That prospect alarmed a community that did not want its waterfront filled with residential buildings and led to the counterproposal for a park. This would prove a hard sell, as neither the bistate Port Authority nor state and city governments saw any reason to build a park. Eventually, as has been recounted here, they were brought around to support a plan that served a broad constituency as well as a broad purpose, and that made it possible for the park to happen.

Inviting the public to participate in the planning was, though not revolutionary, certainly unusual in its scope and scale. In earlier years the New Urbanists had held single twenty-hour public cram sessions (charrettes) at which people expressed their desires in the planning of a new town, but here thousands of people took part in sessions held in various locations over many months. Input was sought not just from neighborhoods closest to the park site, like Brooklyn Heights and Cobble Hill, but also from those farther away, including communities with different characters and interests from the park's immediate neighbors. To win governmental support for the park, it had to be a park for all. This did not necessarily please some residents of the park's proximity, who feared an influx of outsiders into their quiet neighborhood, but it was a condition they had to accept if there was to be a park at all.

Professional planners guided the discussions, but the public did most of the talking. The initial master plan was distilled from those conversations. When the professional designers took over, as they had to, their work reflected what they had heard, even as they dealt with new possibilities and limitations that had not been foreseen and came up with unexpected new ideas.

Nearly a generation has passed since those public meetings, but the stamp the public put on the park is indelible. Going into those meetings, many of the park's sponsors were thinking of the park in conventional terms—green, uniform, and largely passive. But the public wanted more and had a long list of hopes and expectations: recreation and sports, picnics and playgrounds, food and culture, boating and fishing, access to nature and access to the water, diversity and complexity. The people expanded the vision—those who came to the planning sessions and sent ideas to the website, who suggested and requested, who listened and learned, who argued and compromised. They are the true authors of Brooklyn Bridge Park.

As important as community planning was to the very existence of the park, it turned out to be a two-edged sword. Community planning created a wish list that was largely fulfilled, but it also created the expectation that, at every stage of the process, the community would be consulted in advance and that it could have what it wanted. As the park became a reality, as substantial tax dollars were spent on it, the final decisions were made elsewhere—by the professional designers employed to make it happen and by the government paying the bills.

Responding to expectations about the level of continuing community participation became a serious challenge. While some level of public engagement continued throughout the design and construction of the park, there was not enough public input to satisfy everyone. Many accepted the diminished public role as inevitable, but some thought the park's planning had become secretive and duplicitous.

Another reason community consensus eroded over time is that some of the issues that dogged the park most were not discussed in the robust public process that characterized the early stages. While an issue like the Montague Street connection was contentious, it received a lot of attention and there was plenty of opportunity to debate it. Not everyone was satisfied with the outcome, but it did not become the kind of divisive issue that housing did.

The issue of housing, on the other hand, was never really on the table until 2004. Had it been aired in the earlier public process, the pluses and minuses would have been examined at a time when the community was more open to considering the trade-offs necessary to make the park a reality.

The passage of time—fifteen years since the master plan had been created—also allowed some of the considerations that had guided the planning, and that had been accepted, to be forgotten. Many newcomers were not familiar with the ugly reality of the site before its transformation into a park. They had not participated in and did not appreciate the protest against the Port Authority's plans for the area. They thought the alternative to housing was no housing when, in the sweep of time, the alternative to a park had been no park.

Moreover, once the public funds were appropriated and spent and the park was almost complete, it became easier to criticize elements of the plan without seeming to incur the risk of actually killing it. But that would risk depriving the park of adequate funds to maintain itself, which could kill it in a different way. While the consequences might not be felt immediately, the park would eventually deteriorate. Indeed, as the history of the park site makes clear, it could literally disappear into the East River.

Despite unique elements, the Brooklyn Bridge Park experience suggests a number of lessons for other places where manufacturing and commerce have withdrawn from waterways, leaving dead zones that could present opportunities. From Buffalo to Los Angeles, communities across the country see this as a moment to revitalize and connect to their waterfronts.

The financing of park maintenance through housing or other adjacent uses could be applicable elsewhere. Park "purists" often argue that this violates the public nature of parks and goes against the principles of Frederick Law Olmsted, who built the great urban oases in the nineteenth century. Olmsted, at least, was not a purist; he admired Birkenhead in England (near Liverpool), which incorporated housing, and in Riverside, Illinois, he integrated park and housing to insure tax collections would maintain the park.

Moreover, Brooklyn Bridge Park has already demonstrated that relying on a private source for income does not necessarily lead to privatizing the park. When state and city governments have limited funds, it makes sense to employ private means to enable the construction of a public project, so long as the public interest controls the planning and free public access to that project is guaranteed.

As for converting old commercial or industrial sites into parks that retain reminders of their historic character, that is an option available in many places. It is not only waterfronts but also other obsolescent areas that are potential targets for such treatment. It is only a matter of how the site will be treated. A new understanding of what a "park" is may be required for it to be designed in a historically evocative manner, and it may take considerable persuasion to win public support.

Brooklyn Bridge Park grew out of opposition to a powerful government agency's very different plan for the site. This victory may be hard to duplicate elsewhere but it is not impossible. Looking back over the park's history, it required unusual perseverance to beat back the Port Authority's plan and extraordinary savvy and good fortune to replace it with something quite different that was actually funded and built. On the other hand, the Port's plan for commercial development was a stimulus to which the park plan was a response. What was achieved at Brooklyn Bridge Park could encourage other communities to organize and take the initiative to advance important public projects.

Even when park plans originate with agencies of government, the public can and should participate in their development. Indeed, other than the park itself, the success of its public planning is the most important legacy of the park's history. Unusual when it shaped the park's master plan, public participation is now common, almost universal. Such participation, pesky as it may sometimes seem to public officials, is in fact likely to lead to an improved result.

On the face of it, the mechanisms discussed above need not be controversial. Still, as the history of Brooklyn Bridge Park shows, differences can arise at every stage of planning and implementation. Any major undertaking in the public sphere requires finding a workable consensus in an atmosphere filled with competing desires, suspicions, private agendas, and private grievances. Maintaining that consensus becomes harder as time goes on.

It is not just the passage of time; it is also the foreclosure of possibilities. In the case of Brooklyn Bridge Park, as the general gave way to the specific, and as choices were made that could not be unmade, controversy grew. This evolution may be simply a reflection of human nature, which can be controlled to some extent but not completely avoided.

It has been said that genius is the ability to move the layman and simultaneously impress the expert. Considering the controversies and attitudinal changes over the course of time, the extent to which the park as built reflects the principles of the 2000 master plan is remarkable, and the park that descended from that plan has succeeded with visitors and professionals alike. Visitors quite unversed in park design have returned to the park again and again, communicating their delight in it to their family and friends.

Trained professional and architecture critics, who bring a different eye to the park, appreciate it as well. Nicolai Ouroussoff, the *New York Times* architecture critic when the park first opened, wrote, "Much as Central Park embodied Frederick Law Olmsted's vision of American democracy on the eve of the Civil War, Brooklyn Bridge Park, designed by Michael Van Valkenburgh Associates, is an attempt to come to terms with the best and worst of our era; on the one hand, concern for the environment and an appreciation for the beauty of urban life and infrastructure; on the other, the relentless encroachment of private interests on the public realm. Mr. Van Valkenburgh's design engages all of those aspects of contemporary life with a care and balance that make the park one of the most positive statements we've seen in years."[2]

The American Society of Landscape Architects recognized the firm's plan for Brooklyn Bridge Park as "inventive, amazingly clear, and concise."[3] Michael Van Valkenburgh was awarded the Municipal Art Society's Brendan Gill Prize for his

work on the park. The society's president, Vin Cipolla, said that his "careful attention to the site's history and its extraordinary built and natural features has ensured
that this transformation will create an urban destination for generations to come."[4]

In trying to give a blow-by-blow account of the park's creation, it is easy to miss the
almost cataclysmic changes that occurred in Brooklyn in the thirty years following
the first advocacy for a park in the 1980s. Brooklyn went from being something of a
backwater to one of the hottest places in the city, the country, and, some would say,
the world. Previously, taxi drivers routinely refused passengers traveling to the borough—the only place they knew was the River Café, a destination restaurant just
over the Brooklyn Bridge that was likely to produce a return fare. Well-to-do Brook-
lynites tended to shop and dine in Manhattan. Then, in a turnabout, Manhattan
began coming to Brooklyn for culture, food, and cutting-edge stores. With Brooklyn
featured in the travel guides, foreign tourists became ubiquitous.

Demand for boutique commercial space became so strong that in 2013 a
multibuilding Watchtower complex sold for $375 million (with many more Watch-
tower properties to follow).[5] Carefully renovated at considerable cost, these buildings were leased to companies like WeWork as well as thriving tech companies that
outgrew the WeWork model of shared space and wanted their own. In some parts
of Brooklyn new and renovated apartments became as expensive as similar ones in
Manhattan. Brooklyn was seeing new development every day.

This success raised complicated issues. Many Brooklyn old-timers were
challenged by the borough's rebirth. Partly it was economics; the low rents that
had attracted many residents vanished not only from the best neighborhoods but
seemingly from everywhere else as well. The artists, artisans, and restaurateurs
who had come for cheap commercial space found these disappearing, too. But it
was also about the pace and quality of life. The early brownstoners had come to
Brooklyn for its quiet, low-rise communities where they could have a backyard,
raise a family, and send their children to the local school; all this was threatened as
Brooklyn changed.

As a result, many local projects became lightning rods for controversy. Brooklyn Bridge Park was only one example. The Walentas building near the Brooklyn
Bridge on Dock Street provoked concerted opposition but was built anyway. The
closing of Long Island College Hospital, just a long block from Pier 6, was in itself a
traumatic event for the community, but it became a truly major cause of ire when

Figure 21-1 (below). The rendering shows the lower-density alternative offered by Fortis Group, the chosen developers of the former Long Island College Hospital properties, which includes 900,000 square feet of market-rate residential and 225,000 square feet of affordable housing, 10,000 square feet of retail space, and a primary school. Local communities opposed the plan as too tall and too dense in such close proximity to a historic district. (Fortis Group / *Brooklyn Daily Eagle*.)

proposals were made for overwhelmingly tall buildings—one of which could be built as-of-right under existing zoning—to replace the hospital complex (see Figure 21-1). This gave fuel to opponents of the Pier 6 housing, who saw it as proof that the area was becoming overbuilt.

Another project, at the downtown edge of Brooklyn Heights, would replace the local branch library with a thirty-six-story condominium tower housing a new library on the ground floor. This project was fought ferociously as being too tall and a giveaway of public land. The money from the tower was to be used to renovate dilapidated library branches in the borough. Opponents contended that the Brooklyn library system had more money than it acknowledged and did not need this income—an accusation vigorously disputed by library authorities.

Yet another proposal, for a new tower crowding in on the existing Cadman Plaza towers, was voted down by tenants of the tower that owned the prospective development parcel, even though the would-be developer offered each of them a tempting sum in return for his right to build. The anxiety over encroaching residential development colored attitudes toward every project.

Brooklyn Bridge Park had helped propel the change that swept Brooklyn, and in return the change propelled the park. Some welcomed the change; others feared or even hated it. There is no doubt, however, that the change affected how people felt about the park and the residential development that supported it.

When reviewing the park's history, it is tempting to focus on the controversies that swirled around it. Unhappiness often welled up from the community; blogs and forums were filled with anger; recently elected legislators seemed to forsake the

Figure 21-2 (opposite). This is a view of the park south of the Brooklyn Bridge in late summer 2015. The uplands of Pier 5 were being prepared for construction, underwater work was taking place beneath Pier 3, and the uplands of Pier 2 were next on the drawing board. In the next few years 92 percent of the park would be complete. (Alex MacLean.)

project their predecessors had helped develop. It was easy to wonder whether the park would survive the combined effects of democracy and human nature—powerful forces that seemed to rise and fall like the tides against the park's shoreline.

We believe the opposite is true: the park is precisely the product of democracy and human nature. Yes, democracy and human nature turned differences of opinion into lawsuits, disagreements into blood feuds, but it was democracy and human nature that stopped the Port Authority when it was hell-bent on development. Democracy and human nature imagined the park in much its present form when the public and the Local Development Corporation worked out the master plan. Democracy and human nature secured the money necessary to build the park from hard-pressed governments. Democracy and human nature preserved the master plan, preserved the funding, and moved the ball forward through election wins and losses, booms and busts, a terrorist attack, and a superstorm.

In fifty years the story of Brooklyn Bridge Park's creation will likely command mainly academic interest. All the controversy surrounding its emergence will recede, leaving a simple truth: democracy and human nature transformed a maritime wasteland into an urban masterpiece (see Figure 21-2). To see that, all you have to do is spend twenty minutes in the park on a summer day.

ACKNOWLEDGMENTS

The story of Brooklyn Bridge Park is the story of the people who created it. Over more than thirty years, thousands of people touched the park and hundreds made it happen. Without the presence and the actions of the right people at the right time, Brooklyn Bridge Park would not exist. We have written this book as an expression of our gratitude to the people who imagined it, designed it, funded it, and built it.

Success has many fathers—parents, actually, in the case of the park, since so many women played significant roles. In this book we have tried to name the principal players and to indicate their contribution, but we fear that our memories and our sources have failed us in some way. If so, the error is one of omission, not commission.

Many of the same people who created the park helped us write this book. It would have been impossible to tell the story without the generosity and candor of the scores of participants who agreed to be interviewed by us. We quote them in the text and cite them in hundreds of endnotes, where many of the best stories may be found. Some of the best lines in our book came from (and are attributed to) our sources. The story we tell would not have its balance and richness of detail without their personal recollections, and we are grateful for their help.

Thanks also to those who provided us with important documents, including graphic images, and otherwise aided in our research. Those include: Eugene Keilin for his photographs and skillful fine-tuning of images for reproduction; Jonathan Jackson, for always-cheerful computer help and scanning of illustrations; Alexa Hoyer, for her striking photograph of a concert crowd on a Pier 1 lawn; Julius Erdei, for his photograph of Pier 2 awash on the night of Sandy; Mary Frost, for her photograph of a little girl sitting by piles off Pier 1; Brian Merlis, author and archivist, for the 1900 photograph of the Heights waterfront; Wolf Spille, for his information about the history of the piers and the Port Authority maps showing how the pre- and post-1950s piers compared; Cindy Goulder, for sharing the early history of waterfront planning in DUMBO; Otis Pearsall, for his meticulous record-keeping about the park movement's very earliest year; Ahmad ("Jay") Javed of PhotoReal in Brooklyn, for making prints of the bulk of photographs, both from film and digital; and John Dozier Hasty, publisher of the *Brooklyn Heights Press* and *Brooklyn Daily Eagle*, for generously granting blanket permission to reproduce materials from his publications. Thanks also to Tess Colwell and Julie May of the Brooklyn Historical Society; photographers Alex Maclean for his spectacular aerial images and Elizabeth Felicella for opening her archives to us; Regina Myer, Suma Mandel, David

Lowin, Belinda Cape, and Clay Grable of the Brooklyn Bridge Park Corporation; and Nate Trevethan of Michael Van Valkenburgh Associates.

We are also grateful to friends and colleagues who helped us wrestle with organizing the volumes of research material we marshaled, who helped us choose what to include and what to leave out, and who gave us thoughtful and valuable advice along the way.

Special thanks to Fred Nachbaur, director of Fordham University Press, who patiently waited for the manuscript and then helped whip it into shape for a speedy publication, and to Dr. Rosemary Wakeman, director of the Urban Studies Program at Fordham University, who provided thoughtful comments that we incorporated in the manuscript. Constance Rosenblum's editing sharpened and refined the final product, Ann-Christine Racette reviewed all our images for publication and handled the layout, and Eric Newman put it all together and kept us on track.

Despite all the help we got, we have surely made mistakes of fact or judgment, for which we are of course solely responsible.

Finally and fervently, there is no way to thank our families enough for their unfailing good humor and indispensable support. Henrik thanks his spouse, Elaine Krogius, and his son, Sven, for their fortitude, photographs, and good counsel over a period much longer than expected to complete the book. Joanne is grateful to her husband, Eugene Keilin, and her two sons, Greg and Charles, for putting up with her seemingly decadelong preoccupation with this book project and for helping to make it better. Their endless contributions are reflected throughout the final product.

APPENDIX
BROOKLYN BRIDGE PARK THIRTEEN GUIDING PRINCIPLES

July 18, 1992

Mr. Vincent Tese, Chairman
New York State Urban Development Corporation
1515 Broadway
New York, New York 10036

Dear Mr. Tese:

We are pleased to submit to you the planning and development principles
which we hope will guide the transformation and renovation of Brooklyn's
downtown waterfront. This document is the product of a collaborative
effort between the community and its elected officials to define our
shared vision for the rebirth of this area.

We look forward to meeting with you and your staff to discuss the next
steps in drafting the memorandum of agreement and in establishing the
public benefit corporation that will plan, manage and develop the piers.

Sincerely,

Hon. Martin Connor,
State Senator

Hon. Eileen C. Dugan,
Member of the Assembly

Hon. Kenneth K. Fisher,
City Councilmember

Hon. Howard Golden,
President of the Borough of Brooklyn

Hon. Joan Griffin McCabe,
City Councilmember

Hon. Stephen J. Solarz,
Member of Congress

Mr. Anthony A. Manheim, Co-chair
for the Brooklyn Bridge
Park Coalition

cc: Mr. Stanley Brezenoff, Executive Director,
    Port Authority of New York and New Jersey
    Mr. Carl Weisbrod, President
    New York City Economic Development Corporation

THE REDEVELOPMENT OF THE BROOKLYN WATERFRONT SHALL BE GUIDED BY THE FOLLOWING PRINCIPLES:

1. COMPREHENSIVE PLANNING

   a. The Plan shall celebrate the unparalleled vistas and historic nature of the site with a world-class design affording a spectacular entry into Brooklyn.

   b. The Plan shall be conducted by a public entity which holds title to the site which includes Port Authority and other public and private parcels.

   c. The Plan shall encompass the waterfront area between the Manhattan Bridge and Atlantic Avenue including Empire-Fulton Ferry State Park, the Brooklyn Bridge area and the upland of Pier 6.

   d. The overall Plan shall be agreed to before permanent use or construction is authorized.

2. FULL PUBLIC PARTICIPATION AND FULL PUBLIC REVIEW THROUGHOUT THE PLANNING, DEVELOPMENT AND MANAGEMENT PROCESSES

   a. Including representatives of the Brooklyn Bridge Park Coalition, Citywide and Brooklyn groups who have devoted years to public involvement and professional planning for the site.

   b. Including Citywide and Brooklyn area business, labor, civic and educational leaders.

3. RETAIN AND ENHANCE SCENIC VIEWS

   a. Preserve existing street-end view corridors including Atlantic Avenue and Old Fulton Street.

   b. Protect and enhance the view of the Brooklyn Bridge and its towers, the Statue of Liberty and New York Harbor from the adjacent communities and the Promenade.

4. PUBLIC OWNERSHIP TO PLAN, DEVELOP, OPERATE AND MANAGE THE SITE

   a. In accordance with the overall Plan, issue carefully phased sequential requests for proposals for construction and operation through ground leases for commercial developments.

5. MAXIMIZE DEDICATED PARK LAND AND OPEN SPACE FOR YEAR ROUND PUBLIC RECREATION, BOTH ACTIVE AND PASSIVE

   a. The goal for the redevelopment is public access and use in a mixed-use development consisting predominantly of, and including the maximum level of, dedicated park land and open space, for both active and passive recreation.

6. FOSTER PUBLIC ACCESS AND USES FROM BROOKLYN AND THROUGHOUT THE REGION WHILE RESPECTING AND PROTECTING THE CHARACTER OF, AND IMPACTS ON, ADJACENT COMMUNITIES

7. DEVELOP AND PROVIDE FOR ENFORCEMENT OF DESIGN AND CONSTRUCTION GUIDELINES EMPHASIZING DESIGN QUALITY AND PROVIDING ENFORCEABLE LIMITS ON THE HEIGHTS, BULK, MASSING AND FOOTPRINT

8. DEVELOP A FISCALLY PRUDENT PLAN

   a. Specialized commercial uses (e.g. executive conference center/destination resort, restaurants, maritime center) shall be encouraged and residential and office uses shall be discouraged.

   b. The site shall have only so much commercial development in a park-like setting as is necessary to enliven the area, to provide security and to finance ongoing operations.

   c. The revenues from such commercial uses shall be committed to the operation and maintenance of dedicated park and open space areas and contribute to capital development costs.

   d. The development of commercial uses, open space and park areas specified in the overall Plan shall be implemented in an incremental and coordinated manner.

9. FOSTER JOB DEVELOPMENT

   a. Favor development that generates permanent skilled jobs especially based on marine repair, hotel-conference and restaurant services and maritime activities.

10. FOSTER WATER-RELATED DEVELOPMENT

    a. Encourage uses that are enhanced by a waterfront location and/or that will enhance the waterfront.

11. REQUIRE A SCALE AND BUILT FORM THAT RELATES CLOSELY TO THE SURROUNDING NEIGHBORHOODS

12. FOSTER THE RELATIONSHIP BETWEEN THE SITE AND DOWNTOWN BROOKLYN, INCLUDING INCREASED TRANSPORTATION OPPORTUNITIES

    a. Trolleys, buses and other public transportation to connect the site to rail and subway services.

    b. Encourage the provision of pedestrian and bicycle access to, and usage within, the site.

13. MINIMIZE NOISE AND AIR POLLUTION

    a. Minimize vehicular traffic congestion and pollution impact on neighborhoods to the north, east and south.

TIMELINE

1955   The Port Authority of New York acquires the Brooklyn Piers from the
              New York Dock Company, signifying the demise of private con-
              trol of the Brooklyn waterfront.

1963–64   Old finger piers are replaced by wider ones to attract larger ships.

1965   Brooklyn Heights is designated New York City's first historic district.

1974   Special Scenic District protects views from the Brooklyn Heights
              Promenade.

1982–84   Piers 1–5 are closed to commercial shipping.

1985–86   The Port Authority announces its intention to dispose of Piers 1–5
              for commercial uses; the Brooklyn Heights Association (BHA)
              opposes the move.

1987   The BHA suggests a park on the piers.

1988   The Port Authority responds with a plan for dense development.

              The BHA counters with an all-park scheme.

              Community Board 2 rejects the Port Authority's plan and endorses
              the BHA's.

              The Brooklyn Bridge Park Coalition, led by Tony Manheim of the
              BHA, organizes to promote a park plan.

1989–92   Governor Mario M. Cuomo delays several attempts to sell piers to
              private developers.

1992   The Thirteen Guiding Principles for the park are adopted by local
              elected officials and park advocates. These principles envision a
              self-sustaining park that will generate revenue to cover mainte-
              nance and operating costs.

              Brooklyn Borough President Howard Golden proposes a plan called
              "Harbor Market."

1994   George E. Pataki is elected governor, succeeding Mario Cuomo.

1996   The Port Authority leases Pier 3 to a lumber company.

1997   Local elected officials create the Downtown Brooklyn Waterfront Lo-
              cal Development Corporation (LDC) to develop a practical park
              plan.

1998–99   The LDC expands the scope of its park planning to include DUMBO
              and leads a public planning process. Thousands participate
              from many Brooklyn neighborhoods.

              Developer David Walentas promotes a highly commercial plan for
              the DUMBO waterfront, generating strong opposition.

2000	The LDC publishes the master plan for Brooklyn Bridge Park.
	The city commits $65 million to Brooklyn Bridge Park (BBP); the total public cost is estimated to be $150 million.
2001	Governor Pataki commits $85 million of capital funding for the park; commitments now total $150 million.
	Ground is broken on a small city park in DUMBO that the city names "Brooklyn Bridge Park."
	Terrorists destroy the World Trade Center on September 11.
2002	Mayor Michael R. Bloomberg and Governor Pataki create the Brooklyn Bridge Park Development Corporation (BBPDC), with James Moogan as president, to build the park in accordance with the LDC's master plan.
2003	Landscape architect Michael Van Valkenburgh is chosen to design the park.
2004	Wendy Leventer replaces James Moogan as president of the BBPDC.
	Pier 6 is added to Brooklyn Bridge Park.
	Environmental review begins, finding pier pilings in poorer condition than thought and unable to support many uses.
	The park's annual maintenance and operating costs are estimated at $15 million.
	After alternative revenue sources are evaluated, housing becomes the principal funding source for park maintenance and operations.
	Brooklyn Bridge Park Coalition is renamed Brooklyn Bridge Park Conservancy and focuses on public programming.
2005	A revised master plan, containing development sites for housing, is endorsed by the BHA and the Coalition.
	The general project plan and final environmental impact statement are formally approved.
2006	A lawsuit challenges the plan for housing but is dismissed.
2007	Future revenues from development sites are formally dedicated to pay park costs.
	Floating Pool Lady ties up at Pier 2.
	Regina Myer becomes president of the BBPDC.
2008	Park demolition and construction begin in phases.
	The city adds $75 million to the park, the cost of which is now estimated to be $350 million.

	Daniel Squadron is elected state senator, defeating Martin Connor.
2009	Construction begins on Piers 1 and 6.
2010	The city takes control of the park and commits an additional $55 million to its construction.
	A new study of funding alternatives to housing is begun. Local legislators obtain from the city veto power over new housing development.
	Piers 1 and 6 open to the public.
	DUMBO developer David Walentas and his wife donate Jane's Carousel to the park, along with a pavilion to house it and money to maintain it.
	St. Ann's Warehouse, a nonprofit theater company, is chosen to stabilize and renovate the Tobacco Warehouse for cultural and public use, prompting a lawsuit by the BHA and others.
2011	The new study of funding for the park finds no significant new alternatives to housing that would provide a reliable source of revenue. The local legislators surrender their veto power over new developments.
	A judge rules in favor of the plaintiffs in the Tobacco Warehouse lawsuit.
2012	The Tobacco Warehouse litigation is settled, and the structure is leased to St. Ann's Warehouse, which raises $35 million in private funds for the project.
	A joint venture of Starwood Hotels and Toll Brothers is selected as the developer of Pier 1.
	A pop-up pool opens on Pier 2 uplands.
	Pier 5 soccer fields and picnic peninsula open.
	Hurricane Sandy strikes the East Coast.
2013	Plans to close Long Island College Hospital, located near the park, generate prolonged controversy and litigation.
	Squibb Park bridge opens.
	City donates new DUMBO property to the park. The Con Edison site is purchased by the park.
	Developers are selected for Empire Stores and John Street sites.
2014	Ball courts and roller-skating rink open on Pier 2.
	Pier 4 beach and bird sanctuary open.

Newly elected mayor Bill de Blasio adds $40 million in new funds for the park. Total costs may reach $400 million.

De Blasio requires that the development planned for Pier 6 include a component of "affordable housing."

People for Green Space sues to stop development on Pier 6.

Squibb Park bridge closes for repairs.

The scale and height of hotel and housing on Pier 1 generate criticism and new litigation.

2015   The park's financial model is updated and debated.

St. Ann's theater group opens a restored Tobacco Warehouse.

Pier 6 wildflower garden opens.

In DUMBO, new parkland, an education center, and a new park entrance open.

Construction begins on Pier 5 upland and new marina.

A lawsuit is filed by Save the View Now and BHA over the height of structures on Pier 1 but is dismissed by the trial judge.

The Pier 6 lawsuit is settled with an agreement by the park to seek modification of its general project plan.

Brooklyn Bridge Park asks state agencies ESD and BBPDC to consider modification of the general project plan. A public hearing is held, but no action is taken.

A new lawsuit is filed by Save the View and the BHA, claiming that a residential building on Pier 1 pierces the scenic view plane. Plaintiffs' request for a temporary restraining order is denied.

CAST OF MAJOR CHARACTERS

Local Elected Officials

Brooklyn Borough President:	Howard Golden (1997–2001)
	Staff: Marilyn Gelber, Greg Brooks, Jon Benguiat
	Marty Markowitz (2002–13)
	Eric Adams (2014–)
State Senator, 25th District:	Martin Connor (1978–2008)
	Daniel Squadron (2009–)
Assembly Member, 52nd District:	Eileen Dugan (1980–96)
	Joan Millman (1997–2014)
	JoAnne Simon (2015–)
City Council Member, 33rd District:	Kenneth Fisher (1991–2001)
	David Yassky (2002–9)
	Stephen Levin (2010–)
U.S. Representative, 7th District:	Nydia Velázquez (1993–)

State and City Officials

New York State

Governor:	Mario Cuomo (1983–94)
	George Pataki (1995–2006)
	Eliot Spitzer (2007–8)
	David Paterson (2008–10)
	Andrew Cuomo (2011–)

Governors' Appointees:

Vincent Tese, chairman and chief executive officer of the Urban Development Corporation (1985–94); commissioner and vice-chairman of the Port Authority of New York and New Jersey (1991–95)

Charles Gargano, chairman and chief executive officer of the Empire State Development Corporation (formerly the Urban Development Corporation) and vice-chairman of the Port Authority (1995–2007)

Patrick Foye, downstate chairman of the Empire State Development Corporation (2008–9)

Peter Davidson, executive director of the Empire State Development Corporation (2009–11)

Bernadette Castro, commissioner of parks, recreation, and historic preservation (1995–2006)

Carol Ash, commissioner of parks, recreation, and historic preservation (2007–10)

Port Authority of New York and New Jersey

Executive Director: Peter Goldmark (1977–85)
Stephen Berger (1986–90)
Stanley Brezenoff (1990–95)
George Marlin (1995–97)
Robert Boyle (1997–2001)
Christopher Ward (2008–11)

Other Port Staff:

Phil LaRocco, director of world trade and economic development (1970–90)

Lillian Borrone, director of port commerce (1987–2000)

Christopher Ward, chief of planning and external affairs (1997–2002)

Rita Schwartz, external and community affairs official (1983–96)

City of New York

Mayor: Rudolph Giuliani (1994–2001)
Michael Bloomberg (2002–13)
Bill de Blasio (2014–)

Deputy Mayor: Joseph Lhota (1998–2001)
Daniel Doctoroff (2002–8)
Patricia Harris (2002–13)
Robert Lieber (2008–10)
Robert Steel (2011–13)
Alicia Glen (2014–)

Other Mayoral Appointees:

Joshua Sirefman, economic development official (2002–6)

Adrian Benepe, parks commissioner (2002–12)

Joshua Laird, assistant commissioner for planning and parklands (1997–2013)

Seth Pinsky, president of the Economic Development Corporation (2008–13)

Nanette Smith, special assistant to Mayor Bloomberg and chief of staff to Deputy Mayor Patricia Harris (2002–13)

Carolee Fink, senior adviser to Deputy Mayor Robert Steel and Deputy Mayor Alicia Glen (2011–15)

Brooklyn Bridge Park

President:

James Moogan (2002–3)
Wendy Leventer (2004–7)
Regina Myer (2007–)

Professional Staff:

HR&A Advisors, chief consultant to the Local Development Corporation (John Alschuler, Candace Damon, Josh Sirefman)

Urban Strategies (Ken Greenberg, master plan team leader)

Michael Van Valkenburgh Associates, designers and landscape architects for Brooklyn Bridge Park (Michael Van Valkenburgh, Matthew Urbanski, Gullivar Shepard, Paul Seck)

Community Members

Katrin Adams, Fulton Ferry Landing Association
Kenneth Adams, Brooklyn Chamber of Commerce, Local Development Corporation
Jerry Armer, Community Board 6, Cobble Hill Association, Local Development Corporation
Peter Aschkenasy, Brooklyn Bridge Park Development Corporation, Brooklyn Bridge Park Corporation
Sandy Balboza, Atlantic Avenue Betterment Association

Pauline Blake, Community Board 6, Local Development Corporation

Fred Bland, Brooklyn Heights Association

Nancy Bowe, Brooklyn Heights Association, Brooklyn Bridge Park Coalition, Brooklyn Bridge Park Conservancy

Alexandra Bowie, Brooklyn Heights Association

Barbara Brookhart, Community Board 6, Brooklyn Bridge Park Coalition

Steven M. Cohen, Brooklyn Bridge Park Development Corporation, Brooklyn Bridge Park Corporation

John Dew, Community Board 2, Local Development Corporation

Maria Favuzzi, Community Board 6, Brooklyn Bridge Park Coalition

Susan Feldman, St. Ann's Warehouse

Peter Flemming, Brooklyn Heights Association, Willowtown Association

Judi Francis, Willowtown Association, Brooklyn Bridge Park Defense Fund

Doreen Gallo, DUMBO Neighborhood Association

Cindy Goulder, ecological landscape designer

Hank Gutman, Brooklyn Heights Association, Local Development Corporation, Brooklyn Bridge Park Development Corporation, Brooklyn Bridge Park Corporation

Ursula Hahn, Concord Village Neighborhood Association

Irene Janner, Brooklyn Heights Association, Community Board 2, Brooklyn Bridge Park Coalition, Brooklyn Bridge Park Conservancy

Marianna Koval, Brooklyn Heights Association, Brooklyn Bridge Park Coalition, Brooklyn Bridge Park Conservancy

Tony Manheim, Brooklyn Heights Association, Brooklyn Bridge Park Coalition

Shirley McCrae, Community Board 2

Jane McGroaty, Brooklyn Heights Association

Madeline Murphy, Community Board 6, Local Development Corporation

Mary Ellen "Mickey" Murphy, Brooklyn Heights Association, Community Board 2, Brooklyn Bridge Park Coalition

Charlie O'Donnell, Brooklyn Bridge Park Boathouse

Michael "Buzzy" O'Keefe, River Café

Bill Orme, Brooklyn Bridge Park Boathouse

David Offensend, Brooklyn Heights Association, Brooklyn Bridge Park Coalition, Local Development Corporation, Brooklyn Bridge Park Development Corporation, Brooklyn Bridge Park Corporation

Otis Pratt Pearsall, Brooklyn Heights Association

Milton Puryear, Brooklyn Greenway Initiative

Roy Sloane, Cobble Hill Association, Brooklyn Bridge Park Coalition, Local Development Corporation

Julia (Judy) Stanton, Brooklyn Heights Association

Franklin Stone, Cobble Hill Association, LDC

Allen Swerdlowe, Fulton Ferry Landing Association, Brooklyn Bridge Park Coalition, Local Development Corporation

Mary Pat Thornton, Brooklyn Heights Association

Gary VanderPutten, Fulton Ferry, Brooklyn Bridge Park Coalition

William Vinicombe, Community Board 2, Local Development Corporation, Brooklyn Bridge Park Corporation

David and Jane Walentas, DUMBO residents, developers, and philanthropists

John Watts, Brooklyn Heights Association, Brooklyn Bridge Park Coalition, Local Development Corporation, Brooklyn Bridge Park Development Corporation, Brooklyn Bridge Park Conservancy

Nancy Webster, Brooklyn Bridge Park Coalition, Brooklyn Bridge Park Conservancy

Michael Winikoff, Vinegar Hill Neighborhood Association, Local Development Corporation

Joanne Witty, Brooklyn Heights Association, Local Development Corporation, Brooklyn Bridge Park Development Corporation, Brooklyn Bridge Park Corporation

Joan Zimmerman, Fulton Ferry Landing Association

ORGANIZATION AND AGENCY NAMES, ABBREVIATIONS, AND ACRONYMS

Port Authority of New York and New Jersey, a bistate agency responsible for regional transportation and the commercial port, referred to as the Port Authority.

New York State Urban Development Corporation, the state's independent economic development authority, referred to as UDC, now doing business as Empire State Development Corporation; referred to as ESDC, later called ESD.

New York State Department of Environmental Conservation referred to as DEC.

New York State Parks, Recreation, and Historic Preservation referred to as State Parks.

New York City Economic Development Corporation, the city's independent economic development agency, referred to as EDC.

New York City Department of Parks and Recreation referred to as City Parks.

New York City Department of Environmental Protection referred to as DEP.

Community Board 2 and Community Board 6, local district planning boards, referred to as CB 2 and CB 6.

Brooklyn Heights Association referred to as BHA.

Brooklyn Bridge Park Coalition, an advocacy group for the park, referred to as the Coalition; predecessor to the Brooklyn Bridge Park Conservancy, focused on public programming in the park, referred to as the Conservancy.

Downtown Brooklyn Waterfront Local Development Corporation, created by the local elected officials to create a practical plan for a park; referred to as the LDC.

Brooklyn Bridge Park Development Corporation, a subsidiary of ESDC, created to build the park, referred to as BBPDC.

Brooklyn Bridge Park Corporation, a not-for-profit entity created by the city to take over park construction and management, referred to as the Park Corporation.

Citizens Advisory Council, created by the Brooklyn Bridge Park Development Corporation, referred to as the CAC; inactive after the Brooklyn Bridge Park Corporation took over the park project.

Community Advisory Council, created by the Brooklyn Bridge Park Corporation, also referred to as the CAC but with different membership than the earlier CAC.

NOTES

1. The Stage

1   Kevin Bone, *The New York Waterfront: Evolution and Building Culture of the Port and Harbor* (Ann Arbor, Mich.: Monacelli Press, 1997); Peter Hendee Brown, *America's Waterfront Revival: Port Authorities and Urban Development* (Philadelphia: University of Pennsylvania Press, 2009); "A Nation's Waterways," *Brooklyn Waterfront History*, http://www.brooklynwaterfronthistory.org/story/a-nations-waterway/.

2   Ellen M. Snyder-Grenier, *Brooklyn! An Illustrated History* (Philadelphia: Temple University Press, 1996), 69; "Mass Transit, Brooklyn Style," *Brooklyn Waterfront History*, http://www.brooklynwaterfronthistory.org/story/mass-transit-brooklyn-style/.

3   Snyder-Grenier, Brooklyn! 27; "Water's Edge," *Brooklyn Waterfront History*, http://www.brooklynwaterfronthistory.org/story/waters-edge/.

4   Snyder-Grenier, Brooklyn! 83; Brian Cudahy, *Over and Back: The History of Ferryboats in New York Harbor* (New York: Fordham University Press, 1990), 34–36; "Mass Transit, Brooklyn Style," op. cit.

5   Henry R. Stiles, *A History of the City of Brooklyn, 3 vols.* (1867–70; repr., Westminster, Md.: Heritage Books, 2007), 3:220.

6   Ibid., 2:293. To translate into current dollars, see Samuel H. Williamson, "Seven Ways to Compute the Relative Value of a U.S. Dollar Amount, 1774 to Present," *Measuring-Worth*, 2016, https://www.measuringworth.com/uscompare/.

7   Pierrepont Family Papers, Brooklyn Historical Society, Acc. 262, loc. 32B, Box 5.

8   "A Ramp and Two Bridges," *Brooklyn Waterfront History*, http://www.brooklynwaterfronthistory.org/story/a-ramp-and-two-bridges/.

9   The Pierrepont file at the Brooklyn Historical Society, op. cit., contains a February 1853 agreement by the estate of H. B. Pierrepont to pay $30,000 toward "building the archway over Furman St. through the hill at Montague Street, for ferry purposes."

10   Henrik Krogius, *The Brooklyn Heights Promenade* (Charleston, S.C.: History Press, 2011), 29. The author was a resident of Brooklyn Heights at the time.

11   Stiles, *A History of the City of Brooklyn*, 3:575

12   "Warehouse Way," *Brooklyn Waterfront History*, http://www.brooklynwaterfronthistory.org/story/warehouse-way/.

13   *Brooklyn Daily Eagle*, May 29, 1873; "A Working Waterfront," *Brooklyn Waterfront History*, http://www.brooklynwaterfronthistory.org/story/a-working-waterfront/.

14   *Brooklyn Daily Eagle*, January 18, 1888; "Warehouse Way," op. cit.

15   *Brooklyn Daily Eagle*, July 16, 1889.

16   The Spice Mill 30, no. 1 (1907): 30; "Where Coffee Was King," *Brooklyn Waterfront History*, http://www.brooklynwaterfronthistory.org/story/where-coffee-was-king/.

17   "Port Authority to Acquire Vast Brooklyn Dock Area," *New York Times*, June 29,

1955; Montrose Morris, "Past and Present New York Dock Company Warehouses," *Brownstoner*, March 15, 2013.

18   Transcript of hearing, March 10, 1943, New York City Planning Commission on the route and design of the planned BQE, cited in Krogius, *Brooklyn Heights Promenade*, 13–19; letter from Robert Moses to Krogius, May 11, 1953, in which he remarked of the Promenade, "It was adopted in the face of enormous opposition, including quite a few of the property owners who didn't want their back yards taken and bitterly opposed having the common run of folk use this walk" (letter in author's possession).

19   The Port of New York Authority, "1955 Annual Report," http://corpinfo.panynj.gov/files/uploads/documents/financial-information/annual-reports/annual-report-1955.pdf; "Port Authority to Acquire Vast Brooklyn Dock Area," op. cit.

20   Lillian Borrone, interview with authors, February 14, 2014. The power of Local 1814 was shared with other unions active in different parts of New York Harbor, and they rarely had the same interest. Local 1814 was largely Italian; farther north, around the Brooklyn Navy Yard, was an Irish local, as was the local on the west side of Manhattan. A different local covered Port Elizabeth on the New Jersey side of the harbor, and it was ultimately the winner as traffic shifted to the container operations there. "New Jersey [is] part of the United States," State Senator Martin Connor said, by which he meant it had direct physical access through railroads and highways. As a part of Long Island, Brooklyn's access to the mainland passed through bridges and tunnels that were choke points. Martin Connor, interview with authors, January 29, 2015.

21   "Piers below Heights Closed, Area Ripe for Development," *Brooklyn Heights Press*, June 28, 1983.

22   Rita Schwartz, interview with authors, January 30, 2014.

23   Pearsall was a preservationist, but Pierrepont's Montague Street ramp was already gone; many Heights residents feared that a new connection to the piers would become a thoroughfare and change the character of their quiet neighborhood.

24   Scott M. Hand and Otis Pratt Pearsall, "The Origins of Brooklyn Bridge Park, 1986–1988" (unpublished manuscript, 2014), 23–24, http://brooklynhistory.org/docs/OriginsBrooklynBridgePark.pdf.

25   As with many volunteer community organizations, the BHA officers had relatively short tenures, and a succession of BHA presidents will appear in our story.

26   Fred Bland, interview with authors, May 27, 2014.

2. All Hell Breaks Loose

1   Henrik Krogius, *The Brooklyn Heights Promenade* (Charleston, S.C.: History Press, 2011), 44–45. The author attended a "town hall" meeting in Brooklyn's Borough Hall on May 7, 1953, at which a large crowd challenged public officials on the Port Authority's intent.

2   Ibid.

3   Peter Goldmark, interview with authors, March 5, 2014.

4   Ibid.

5   Stephen Berger, interview with authors, December 21, 2013.

6   Ibid.

7   "Brooklyn Piers 1–6: A Framework for Discussion," final version, February 1986; Halcyon Ltd., "Development Concepts for the Brooklyn Piers: Prepared for the Port Authority of New York and New Jersey," December 1985.

8   "Brooklyn Piers 1–6: A Framework for Discussion," op. cit., 7–8, identified the following opportunities to fulfill the objective: "Squibb Park, located below Columbia Heights at the western end of Middagh Street, which already represents a 'stepping stone' elevation between Brooklyn Heights and the Pier site; [t]he Montague Street commercial corridor, which leads to the visual center over the Piers site on the Brooklyn Heights Promenade; Joralemon Street, which is presently the only direct traffic link through Brooklyn Heights to the Piers."

9   "'No Vision in Pier Study' Says Guest BHA Panel," *Brooklyn Heights Press*, February 27, 1986; "Piers Panel Throws Cold Water on Halcyon Port Authority and Opts for Housing," *The Phoenix*, March 6, 1986.

10   Photocopies of letters dated March 19, 1986, from Carl Geupel to Earl Weiner and Edward Logue (with other panelists copied).

11   Photocopies of replies sent to Carl Geupel by Edward Logue dated March 27, 1986, and by Tony Manheim dated April 11, 1986.

12   Photocopy of reply to Carl Geupel by Robert Campbell dated March 31, 1986.

13   "BHA to Do Own Study and Design for Piers 1–6," *Brooklyn Heights Press*, November 10, 1986.

14   "BHA Pier Study Revealed before Audience of 400," *Brooklyn Heights Press*, February 26, 1987.

15   Buckhurst, Fish, Hutton & Katz, "The Future of the Piers: Planning and Design Criteria for Brooklyn Piers 1–6," prepared for Brooklyn Heights Association, June 1987.

16   Port Authority, "Draft Request for Consulting Services," August 13, 1987; "Port Authority Moves to Open Pier Area for Development," *The Phoenix*, November 19, 1987.

17   "Piers Consultant Terms PA Site Best Suited for Residential Use," *Brooklyn Paper*, February 6–12, 1988; "PA Puts Secrecy Lid on Developer Search," *Brooklyn Paper*, May 3–9, 1988.

18   Hardy Adasko, interview with authors, January 22, 2014.

19   "Hearing Debates Waterfront Planning," *Brooklyn Paper*, October 3–9, 1987.

20   "City Announces Timetable for Piers below Promenade," *Brooklyn Heights Press*, July 24, 1986.

21   Otis Pearsall, interview with Henrik Krogius., February 14, 2013. Following brief interviews on that date and March 21, 2013, with Henrik Krogius, Pearsall was prompted to

do his own further research, together with Scott Hand, resulting a year later in their issuing a hundred-page paper, "The Origins of Brooklyn Bridge Park, 1986–1988" (unpublished manuscript, 2014), http://brooklynhistory.org/docs/OriginsBrooklynBridgePark.pdf, covering the period of their close involvement with the Heights waterfront question.

22   William Vinicombe, interview with authors, April 28, 2014.

23   Rita Schwartz, interview with authors, January 30, 2014.

24   "'American Landscape' Plan Is Unveiled for Piers Here," *Brooklyn Heights Press*, August 4, 1988.

25   Ibid.

26   Ibid.

27   "PA Rejects Pier Park Plan," *Brooklyn Paper*, August 6–12, 1988.

28   Pearsall, op. cit.

29   Ibid.

30   Hand and Pearsall, "Origins of Brooklyn Bridge Park," 64–65.

31   Ibid. 78.

32   Pearsall, op. cit.

33   Scott Hand memo, January 1, 1989.

3. The Manheim Years

1   Roy Sloane of Cobble Hill, a graphic designer, is generally credited with creating the organization's name and logo. In 1985, when the loosely organized Coalition members decided they needed a more formal body, they took an existing but dormant not-for-profit corporation called "Friends of Fulton Ferry Landing" (as distinguished from "Fulton Ferry Landing Association," the active organization for that community then and subsequently) and renamed it the "Brooklyn Bridge Park Coalition."

2   John Watts, interview with authors, November 11, 2014.

3   Alex Garvin, interview with authors, January 29, 2014.

4   Stephen Berger, interview with authors, December 21, 2013.

5   Scott M. Hand and Otis Pratt Pearsall, "The Origins of Brooklyn Bridge Park, 1986–1988" (unpublished manuscript, 2014), 31, http://brooklynhistory.org/docs/OriginsBrooklyn BridgePark.pdf.

6   Ibid.

7   Martin Connor, interview with authors, January 29, 2015.

8   Ibid.

9   "Officials to Stop Heights 'Sweetheart Deal,'" *Brooklyn Heights Press*, November 23, 1989; "Does Port Authority's 'Secret Deal' Bypass Planning Process for Piers?" *Brooklyn Heights Press*, November 23, 1989; "What a Deal!" *Brooklyn Paper*, November 30–December 6, 1989.

10   "Officials to Stop Heights 'Sweetheart Deal,'" op. cit.; Margaret Daly, "Outrage: Politicians and Civic Leaders Denounce the Port Authority," *Brooklyn Paper*, November 30–December 6, 1989.

11   Ibid.

12   "What a Deal!" op. cit.; reprints of Manheim correspondence.

13   "Cuomo Demands Port Authority Delay Vote on Heights Piers," *Brooklyn Heights Press*, December 29, 1989.

14   "Parks Coalition Says PA Lied on Piers," *Brooklyn Paper*, July 27–August 2, 1990.

15   "Consultant Awarded $150,000 to Study Heights Uses," *Brooklyn Heights Press*, September 20–27, 1990; "PA Backs Off on Pier Deal," *Brooklyn Paper*, March 8, 1990.

16   "Governor Supports Park on Piers below Promenade," *Brooklyn Heights Press*, November 1–7, 1990.

17   Ken Fisher, interview with authors, February 27, 2014.

18   Martin Connor, interview with authors, January 29, 2015.

19   Hack later served as dean of the University of Pennsylvania's School of Design from 1996 to 2008.

20   "Piers Study Says Park Plan Too Costly," *Brooklyn Paper*, January 18–24, 1991.

21   For more on Westway see note 20 in Chapter 9.

22   "Despite Opposition Agency Plans to Sell Piers to Private Developers," *New York Times*, April 3, 1992.

23   "B'kyn Piers on Block," *New York Newsday*, April 2, 1992; "Port Authority Moves to Unload Piers," *Brooklyn Heights Press*, April 2, 1992.

24   "Port Authority Pulls Back from Sale of Waterfront," *New York Times*, April 8, 1992; "Port Authority Flipflop," *Brooklyn Paper*, April 10–16, 1992; "Cuomo Docks Sale of Piers," *New York Newsday*, April 18, 1992.

25   Marilyn Gelber, interview with authors, February 12, 2014.

26   Ibid.

27   The Thirteen Guiding Principles are reproduced as an appendix.

28   Dumbo is an acronym for "Down Under the Manhattan Bridge Overpass." It is reported by Crane Davis to have originated with residents who thought an unattractive name would deter development. Jeff Scherer, "What Does DUMBO Stand for, Revisited," DUMBO NYC, November 11, 2015, http://dumbonyc.com/blog/2015/11/11/what-does-dumbo-brooklyn-stand-for/.

29   "Pier Development Will Now Fall under City Advisory Board," *Brooklyn Heights Press*, May 14–20, 1992; "City: Heights Piers Will Be Part of Citywide Plan," *Brooklyn Paper*, July 17–23, 1992; Gelber, op. cit.

30   "City's Waterfront Plan Called Respectful of Local Efforts," *Brooklyn Heights Press*, July 30, 1992.

31   Department of City Planning, City of New York, "New York City Comprehensive Waterfront Plan: Reclaiming the City's Edge," 1992, http://www1.nyc.gov/assets/planning/download/pdf/about/publications/cwp.pdf.

32   "City's Waterfront Plan Worries Park Coalition," *Brooklyn Heights Press*, August 27, 1992.

33   "Brooklyn Harbor 1992 Proposal," Office of the Brooklyn Borough President.

34   "Golden's Aide Assures CB6 on Piers," *Brooklyn Heights Press*, June 4, 1992.

35   Ibid.

36   "Golden Pushes Pier Plan," *Brooklyn Paper*, June 12–18, 1992.

37   Fisher, op. cit.

38   "National Park is Urged for Piers," *Brooklyn Heights Press*, March 11, 1993.

39   "Title Appears Transferred to State UDC" (erroneously reported), *Brooklyn Heights Press*, September 15, 1993.

40   Governor Cuomo's State of the State address, January 5, 1994.

41   "Further Delays Seen Likely for Heights Piers Plan," *Brooklyn Heights Press*, August 25, 1994.

42   "Piers 1–5 Task Force: A Last Moment in the Sun for Cuomo," *Brooklyn Heights Press*, November 10, 1994.

43   "Manheim: Cuomo's Loss Didn't Help," *Brooklyn Heights Press*, November 10, 1994.

44   "Park Coalition Plans Session to Revive Project for Piers," *Brooklyn Heights Press*, May 4, 1995; "Noted Downtown Shaper Ed Logue Calls Pataki Key to Piers Park Hope," *Brooklyn Heights Press*, June 5, 1995.

45   Lillian Borrone, interview with authors, February 14, 2014.

46   Ibid.

47   Ibid. As it turned out, Brooklyn Bridge Park would be nearly completed before significant development took place on Governors Island.

48   George Pataki, interview with authors, February 25, 2014.

49   Letters, February 9, 1996, from Howard Golden to Charles Gargano; February 15, 1996, from Eileen Dugan and Martin Connor to Gargano; February 16, 1996, from Anthony Manheim to Lillian Borrone; "State Won't Acquire Piers," *Brooklyn Heights Press*, February 19, 1996.

50   Piers 1 and 5 were leased for storage of cocoa beans and paper, respectively, and the Jehovah's Witnesses and U.S. Marshals leased space for parking cars.

51   David Offensend, letter published in *Brooklyn Heights Press*, March 21, 1996, with the story "Community Mounts Attack on Strober Lease of Pier 3."

52   Borrone, op. cit.

53   Offensend, op. cit.

54   The Praedium Group Ltd., Ernst & Young, and Federman Design + Construction Consultants Inc., "Economic Viability Study Piers Sector, Brooklyn Bridge Park: Prepared for Brooklyn Bridge Park Coalition," February 1997.

55   Ibid., 5. The study concluded that the projected uses would generate a little under $5 million a year toward the park's maintenance.

56   "Shakeup in Piers 1–5 Effort," *Brooklyn Heights Press*, December 18, 1997.

57   "Heights Worries about Its Waterfront," *Brooklyn Heights Press*, January 15, 1998.

58   Ibid.

59   "Piers Plan Needs Park Coalition," *Brooklyn Heights Press*, January 15, 1998.

60   "Politicians and the Piers," *Brooklyn Heights Press*, January 22, 1998.

61   "Park Coalition Names Director," *Brooklyn Heights Press*, November 5, 1998; "Coalition Chief Hopes to Sell Piers Park Vision to World," *Brooklyn Heights Press*, January 21, 1999.

4. A New Game with a Fresh Team

1   Hardy Adasko, interview with authors, January 22, 2014.

2   Martin Connor, interview with authors, January 29, 2015.

3   Gary VanderPutten, interview with authors, April 27, 2014. Tony Manheim said, "She lived and breathed the community." Manheim, interview with authors, February 21, 2014.

4   Connor, op. cit.

5   Ibid. A number of sources have told the authors that Dugan was clear that the money should be spent to advance the park but that it should not be given to the Coalition.

6   Wendy Froede, "LDC Reveals Waterfront Plan," *Brooklyn Paper*, October 22, 1999.

7   "BHA Sets Principles of Cooperation," *Brooklyn Heights Press*, March 4, 1999.

8   Ken Fisher, interview with authors, February 27, 2014.

9   Noting that many brownstones in Cobble Hill were single-family houses, rather than broken up into apartments as were many in Brooklyn Heights, Franklin Stone said, "Our per capita is probably higher than your per capita. Those of us who live there do not feel second-class. In fact, we feel first-class." Stone, interview with authors, January 30, 2014.

10   Walentas told the authors he first heard about DUMBO when he was developing buildings in SoHo and NoHo, at the time artistic communicates in Manhattan, and someone said to him that DUMBO would be next.

11   "Shakeup in Piers 1–5 Effort," *Brooklyn Heights Press*, December 18, 1997.

12   Hank Gutman also fought off suggestions that the BHA boycott the LDC because he thought the local officials who created it might actually have good intentions. "My only reason for believing that . . . was I had never met an elected official who wouldn't rather

pose at the ribbon cutting for a park than a sewage treatment center," he told the authors. Gutman, interview with authors, March 2, 2014.

13 In retrospect, Fisher realized that he had not known the Coalition that well. "We hadn't completely peeked behind the curtain," he said. Later on he saw that the Coalition was not broadly representative, that it was run by "Brooklyn Heights Brahmins" and that the other members were just signatories without playing a real role. Fisher, op. cit.

14 After redistricting in 2000, the Brooklyn piers fell within the district of Congresswoman Nydia Velázquez, who chose Betty Williams, later elected a justice of the Supreme Court in Kings County.

15 The three staff appointees displayed no other agenda than to help the process along. The experience and authority of both Brooks and Benguiat were invaluable.

16 William Vinicombe, interview with authors, April 28, 2014.

17 Lillian Borrone, interview with authors, February 14, 2014.

18 Ibid.

19 Ibid. Peter Goldmark remembers that the union was waning in those days, but it was still powerful with the Brooklyn borough president. Goldmark, interview with authors, March 5, 2014.

20 David Offensend, interview with authors, April 16, 2014.

5. Strange Bedfellows

1 January 12, 1999, minutes of regular meeting of the Board of Governors of the BHA.

2 David Offensend, interview with authors, April 16, 2014. Irene Janner, interview with authors, June 12, 2014. Fred Bland remembered taking Tony out for a drink to persuade him to resign, but Tony said, "That's too bad that you're going to [have to] fire me. Let's have another martini." "So we did," Bland said. "We could hardly walk out of there." Bland, interview with authors, May 27, 2014.

3 "An Immodest Proposal," *Brooklyn Bridge*, January 1999, 48–53.

4 "New Life for the Fulton Ferry Area: Victorian Bustle under the Brooklyn Bridge Might Return," *Phoenix*, May 24, 1979; e-mail messages from Cindy Goulder to Henrik Krogius, May 2 and 9, 2013; Judy Stanton, interview with authors, May 4, 2013.

5 Goulder, op. cit.

6 "Developer Pursues Plan for Complex along Brooklyn Waterfront," *New York Times*, May 8, 1999; "A Stunning Pier Hotel Design Stands Out among Flawed Plan," *New York Times*, May 24, 1999; "World-Class Hotel Keystones Walentas' New DUMBO Plan," *Brooklyn Heights Press*, May 27, 1999; "The 1999 New York Awards," *New York*, http://nymag.com/nymetro/news/nyawards/1710/.

7 David and Jane Walentas, interview with authors, March 25, 2014.

8   Gary VanderPutten thought the LDC put the Coalition out of business but gives fellow Coalition board member Maria Favuzzi credit for focusing on the Walentas plan; VanderPutten himself had previously created a document that attacked the plan. Vander-Putten, interview with authors, April 27, 2014.

9   June 8, 1999, minutes of the regular meeting of the Board of Governors of the BHA.

10   The Brooklyn Heights Association had never limited its concerns or actions to its neighborhood alone. It had opposed many projects outside the historic district, including the Morgan Stanley Building at One Pierrepont Plaza, Brooklyn Law School's dormitory on State Street, the Court Street movie theater, and the Federal Courthouse.

11   Franklin Stone, interview with authors, January 30, 2014.

12   Jerry Armer, interview with authors, January 15, 2014; Stone, op. cit.

13   "Park Coalition Names Albert Butzel President," *Brooklyn Heights Press*, October 14, 1999.

14   "Resolution Affirms Primacy in Piers Park Plan," *Brooklyn Heights Press*, November 4, 1999.

15   "Plug Pulled on DUMBO Proposal," *New York Times*, December 12, 1999.

16   In 2014 David Walentas was listed as Number 380 on the *Forbes* 400 list with a net worth of $1.73 billion.

17   Walentas was not selected as the developer for Pier 1 either. He seemed to think that these decisions were personal; Brooklyn Bridge Park President Regina Myer said the park's decisions were based entirely on the numbers. Myer, interview with authors, February 27, 2014.

18   When Marianna Koval was president of the Coalition, the location of the carousel was vigorously disputed, with Koval arguing that it should be located elsewhere in the park.

19   Myer, op cit. Many years after he left the leadership of the Coalition, Tony Manheim would celebrate his seventy-fifth birthday with a party at Jane's Carousel. John Watts, interview with the authors, November 11, 2014.

6. Public Planning

1   Harvey Schultz had also served as commissioner of environmental protection in the administration of Mayor Ed Koch and, before that, in multiple capacities at the New York City Department of City Planning. Martha Holstein began her career in government relations in the administration of Mayor John Lindsay.

2   Discussion in this chapter is based on notes and recollections of Joanne Witty.

3   Bill Farrell, "Heights of Park Planning," *New York Daily News*, August 3, 1999.

4   Candace Damon, interview with authors, March 21, 2014.

5   "Planner Tabbed for Piers," *Brooklyn Paper*, September 3, 1999; "Design Team Selected for Waterfront Complex," *New York Daily News*, September 7, 1999.

6   "Who Was There Was What Mattered at Planning Session," *Brooklyn Heights Press*, November 11, 1999; "Let the Planning Begin!" *Brooklyn Paper*, November 12, 1999.

7   Michael Van Valkenburgh, interview with authors, February 11, 2014.

8   "Hundreds Attend Planning Session for Piers Park," *Brooklyn Heights Press*, November 11, 1999; Julian Barnes, "Disparate Visions for a New Park," *New York Times*, December 12, 1999.

9   "Piers Park Tour Hears More Than One Kind of Buzz," *Brooklyn Heights Press*, December 16, 1999.

10   Dennis Holt, "Bridge Park Development Corp Plans New Round of Workshops," *Brooklyn Daily Eagle*, January 10, 2000; Bill Farrell, "More Input Sought for Bridge Park," *New York Daily News*, January 14, 2000.

11   "Park Planning Process Looks Increasingly Persuasive," *Brooklyn Heights Press*, January 27, 2000.

12   "Port Authority Agrees to Piers 1–5 Park Study," *Brooklyn Heights Press*, February 10, 2000; "Port Authority Agrees to Let Piers Be Used for Brooklyn Bridge Park," *New York Times*, February 11, 2000; "Port Authority, Pataki Get behind Waterfront Park on Piers," *Brooklyn Daily Eagle*, February 11, 2000; Bill Farrell, "Heights Piers Set Aside for Waterfront Parkland," *New York Daily News*, February 14, 2000; "Brooklyn Bridge Park Clears Another Hurdle," *Brooklyn Heights Courier*, February 14, 2000.

13   "Piers Park Hopes Here May Be Affected by Governors Island," *Brooklyn Heights Press*, January 6, 2000.

14   "Olympics Plan Jolts Park Planners," *Brooklyn Heights Press*, March 23, 2000.

7. Public Planning Continues

1   "Reactions Mix Puzzlement with Joy over Park Plans," *Brooklyn Heights Press*, March 2, 2000; "Strong Show of Interest for Park Planners' Ideas," *Brooklyn Heights Press*, March 2, 2000; "Planners Set Third Meeting," *Brooklyn Paper*, March 13, 2000.

2   Discussion of opinions and debate within the LDC board are drawn from notes and recollections of Joanne Witty.

3   Hank Gutman, interview with authors, March 2, 2014. Interestingly, Montague Street merchants and the Chamber of Commerce did not seem to care one way or another.

4   The Clark Street platform extension would be examined in detail in the LDC's later transportation study and be found impractical.

5   "Draft 'Master Plan' for Park Revealed," *Brooklyn Heights Press*, April 27, 2000.

6   "Joralemon Resident Sees Park Benefit," *Brooklyn Heights Press, April 27, 2000.*

7   "Enviable Joralemon," *Brooklyn Heights Press*, April 27, 2000. This proved to be the case. When the park was nearly complete, Peter Flemming sold his house on Joralemon Street and moved to Columbia Heights. "I don't think my neighbors could complain about

the park having depreciated their value," he said. Flemming, interview with authors, February 26, 2014.

8   "Draft 'Master Plan' for Park Revealed," op. cit.

9   Ibid.

10   "Hopeful Air Marks Further Park Discussion," *Brooklyn Heights Press*, May 4, 2000.

11   Julian E. Barnes, "As Some Fight a Park Plan, Its Supporters See Elitism," *New York Times*, August 16, 2000; Dennis Holt, "*Times* Article Has Wrong Stress," *Brooklyn Heights Press*, August 24, 2000.

12   "Critics of Park Plan Offer Alternatives," *Brooklyn Paper*, October 9, 2000.

13   Although considerable work was done on the cost estimates, it was not possible to make a precise or accurate estimate of a concept. At the end of the analysis, the consultants did a reality check. HR&A's Josh Sirefman explained that the number "sounded big enough to be ambitious, and manageable enough to not get thrown out of a room." Sirefman, interview with authors, February 17, 2014. Of course, the actual costs were much higher and the park actually built was larger and more complex than the concept plan.

14   "No Big Surprises in Final Version of Park Master Plan," *Brooklyn Heights Press*, June 29, 2000.

15   Ibid.

16   Letter from Gabrielle Belson Rattner to Governor George Pataki, July, 21, 2000, transmitting petitions, letters, and a press kit on behalf of Waterfront Development Watch.

17   Letter and supporting material from Gabrielle Rattner to Henrik Krogius as editor of *Brooklyn Heights Press*, January 3, 2001.

18   Barnes, op. cit. Not all park supporters were so charitable. "My answer to them was, 'Move to Greenwich. If you want to live in a gated community, move to Greenwich, not Brooklyn.' No offense to my friends in Greenwich," one park supporter told the authors. Gutman, op. cit.

19   "Park Plan Hits Snag over DUMBO Marsh Element," *Brooklyn Heights Press*, October 19, 2000; Goulder was a consistent champion of natural elements in the park. Dennis Holt, "Brooklyn DUMBO Cove Has Wealth of Information," *Brooklyn Heights Press*, October 9, 2003.

20   Statement from Brooklyn Heights Association under the headline "Heights Association Endorses Plan," *Brooklyn Heights Press*, June 29, 2000.

21   Wendy Froede, "City Backs Waterfront Park," *Brooklyn Paper*, June 12, 2000.

22   Franklin Stone, interview with authors, January 30, 2014.

8. Money and Political Gamesmanship

1   Like his father, Harold Fisher, who was described in an obituary in the *New York Post* in 1999 as a "legendary Brooklyn Democratic power broker." "Former MTA Boss Fisher Dies," *New York Post*, December 27, 1999.

2   Ken Fisher, interview with authors, February 27, 2014.

3   Ibid.

4   Sirefman had come to take a leading role on the HR&A team and will play a key role later in the story.

5   Fisher, op. cit. It may have helped that Amy Klein had also been chief of staff for the Council's finance committee, which was chaired by Brooklyn City Councilman Herb Berman. Berman had helped Giuliani with the mayor's plan for a sports facility in Coney Island and, according to Hardy Adasko, had control of a pot of money that could be used for Brooklyn projects. Adasko, interview with authors, January 22, 2014.

6   Wendy Froede, "Rudy Snubs Howie over Bridge Park," *Brooklyn Paper*, July 30, 2001.

7   Fisher, op. cit.

8   Ibid. "Park Gets a $64 Million Pledge," *New York Times*, June 8, 2000; "Surprise! City Provides $61 Million for Piers Park," *Brooklyn Heights Press*, June 8, 2000; "City Backs Waterfront Park," *Brooklyn Paper*, June 12, 2000.

9   Christopher Ward would later become executive director of the Port Authority himself, serving from 2008 to 2011. He was helpful to the park in accelerating release of Port Authority funds as park construction took off.

10   Notes and recollection of Joanne Witty.

11   Memo from Senator Martin Connor to Governor George Pataki, January 3, 2001.

12   "Governor Announces $85 Million for Brooklyn Bridge Park: Key Parcel Acquired from Con Edison; $2 million to Restore Fulton Ferry State Park," Press Release from Governor George Pataki, January 5, 2001.

13   Gregg Birnbaum, "Pataki Boosts PA Park Plan in Slap at Giuliani," *New York Post*, January 6, 2001, http://nypost.com/2001/01/06/pataki-boosts-pa-park-plan-in-slap-at-giuliani/.

14   Wendy Froede, "Gov's Slap at Mayor Nets $85 Million for Bridge Park," *Brooklyn Paper*, January 15, 2001.

15   "Long a Dream, Brooklyn Park Nears Reality," *New York Times*, January 6, 2001.

16   Editorial, *New York Daily News*, October 10, 2000.

17   Memo from Connor, op. cit.

18   Joanne Witty notes from meeting of July 20, 2000.

19   The New York State Parks Department's use of these funds, a mix of state and federal money, would come back to haunt the park. See Chapter 15.

20   See Chapter 11 and related notes.

21   "Polytech Plan 'Incubator' Topped by Roof Garden," *Brooklyn Heights Press*, February 1, 2001.

22   See Chapter 15.

23   "Montague St. Gateway," *Brooklyn Paper*, March 12, 2001; "Monumental Montague Park Entry Mostly Opposed by Local Groups," *Brooklyn Heights Press*, March 22, 2001.

24   "Rudy: Tear Down Purchase Building," *Brooklyn Paper*, August 6, 2001; "An Artist Makes Case for Purchase Building," *Brooklyn Heights Press*, August 9, 2001; "The Purchase Building" (editorial), *Brooklyn Heights Press*, August 9, 2001; "A Landmark for New York City: Brooklyn Bridge Park" (full-page advertisement urging demolition of Purchase Building), *Brooklyn Heights Press*, August 9, 2001.

25   "A B'klyn Base: Emergency Offices Find a New Home," *Newsday*, February 21, 2002.

26   "Daffodil Beds in Shape of Twin Towers Planted at Pier 4," *Brooklyn Heights Press*, November 1, 2001.

9. Breaking the Logjam

1   Phillip Lentz, "Brooklyn Bridge Park Back on Track," *Crain's New York Business*, March 22, 2002; Martin Connor, interview with authors, January 29, 2015; notes and recollections of Joanne Witty.

2   Alex Garvin, interview with authors, January 29, 2014.

3   Dan Doctoroff, interview with authors, April 2, 2014.

4   Josh Sirefman, interview with authors, February 17, 2014.

5   Charles Fox was Governor Pataki's deputy secretary for environmental issues, reporting to John Cahill, secretary (or chief of staff) to the governor.

6   Charles Fox, interview with authors, April 8, 2014.

7   Phillip Lentz, "Brooklyn Bridge Park Deal," *Crain's New York Business*, May 1, 2002.

8   Patrick Gallahue, "Who's Who on Bridge Park Board," *Brooklyn Paper*, May 13, 2002. The board had eleven members. Charles Gargano, chair of Empire State Development Corporation, chaired the new board. The vice-chair was Dan Doctoroff, New York City deputy mayor for economic development and rebuilding. Other gubernatorial appointees were State Parks Commissioner Bernadette Castro; Julio Mercado, senior pastor of a church running community programs in Williamsburg and Bushwick; and Valerie Lancaster Beal, an investment banker. Other city appointees were Deputy Mayor Patricia Harris, New York City Parks Commissioner Adrian Benepe, and Gilbert Rivera, a Park Slope resident and owner of a building supply and restoration company in Brooklyn.

9   Bill Farrell, "Bridge to a New Park View," *New York Daily News*, May 3, 2002.

10   Ibid.

11   The New York State Environmental Quality Review Act requires all state and local government agencies to consider environmental impacts when deciding whether to take a

discretionary action. The SEQRA process is designed to identify potential impacts related to a proposed action and to avoid or mitigate them.

12   "Moving toward Brooklyn Bridge Park Reality," *Brooklyn Heights Press*, July 11, 2002; "Residents to Get Say on Park Development Plan," *Brooklyn Paper*, July 15, 2002.

13   Memorandum, December 4, 2002, from Adam Zalma of the Economic Development Corporation to President James Moogan, Brooklyn Bridge Park Development Corporation and Deputy Mayor for Economic Development Dan Doctoroff, analyzing the bids received from Two Trees and Boymelgreen Developers. Despite Boymelgreen's higher bid, there were doubts about his capacity to follow through. With reservations, the board of the development corporation voted to designate Boymelgreen and require a $1 million performance bond. Minutes of the Board of Directors of the Brooklyn Bridge Park Development Corporation, December 19, 2002. In the event, Boymelgreen abandoned the project. More than ten years later, his performance bond was returned to him.

14   "Planners Say Pier 6 Is Part of Park," *Brooklyn Heights Press*, May 23, 2003.

15   "The Park Concept Plan" (editorial), *Brooklyn Heights Press*, May 23, 2003.

16   Dennis Holt, "Review Begins on Impact of Plan for Brooklyn Bridge Park," *Brooklyn Heights Press*, July 3, 2003; "Elements Not Yet Decided on Crucial to Park Impact Study," *Brooklyn Heights Press*, July 3, 2003; "Down by the Waterside" (editorial), *Brooklyn Heights Press*, July 3, 2003.

17   Holt, "Review Begins on Impact of Plan for Brooklyn Bridge Park."

18   Ibid.

19   Wendy Leventer, interview with authors, February 28, 2014.

20   Westway was an ambitious plan to replace the lower portion of Manhattan's aging elevated roadway along the Hudson River with a new highway buried along the water's edge and funded with money from the Interstate Highway Trust Fund. It was vigorously attacked by environmentalists and many adjacent communities, and was defeated in the federal courts when Judge Thomas Griesa famously found that its construction would harm striped bass in the river. The decision would have an impact on Brooklyn Bridge Park more than thirty years later when the New York State Department of Environmental Conservation objected to plans for the floating swimming pool and floating walkways because their shadows would affect the fish.

10. Reality Sets In

1   Lindsey Gruson, "In Cleaner Harbor, Creatures Eat the Waterfront," *New York Times*, June 27, 1993; Christopher Bonanos, "Secrets of the Deep," *New York*, May 10, 2009; Lisa W. Foderaro, "Cleaner Harbor Has Downside: Pests That Plagued Park Construction," *New York Times*, August 23, 2011.

2   Dennis Holt, "Brooklyn Bridge Park Head Gives Heavy Cost Estimate," *Brooklyn Heights Press*, August 5, 2004.

3   Ibid.

4   Wendy Leventer, interview with authors, February 28, 2014.

5   Ibid.

6   Ibid.

7   "Can Park Plan's Merits Trump Bad Presentation?" (signed editorial by Henrik Krogius), *Brooklyn Heights Press*, February 10, 2014.

8   Photocopy of letter dated March 1, 2006, from the Brooklyn Bridge Park Conservancy to John Cahill, secretary and chief of staff to the governor.

9   Ariella Cohen, "Big Shakeup—and Big Costs—at 'Brooklyn Bridge Park,'" *Brooklyn Paper*, March 17, 2007, http://www.brooklynpaper.com/stories/30/11/30_11parkshakeup.html.

10   "Hastily Drawn Park Plan" (letter from Robert Stone for Willowtown Association Park Committee), *Brooklyn Heights Press*, June 9, 2005.

11   Elizabeth Hays, "State Stalled on Brooklyn Bridge Park," *New York Daily News*, November 26, 2007, http://www.nydailynews.com/new-york/brooklyn/state-stalled-bridge-park-new-leader-spur-building-150m-waterfront-article-1.261483.

12   Leventer, op. cit.

13   Josh Sirefman, interview with authors, February 17, 2014.

14   James Whalen, interview with authors, May 20, 2014.

15   Michael Van Valkenburgh, interview with authors, February 11, 2014.

11. Housing "in the Park"

1   The trial court's decision can be found as *Brooklyn Bridge Park Legal Defense Fund v. New York State Urban Development Corporation*, 14 Misc. 3d 515, 828 N.Y.S. 2d 347 (2006); 2006 N.Y. Misc. LEXIS 3418; 2006 NY Slip Op. 26466. See also Elizabeth Stull, "Court Dismisses Suit against Plan for Piers Park," *Brooklyn Heights Press*, November 30, 2006.

2   George Pataki, interview with authors, February 25, 2014.

3   Ken Fisher, interview with authors, February 27, 2014.

4   Robert Lieber, interview with authors, March 4, 2014.

5   Dan Doctoroff, interview with authors, April 2, 2014.

6   To be clear, the communities were not enthusiastic about the need to produce revenue. The principles called for "*only* so much" revenue as might be necessary (emphasis added).

7   Michael Van Valkenburgh, interview with authors, February 11, 2014.

8   Dennis Holt, "Time to Start Over?" *Brooklyn Heights Press*, August 4, 2004.

9   This is confirmed by internal minutes of the Brooklyn Bridge Park design meeting on December 11, 2003, circulated among its members.

10   Signe Nielsen of Mathews Nielsen Landscape Architects.

11   "Should private development occur on the site, the land use offering the highest potential economic return at least risk is market-rate housing. . . . As a non-peak use, problems of traffic and access are minimized. Furthermore, residential uses help create day/night activities, contributing to safer and more effective public spaces." Buckhurst Fish Hutton Katz, "The Future of the Piers: Planning and Design Criteria for Brooklyn Piers 1–6," prepared for Brooklyn Heights Association, June 1987, 40.

12   *Waterfront Matters* 7, no. 1 (2008): 8.

13   Gary VanderPutten, interview with authors, April 27, 2014.

14   This was the site that Con Edison had promised to contribute to the park for its use. At this point the Con Ed site was not yet in park hands. After part of the property was designated a development site, Con Ed would claim that it was entitled to be paid a market price for it; despite the earlier promise, Con Ed refused to negotiate this point, and the city agreed to pay Con Ed $9.2 million out of the proceeds from the eventual development deal.

15   Andrew Jackson Downing and Frederick Law Olmsted were both inspired by Birkenhead Park near Liverpool, England, in that "its shrewd exploitation of real estate around the edges of its parkland made it an especially apt model for Americans to imitate." John Dickson Hunt, "The Influence of Anxiety," in *Public Nature*, edited by Ethan Carr, Shaun Eyring, and Richard Guy Wilson (Charlottesville: University of Virginia Press, 2013), 23–24.

16   "Court Dismisses Suit against Park Plan," *Brooklyn Heights Press*, November 30, 2006.

17   The Agreement of Lease between Brooklyn Bridge Development Corporation and 360 Brooklyn Investors LLC, as of February 29, 2008, contained the provisions to include 360 Furman in the general project plan and to require payments to the park. State legislation was necessary to permit the park development corporation to collect PILOT payments. That legislation was adopted on July 26, 2006, and amended Chapter 428, Laws of New York, sec. 16n. Jess Wislowski, "Bill Paves Way for A-Park-Ments," *Brooklyn Paper*, July 2–9, 2005.

18   The scenic view plane never protected the views west and north from Columbia Heights north of the Promenade.

19   Fulton Ferry Landing was at grade between Brooklyn Heights and DUMBO. Any development on the Pier 1 site would affect this community, not just by its bulk but by the traffic it would generate.

20   Lisa W. Foderaro, "By Blocking Views of a Bridge, a Building Incites a Brooklyn Heights Battle," *New York Times*, January 25, 2015. For a discussion of this controversy, see Chapter 16.

21   Ken Fisher, interview with authors, February 27, 2014.

22   This number was projected as early as the summer of 2004. "Brooklyn Bridge Park Head Gives Heavy Cost Estimate," *Brooklyn Heights Press*, August 5, 2004.

23   "Debate Rages on Housing at Planned Brooklyn Park," *New York Times*, July 23, 2006; "The Battle of Renderings," *Brooklyn Heights Press*, July 21, 2005.

24   "Heights Association Gives Qualified Approval to Brooklyn Bridge Park Plan," *Brooklyn Heights Press*, March 24, 2005; "Fulton Ferry Group Backs Park Plan" (letter from Gary VanderPutten, Allen Swerdlowe, and Katrin Adams), *Brooklyn Heights Press*, February 9, 2005; "Park Conservancy Refutes Criticism of Current Plan," *Brooklyn Heights Press*, August 4, 2005; "Selling Brooklyn Bridge Park," *New York Times*, February 13, 2005.

25   "Park Conservancy Refutes Criticism of Current Plan," op. cit.

26   Notice of Petition, *Brooklyn Bridge Park Legal Defense Fund Inc. and Judith A. Francis and Robert Stone, Individually v. New York State Urban Development Corporation and Brooklyn Bridge Park Development Corporation*, May 9, 2006.

27   Decision of Justice Lawrence S. Knipel, *Brooklyn Bridge Park Legal Defense Fund v. New York State Urban Development Corporation*, op. cit. at 524 and 355; Slip Op. at 17.

28   *Matter of Brooklyn Bridge Park Legal Defense Fund Inc. v. New York State Urban Dev. Corp.*, N.Y. App. Div. LEXIS 3533 (N.Y. App. Div. 2d Dep't, April 22, 2008).

29   Irene Janner and Judy Stanton, interview with authors, June 12, 2014.

30   See Chapters 13 and 19.

12. At Long Last, Shovels

1   *Brooklyn Bridge Park Dev. Corp. v. Strober Bros. Bldg. Supply Ctrs.*, Index No. 100876 (Kings Cnty. Civ. Ct.).

2   Spitzer and Gutman's wife, Karoly, had both clerked for U.S. District Court Judge Robert Sweet. At the time Spitzer was elected governor, Gutman was chairing the LDC and managing a transportation study concerning access to the park.

3   Foye was a former Nassau County economic development official, a former member of the Conservative Party, and a donor to Republican candidates; he had known Spitzer's wife, Silda, when they both practiced law at Skadden, Arps, Slate, Meagher & Flom.

4   Charles E. Bagley, "New York Official Resigns Post amid Shift in Leadership," *New York Times*, March 18, 2007.

5   Josh Sirefman, interview with authors, February 17, 2014.

6   Ariella Cohen, "Big Shakeup—and Big Costs—at Brooklyn Bridge 'Park,'" *Brooklyn Paper*, March 17, 2007.

7   In succeeding years the Floating Pool Lady was moved to the Bronx.

8   "Velazquez Gets Funds to Study Piers Park Access," *Brooklyn Daily Eagle*, December 6, 2001.

9   Sam Schwartz PLLC and HDR-Daniel Frankfurt, *Brooklyn Bridge Park Transportation + Access Study Prepared for the Downtown Brooklyn Local Development Corporation*, March 2008, http://www.brooklyncb6.org/; "Comprehensive Traffic-Calming Plan Re-

leased," *Brooklyn Heights Press*, December 6, 2001; "Million Dollar Study to Improve Bridge Park Access," *Brooklyn Heights Courier*, December 10, 2001.

10   Ash received complaints from a number of civic groups concerning access to the Tobacco Warehouse during its management by the Conservancy. Among them were Arts at St. Ann's, BKLYN Designs, Brooklyn Arts Council, Creative Time, Czechoslovak American Marionette Theater, DUMBO Arts Center, Galapagos, Jazzreach, New York Photo Festival, powerHouse Books and Arena, and a number of artists and galleries. Letter from League for Excellence in the Arts in DUMBO to Carol Ash, August 7, 2007. Ash terminated the Conservancy's exclusive permitting rights. Letter from Commissioner Carol Ash to Brooklyn Bridge Park Conservancy, February 11, 2009.

11   Ash also cut through a bureaucratic tangle that allowed the park to accelerate demolition of the Cold Storage Warehouse and salvage the durable longleaf pine that lined its interior. Regina Myer, interview with authors, February 27, 2014.

12   Myer's approach can be compared to that of her predecessor, Jim Moogan, for whom the first order of business was to publish a request for proposals for development of the Empire Stores. At that time, the winning bidder offered a stream of payments valued at $54 million but could not complete the transaction. In 2013 the Empire Stores was the subject of a spirited auction that produced more than $127 million for the park.

13. The Politics of Housing

1   "New Generation Leads Cobble Hill Association," *Brooklyn Heights Press*, May 15, 2008; "Park Foes Now Target Connor," *Brooklyn Heights Press*, July 3, 2008; "New Park 'Advocacy' Group Is Just the Old Opposition," *Brooklyn Heights Press*, October 22, 2008.

2   Irene Janner and Judy Stanton reported quite a few planning meetings held by Judi Francis and many others from the south to devise their own plan for Pier 6. Janner and Stanton, interview with authors, June 12, 2014.

3   We put the phrase "in the park" in quotation marks, because Judge Knipel had previously ruled that the housing sites were not parkland and never had been. Despite his decision, the phrase continued to be used.

4   United States Senator Charles Schumer endorsed Daniel Squadron and actively supported him in the race against Connor. See "Chuck Schumer Backs Former Aide over Veteran Pol in Heated State Senate Race," *New York Daily News*, April 6, 2008, http://www.nydailynews.com/news/chuck-schumer-backs-aide-veteran-pol-heated-state-senate-race-article-1.282988. In Connor's Senate district the decisive voting block had always resided in Hasidic Williamsburg, not any of the brownstone communities. Connor had a good relationship with the religious leaders there and had received their political support in the past. This time, with the help of Schumer and Mayor Bloomberg, Squadron took votes from Connor in Williamsburg; Connor believed those votes made the difference.

5   Issuance of general obligation bonds requires a statewide referendum, which is seldom proposed and often fails.

6   Robert Lieber, interview with authors, March 4, 2014.

7   Peter Davidson, interview with authors, February 24, 2014.

8   Ibid.

9   Lieber, op. cit.

10   Term sheet dated March 8, 2010, among the City of New York, the State of New York, and the New York State Urban Development Corporation with regard to the restructuring of the Brooklyn Bridge Park and Jacob K. Javits Convention Center projects.

11   Lieber, who had been an investment banker and was new to government, observed that disputes in government were hard to handle because they were seldom resolved on the merits: "There's always some other backroom trade . . . that is important to one side of the equation to try and extract from the other commitments to do other things, and that would create a lot of the slowdown." Lieber, op. cit.

12   Ibid.

13   Ibid.

14   Henrik Krogius, "City Largely Keeps Brooklyn Bridge Park Team in Place," *Brooklyn Heights Press*, July 29, 2010.

15   The John Street site, at the northern end of the park, was on part of the previously mentioned Con Edison lot.

16   Lisa W. Foderaro, "Housing Deal Ensures Park in Brooklyn Will Expand," *New York Times*, August 2, 2011; Dennis Holt, "Housing Deal Set for Brooklyn Bridge Park," *Brooklyn Heights Press*, August 4, 2011; "Building a Real, World-Class Brooklyn Bridge Park" and "Update on Brooklyn Bridge Park," undated but issued in August–September 2011 by State Senator Daniel Squadron.

17   Foderaro, "Housing Deal Ensures Park in Brooklyn Will Expand"; Holt, "Housing Deal Set for Brooklyn Bridge Park."

14. The Park Begins to Materialize

1   Erin Durkin, "First Look at First Stage—Finally!" *New York Daily News*, July 21, 2009; Dennis Holt and Henrik Krogius, "The Hills Are Alive at Brooklyn Bridge Park," *Brooklyn Daily Eagle*, October 29, 2009.

2   As it turned out, Walentas also paid to repair the damage to the Carousel wrought by Superstorm Sandy. Regina Myer, interview with authors, February 27, 2014.

3   Ibid.; Michael Van Valkenburgh, interview with authors, February 11, 2014.

4   Myer, op. cit.

5   David Lowin, interview with authors, February 27, 2014.

6   Myer, op. cit.

7   Nicolai Ouroussoff, "The Greening of the Waterfront," *New York Times*, April 2, 2010.

8   "Mayor, Governor Open Brooklyn Bridge Park," *Brooklyn Heights Press*, March 25, 2010.

9   Ibid.

10   Lowin, op. cit.

11   Myer, op. cit.

12   Lowin, op. cit.

13   Myer, op. cit.

14   "The Park: What to Expect," *Brooklyn Heights Press*, March 25, 2010.

15   Joyce Wadler, "A Ride with Head-Spinning Views," *New York Times*, September 2, 2011; "Family Attractions in NYC: The 50 Best Sites and Attractions," *Time Out New York Kids*, November 6, 2014, http://www.timeout.com/new-york-kids/attractions/family-attractions. Both the park itself and Jane's Carousel are listed. Brooklyn Bridge Park ranks first in *Time Out*'s list of the city's best parks. See Jillian Anthony, "The Best NYC Parks," *Time Out New York*, March 30, 2016, http://www.timeout.com/newyork/attractions/10-best-parks-in-new-york-city-parks-gardens.

16   Mary Frost, "First Look at Redesigned Pierhouse in Brooklyn Bridge Park," *Brooklyn Heights Press*, June 6, 2013.

15. Deep Differences over a Nineteenth-Century Relic

1   Brooklyn Bridge Park Project Final Environmental Impact Statement, December 2005, S-8, http://www.brooklynbridgepark.org/pages/project-approvals-and-presentations.

2   The study was conducted by Nanette Rainone, former director of BRIC (Brooklyn Information and Culture).

3   Patrick Gallahue, "Tobacco Playhouse," *Brooklyn Paper*, April 29, 2002.

4   Tobacco Warehouse Summer Series Proposal, Brooklyn Bridge Park Coalition and Arts at St. Ann's.

5   Susan Feldman, interview with authors, February 20, 2014; Marianna Koval, interview with authors, May 28, 2014.

6   Revocable permit dated June 22, 2004, between the Office of Parks, Recreation, and Historic Preservation and the Brooklyn Bridge Parks Conservancy.

7   Letter from League for Excellence in the Arts in DUMBO (LEAD) to Carol Ash, August 7, 2007.

8   Koval, op. cit.

9   Letter from Commissioner Carol Ash to Brooklyn Bridge Park Conservancy, February 11, 2009.

10   Samara Daly, interview with authors, March 4, 2014.

11   Tobacco Warehouse request for proposal presentation, November 15, 2010, http://www.brooklynbridgepark.org/pages/project-approvals-and-presentations.

12   The project would cost $35 million, all of which had to be raised by St. Ann's.

13   *Brooklyn Heights Association et al. v. National Parks Service et al.*, CV-11-0226, Eastern District of New York, January 11, 2011.

14   *In the matter of the application of Brooklyn Heights Association et al. v. New York State Office of Parks, Recreation, and Historic Preservation et al.*, Index No. 1120/11, January 19, 2011.

15   Hank Gutman, interview with authors, March 2, 2014.

16   Gutman, who later played a key role in settling the lawsuit, told the authors, "I understood that there were people who loved that building in its God-given state ever since God caused the top two floors and the ceiling to collapse." Ibid.

17   *Brooklyn Heights Association et al. v. National Parks Service et al.*, op. cit. Memorandum of Law of Defendant-Intervenor Brooklyn Bridge Park Corporation in Opposition to Plaintiffs' Motion for Preliminary Injunction (March 14, 2011) and Memorandum in Support of Its Cross-Motion and Motion to Dismiss the Verified Petition and Complaint (May 10, 2011).

18   Koval, op. cit.

19   Feldman, op. cit.

20   Gutman, op. cit.

21   Both buildings were seriously flooded by the storm, as were the private buildings included in the map.

22   The final agreement had created a number of advisory groups to participate in determining the use and design of the property newly acquired for the park.

23   That building houses an environmental education center, a maintenance facility for the park, bathrooms for the public, and display space for art projects.

24   Koval, op. cit.

25   The project received the AIANY Architecture Honor Award; the ULI Global Award for Excellence in Institutional Development; the MASterworks Award for Adaptive Reuse; and the *Architect's Newspaper* Best of Design Award.

16. A Hurricane Has Unexpected Consequences

1   Andrew Freedman, "Statistics Show Hurricane Sandy's Extraordinary Intensity," Climate Central, November 1, 2012, http://www.climatecentral.org/news/statistics-show-just-how-intense-hurricane-sandy-was-15196; Andrew Freedman, "32-Foot-Plus Waves From Hurricane Sandy Topple Records," Climate Central, November 14, 2012, http://www.climatecentral.org/news/32-foot-wave-from-hurricane-sandy-topples-records-noaa-finds-15241; Alan Duke, "Superstorm Sandy Breaks Records," *CNN*, October 30, 2012, http://www.cnn.com/2012/10/30/us/sandy-records/.

2   Regina Myer, interview with authors, March 27, 2014.

3   Matthew DeLuca, "Jane's Carousel Survives a Very Close Call with Hurricane Sandy," *The Daily Beast*, November 1, 2012, http://www.thedailybeast.com/articles/2012/11/01/jane-s-carousel-survives-a-very-close-call-with-hurricane-sandy.html; "Flooded in Sandy, Jane's Carousel Gets Extra Protection," *Brooklyn Daily Eagle*, September 18, 2013.

4   Jennifer Peltz, "Mayor Praises Brooklyn Bridge Storm Prevention," *Brooklyn Daily Eagle*, June 13, 2013.

5   Matthew Urbanski in response to query by authors.

6   "Brooklyn Bridge Park: Storm Resilience through Design," Brooklyn Bridge Park Corporation, December 31, 2012; Michael Van Valkenburgh, "How My Firm Saved Brooklyn Bridge Park from Sandy's Fury," *Innovation by Design*, October 25, 2013, http://www.fast-codesign.com/3020633/innovation-by-design/perspective-how-i-saved-brooklyn-bridge-park-from-sandys-fury; "Sandy Success Stories," produced by Happold Consulting on behalf of an alliance of environmental organizations, June 2013.

7   Van Valkenburgh, "How My Firm Saved Brooklyn Bridge Park"; Rebecca McMackin, "Weathering the Storm: Horticulture Management in Brooklyn Bridge Park in the Aftermath of Hurricane Sandy," *Stormwater Management*, January 15, 2013.

8   See "Region II Coastal Analysis and Mapping," *Federal Emergency Management Agency*, http://www.region2coastal.com/.

9   Mireya Navarro, "New Building Codes Pass after Lessons from Hurricane Sandy," *New York Times*, November 14, 2013; New York City Building Code, Appendix G, Flood Resistant Construction.

10   New York City Building Code, Appendix G, Section G201.2.

11   Jonathan Marvel, interview with authors, March 28, 2014.

12   Joann Plockova, "Storm-Proofing Pier House," *Green Building and Design*, November–December 2014.

13   Some later argued that it made no sense to apply city rules on state property, but this apparently reflected ESDC's long-standing policy to follow local rules, including local zoning codes, unless otherwise stated in the general project plan.

14   Assembled by Otis Pearsall, "Factual Record of the Brooklyn Heights Association's Fall 2005 Campaign for Brooklyn Bridge Park's Pier 1 Height Limitation," August 30, 2014.

15   Ibid.

16   Ibid.

17   Brooklyn Bridge Park Project, Final Environmental Impact Statement, December 2005, 24–90, http://www.brooklynbridgepark.org/; "Development Sites at Brooklyn Bridge Park, Design Guidelines," Holliday Fenoglio Fowler, 29–30.

18   The point from which the height should have been measured became another point of contention. Pearsall claimed that the measurement should have been from the southeast corner of the tallest of the cold storage buildings at Furman Street. He did not know what that elevation was, but we now know that it was approximately 7.75 feet above sea level. A building height of 100 feet from that point would put it at elevation 107.75 feet. The New York City Zoning Resolution, which ESDC advised should be followed, contained a different starting point. It said to use the average elevation along the frontage of the building or the 100-year flood plain, whichever was greater. Before Sandy, the average el-

evation was greater than the flood plain; at 10.25 feet, it was 2.5 feet higher than the point Pearsall chose. After Sandy, the 100-year flood plane was higher, raising the elevation another 3.5 feet for a total elevation of 13.75 feet. It was from this base plane that the 100-foot height was measured, putting the building's roof slab at elevation 113.75 feet, or 6 feet taller than Pearsall was expecting.

19   Toll Brothers and Starwood Hotels formed a joint venture for purposes of the project.

20   Mary Frost, "Brooklyn Heights 'Save the View Now' Meeting Draws Large Crowd," *Brooklyn Heights Press*, January 8, 2015.

21   The southern wall of the northern building was approximately fifty-five feet south of the tallest wall of the cold storage buildings. This represents a shift south of that building from what was shown in the final environmental impact statement, and a portion of the building viewed from Columbia Heights is about thirty feet taller than the previous buildings. Guterman claimed this was a violation of the FEIS; the Park Corporation pointed to Comment 216, which includes the statement, "BBPDC has made no commitment that the buildings to be built on the Pier 1 uplands would occupy the footprint of the existing Cold Storage Buildings" (FEIS, op. cit.).

22   Frost, "Brooklyn Heights 'Save the View Now' Meeting Draws Large Crowd."

23   *Save the View Now v. Brooklyn Bridge Park*, Index No. 504785/15 (Kings Cnty. Sup. Ct. June 10, 2015) (Knipel, J.); 2015 NY Slip Op. 31047 (U).

24   2015 NY Slip Op. 31047 (U), 13–14. Justice Knipel also found that the time to bring a case had expired.

25   Connie Fishman, interview with author, February 11, 2015.

17. The Growing Experience

1   Regina Myer, interview with authors, February 27, 2014.

2   Tony Manheim, interview with authors, February 21, 2014.

3   Lore Croghan, "Critics Throw Stones at Empire Stores' Glass Rooftop Plan," *Brooklyn Eagle*, December 18, 2013.

4   Ibid.

5   Lana Bortolot, "From Roofless Warehouse to Theater Home," *Wall Street Journal*, November 12, 2013.

6   "Bridge Too Far? Squibb-to-Bklyn-Bridge-Park Footpath Costs Soar," *Brooklyn Paper*, December 6, 2011.

7   "The Squibb Park Bridge Winds a New Path to Brooklyn Bridge Park," *Time Out New York*, March 27, 2013; "Plaudits for New Squibb Bridge from Heights to Bridge Park," *Brooklyn Eagle*, March 25, 2013.

8   Lisa W. Foderaro, "A New Bridge Bounces Too Far and Is Closed until Spring," *New York Times*, October 3, 2013. If there was any doubt about its popularity, it was resolved by the many complaints voiced when the bridge was closed for repair.

9   *Brooklyn Bridge Park Corporation v. HNTB Corporation et al.*, Index No. 450115/2016, NY Supreme Court (NY County), filed January 22, 2016; ARUP, a global engineering consulting firm, was hired to assess the Squibb Park bridge deficiencies and correct them.

10   "BQE Barrier, Emblem of Bisected Waterfront, Becomes Beacon for B'klyn Bridge Park Traffic," *Brooklyn Eagle*, October 10, 2013.

11   "Brooklyn Bridge Park Celebrates Opening of New Parkland," *Brooklyn Eagle*, November 19, 2013.

12   "First Look at Redesigned 'Pier House' in Brooklyn Bridge Park," *Brooklyn Eagle*, June 6, 2013; "Condos That Fund a Brooklyn Park," *New York Times*, November 23, 2013.

13   Michael Kimmelman, "A Step Up for Brooklyn Bridge Park," *New York Times*, September 17, 2013.

14   "Update Coming on Proposed Brooklyn Bridge Park Marina, Roller Skating Rink," *Brooklyn Eagle*, November 18, 2013.

18. Learning from the Site

1   Matthew Urbanski, interview with authors, February 11, 2014.

2   William S. Saunders, "The Urban Landscaper," *Harvard Magazine*, November–December 2013, 33.

3   Mary Billard, "Robert Hammond: Leaving the High Life," *New York Times*, November 27, 2013.

4   Saunders, "Urban Landscaper," 94. Van Valkenburgh is also quoted as saying, "If I had seven days to live, I'd spend the first at a tree farm." The tree species chosen by Van Valkenburgh for Brooklyn Bridge Park are listed in Chapter 14.

5   Anne Raver, "Hey, Mister, I've Got a Park I Can Sell You," *New York Times*, July 25, 2014.

6   Ibid.

7   Ibid.

8   Ibid.

9   Michael Van Valkenburgh, interview with authors, February 11, 2012. Still, Van Valkenburgh has often pointed to the community's role in focusing the design process. "Contemporary park users are different and need different things in a park," he has said. "Our team learned a great deal about this at our storefront sessions where neighbors walked in and talked to the design team about their personal aspirations for the park."

10   Some observers were not happy with the berm, finding it featureless and unnatural. One Heights architect would have preferred a wall, the traditional method of sound deadening along interstate highways.

11   Urbanski, op. cit.

12   Van Valkenburgh, op. cit.

13   Ibid.

14   Saunders, "Urban Landscaper," 33

15   Van Valkenburgh, op. cit.

16   Urbanski, op. cit.

17   Jonathan Marvel, interview with authors, March 28, 2014.

18   Ibid. The use of corridors on alternate floors derives from Le Corbusier's 1952 Unité d'Habitation, a large apartment building in Marseille, much admired though rarely copied.

19   Saunders, "Urban Landscaper."

20   Van Valkenburgh, op. cit.

21   Ibid.

22   Urbanski, op. cit.

23   Gullivar Shepard, interview with authors, February 11, 2013.

24   Admiration for the light poles was not universal. "I don't love the light poles," Ken Fisher told one of the park's designers. "Please tell me that you didn't design them that way as some kind of allusion to the waterfront's industrial past." Fisher, interview with authors, February 27, 2014.

25   Raver, "Hey, Mister, I've Got a Park I Can Sell You." Van Valkenburgh repeatedly credited the public planning process with establishing a priority for direct access to the water, which he provided at numerous points along the shore.

26   Hank Gutman, interview with authors, March 2, 2014.

19. The Politics of Housing, Continued

1   Daniel Doctoroff, interview with authors, April 2, 2014.

2   Ibid.

3   Marianna Koval, interview with authors, May 28, 2014.

4   "BBP Financial Model Update," Board of Directors, October 21, 2013, http://brooklynbridgepark.org/pages/project-approvals-and-presentations. This URL will take the reader to a long list of documents available to the public concerning financial studies, park development projects, marine structures, and transportation issues.

5   Adrian Benepe, interview with author, May 2, 2014.

6   Liz Robbins, "The Battle of Brooklyn Bridge Park," *New York Times*, August 1, 2014.

7   Josh Barbanel, "Affordable Units for Park Draw Ire," *Wall Street Journal*, May 9, 2014; "Brooklyn Development Plans Stirs Debates on Affordable Housing and Park Funding," *New York Times*, May 13, 2014; "Affordable Units Planned for Brooklyn Bridge Park, but Opposition Remains," *Brooklyn Eagle*, May 20, 2014.

8   Letter dated April 7, 2014, to Mayor Bill de Blasio from State Senator Daniel Squadron, Assembly Member Joan Millman, Councilmen Stephen T. Levin, Congresswoman Nydia Velázquez, and Councilman Brad Lander. They also asked for "more sustainable and re-

sponsible alternatives" without spelling out what these might be. Lisa W. Foderaro, "De Blasio Is Urged to Alter Housing Plans at Brooklyn Bridge Park," *New York Times*, April 9, 2014.

9   "Affordable Units Planned for Brooklyn Bridge Park, but Opposition Remains," *Brooklyn Eagle*, May 20, 2014.

10   Charles B. Bagli, "Brooklyn Development Plan Stirs Debate on Affordable Housing and Park Funding," *New York Times*, Mary 13, 2014. To such critics, Doctoroff said he did not "believe that somehow you have to preserve these pristine edges of every park. Instead what I would worry about . . . is the sustainability of funding to maintain the park." "I never viewed having building on the edge as any sort of violation of principle," he said, but "even if you concede it, that the park is negatively impacted by the buildings, the worst thing that could happen to a park is if it falls into disrepair because of the vicissitudes of the city's funding streams" (Doctoroff, op. cit.).

11   Robbins, "Battle of Brooklyn Bridge Park."

12   Ibid.

13   Barbanel, "Affordable Units for Park Draw Ire."

14   Robbins, "Battle of Brooklyn Bridge Park."

15   Benepe, op. cit.

16   "Judge Blocks Brooklyn Bridge Park from Approving Pier 6 Towers, for Now," *Brooklyn Eagle*, July 18, 2014, http://brooklyneagle.com/articles/2014/7/18/judge-blocks-brooklyn-bridge-park-approving-pier-6-towers-now.

17   Press release, June 30, 2015, announcing the conditional designation and the plan to seek a modification of the general project plan to reduce each building by thirty feet in height, to include a seventy-five-seat pre-K, some retail and community space, 30 percent of residential units affordable, and an increase in parkland by virtue of closing an internal park road. See http://www.brooklynbridgepark.org/press/plans-unveiled-for-pier-6-residential-buildings-at-bbp.

18   Rich Calder, "Battle over Pier 6 Luxe and Affordable Housing Heats Up," *New York Post*, July 30, 2015, http://nypost.com/2015/07/30/battle-begins-over-luxe-and-affordable-housing-plan-at-pier-6/; Erin Durkin, "Local Groups Blast Brooklyn Park Tower Plans," *New York Daily News*, August 31, 2015, http://www.nydailynews.com/new-york/brooklyn/local-groups-blast-brooklyn-park-tower-plans-article-1.2343741; "Public Advocate Latest to Join Fight against Pier 6," *The Real Deal*, September 1, 2015, http://therealdeal.com/2015/09/01/public-advocate-letitia-james-the-latest-to-join-pier-6-opposition/.

19   Peter Flemming, interview with authors, February 26, 2014.

20   The first CAC resolution, adopted May 27, 2014, read, "The CAC would like to have a review of the GPP, including but not limited to, the uplands of Pier 6, including the street grid, beginning with an immediate solicitation of public comments at a hearing and a review by DOT of the traffic flow, followed by a public presentation to the public and pub-

lic comment on an expedited basis, including building envelopes, surrounding plazas, and all related design elements of the Pier 6 uplands. This review does not mandate or preclude ULURP." The second read, "The CAC urges a full scale public review of the existing GPP (and/or its succession by ULURP) to include financial parameters and environmental considerations that have evolved since 2004."

21 Elected officials like Senator Squadron and many members of the CAC had always opposed housing because they thought those living near the park might "privatize" it and feel entitled to dictate what happened there. Since they were supporting the arguments and the campaign organized by residents of 360 Furman, it seemed ironic that they were now allied with residents who lived in the park and were trying to keep others from doing so.

22 "Fractious Board Meeting Pulls Pier 6 in Different Directions," *Brooklyn Eagle*, June 9, 2014; "Not in Brooklyn's Front Yard," *Brooklyn Paper*, June 13–19, 2014.

23 The representatives of Senator Squadron, Assembly Member Simon, and Council Member Levin were the minority votes; the representative of Borough President Adams voted the other way.

24 "Brooklyn Bridge Park Financials," People for Green Space Foundation, prepared for BBPC Board Meeting on November 7, 2014.

25 "Brooklyn Bridge Park Response to People for Green Space Foundation Inc.," released November 25, 2014.

26 Brooklyn Bridge Park Financial Model Update, public presentation, July 9, 2015, http://brooklynbridgepark.org/pages/project-approvals-and-presentations.

27 When asked why a large private gift to Hudson River Park could not be better spent on repairing deteriorated marine structure than on new park, Madelyn Wils, president and CEO of the park, replied, "If anyone knows a donor willing to cover the cost of pile repairs, we're all ears." Lisa W. Foderaro, "How Diller and von Furstenberg Got Their Island in Hudson River Park," *New York Times*, April 3, 2015.

28 The Denham report, titled, "Report on Brooklyn Bridge Park's Financial Model," was released by the park corporation on July 29, 2015, and can be found at http://www .brooklynbridgepark.org/pages/project-approvals-and-presentations.

29 Letter from People for Green Space Foundation Inc. to Members of the Board, Brooklyn Bridge Park Corporation, dated November 3, 2015.

30 Memorandum to Members of the Board of Directors of Brooklyn Bridge Park from Regina Myer, dated December 1, 2015.

31 Robbins, "Battle of Brooklyn Bridge Park."

32 Michael Randazzo interview with Lori Schomp, *Brooklyn Heights Blog*, September 17, 2014, http://brooklynheightsblog.com/archives/70314.

33   Adrian Benepe, interview with authors, November 3, 2015.

34   Tupper Thomas, interview with authors, July 23, 2014.

35   Elizabeth Barlow Rogers, interview with authors, March 25, 2014..

36   In response to requests to the comptrollers of the city and the state by Senator Squadron and others, both opined that while perhaps legally possible, either the park corporation or the Brooklyn Bridge Park Development Corporation would probably have to borrow through another entity and obtain various approvals, to say nothing of the credit issues that were specifically noted but not addressed. The City of New York's Office of Management and Budget, by letter to Regina Myer dated December 3, 2015, was very clear that it would not support borrowing for many reasons, among them that the "debt of BBP would be perceived as a moral obligation of the City, which would pose severe risk to the City's borrowing program in the event of a default."

37   The Brooklyn Heights Association had always been a staunch supporter of the Grand Bargain. As recently as August 2014, Alexandra Bowie, president of the BHA, said, "We have always had the position that housing is the best way to support the park. Robbins, "Battle of Brooklyn Bridge Park." Bowie's successor, Patrick Killackey, has set that history aside and been surprisingly hostile to the park, as has the BHA's representative to the CAC, Carolyn Ziegler.

38   Letter of February 24, 2015, from Shirley A. McRae, chairperson of Community Board 2, to Regina Myer, president of the Brooklyn Bridge Park Corporation

39   Dana Rubinstein, "'Dysfunctional Dynamic' Sparks Battle at Brooklyn Bridge Park," *Politico New York*, March 3, 2015, http://www.capitalnewyork.com/tags/brooklyn-bridge-park.

40   Sally Goldenberg, "State Delays Controversial de Blasio Backed Housing Plan, *Politico New York*, January 21, 2016, http://www.capitalnewyork.com/article/city-hall/2016/01/8588677/state-delays-controversial-de-blasio-backed-housing-plan; Josh Barbanel, "For Brooklyn Par, Agreement That's a Bridge Too Far," Wall Street Journal, February 26, 2016, http://www.wsj.com/articles/for-brooklyn-park-agreement-over-housing-is-a-bridge-too-far-1456536357; "Levine Tells State to Hurry Up and Approve BK's Pier 6 Project," *The Real Deal*, March 21, 2016, http://therealdeal.com/2016/03/21/robert-levine-pushes-for-state-approval-for-brooklyn-bridge-parks-pier-6/.

20. Waterfront, Parks, and Community Planning

1   "Coastal Zone Management Act of 1972, as Amended through Pub. L. No. 109-58, the Energy Policy Act of 2005," https://coast.noaa.gov/czm/media/CZMA_10_11_06.pdf.

2   The "Vision 2020" page, now defunct, was available at http://www.nyc.gov/html/dcp/html/cwp/cwp_2.shtml.

3   Lisa W. Foderaro, "Correction Seen after Years of Disinvestment in Neighborhood Parks," *New York Times*, October 8, 2014.

4   Laura Kusisto, "City Looks at Life beyond Housing," *Wall Street Journal*, October 28, 2014. In some quarters, de Blasio was criticized for scoring "cheap political points" and not doing more. Reflecting the complaints, the architecture critic Michael Kimmelman noted that the Bloomberg administration had in fact advanced $80 million of de Blasio's $130 million program and had "poured $5 billion in capital investment into parks, most of which were in the Bronx, Brooklyn, Queens and Staten Island." See "Mayor de Blasio's Plan for Parks Needs to Grow," *New York Times,* October 28, 2014.

5   Lisa W. Foderaro, "New York City's Low-Profile Parks to Get Conservancies' Help, and Some Cash," *New York Times*, November 13, 2015.

6   Michael Kimmelman, "Room to Grow in Mayor's Plan for City Parks," *New York Times*, October 29, 2014.

7   Foderaro, "New York City's Low-Profile Parks."

8   Danielle Furfaro, "Stuck in Park: Williamsburg, Greenpoint Residents Take Waterfront Fight to City Hall," *Brooklyn Paper*, March 13, 2015, http://www.brooklynpaper.com/stories/38/12/dtg-bushwick-inlet-park-protest-2015-03-20-bk_38_12.html; Evan Bindelglass, "Bushwick Inlet Park Advocates Chant 'Where's Our Park?'" *Curbed New York*, March 13, 2015, http://ny.curbed.com/2015/3/13/9981332/bushwick-inlet-park-advocates-chant-wheres-our-park.

9   James. S. Russell, "The Price of Thomas Heatherwick's Imagination," *New York Times,* July 30, 2015.

10   "River Park Gets $100 Million Launch," *Wall Street Journal*, November 7, 2014; "A Billionaire's Hudson River Project" (editorial), *New York Times*, November 22, 2014; David Callahan, "The Billionaires' Park" (op-ed), *New York Times*, December 2, 2014.

11   Lisa W. Foderaro, "Queens Wants to Transform an Abandoned Railway into a Park," *New York Times*, January 8, 2013.

12   See "WDC History," *Louisville Waterfront Park*, http://www.louisvillewaterfront.com/aboutUs/wdcHistory/.

13   Candace Damon, interview with authors, March 21, 2014, and December 5, 2015; "Overview," *Waterfront Seattle*, http://waterfrontseattle.org/overview.

14   The New York Independent Budget Office produced an interesting analysis of tax increment financing. See "Learning from Experience: A Primer on Tax Increment Financing," *IBO Fiscal Brief,* September 2002.

15   "The Plan of Chicago," *Burnham Plan Centennial*, http://burnhamplan100.lib.uchicago.edu/history_future/plan_of_chicago/; Julia S. Bachrach, "Daniel H. Burnham and Chicago's Parks," http://www.chicagoparkdistrict.com/assets/1/23/burnham.pdf.

16   Shia Kapos, "By Any Other Name, Would Millennium Park Smell as Sweet?" *Crain's Chicago Business*, September 13, 2014, http://www.chicagobusiness.com/article/20140913/

ISSUE09/309139978/by-any-other-name-would-millenium-park-smell-as-sweet; "Millennium Park without the Pritzker Pavilion? It Almost Happened," *DNAinfo*, November 2, 2015, https://www.dnainfo.com/chicago/20151102/downtown/millennium-park-without-pritzker-pavilion-it-almost-happened; Dawn Reiss, "10 Years of Millennium Park History," *Michigan Avenue*, August 1, 2014, http://michiganavemag.com/10-years-of-millennium-park-history.

17   Rachel Nania, "D.C.'s First Elevated Park Designed to Bridge Community Gap," *WTOP Living News*, February 9, 2015, http://wtop.com/living/2015/02/d-c-s-first-elevated-park-designed-bridge-community-gap/slide/1/; "11th Street Bridge Park," http://www.bridgepark.org/; "11th Street Bridge Park," *Anacostia Waterfront Initiative*, https://www.anacostiawaterfront.org/awi-transportation-projects/11th-street-bridge/.

18   Rebecca Cooper, "11th Street Bridge Park, D.C.'s Answer to the High Line, Lands First Seven-Figure Donation," *Washington Business Journal*, September 29, 2015, http://www.bizjournals.com/washington/blog/top-shelf/2015/09/11th-street-bridge-park-d-c-s-answer-to-the-high.html.

19   Jonathan O'Connell, "Can D.C. Build a $45 Million Park for Anacostia without Pushing People Out?" *Washington Post Magazine*, January 21, 2016, https://www.washingtonpost.com/lifestyle/magazine/can-dc-build-a-45-million-park-for-anacostia-without-pushing-people-out/2016/01/20/d96e9cde-a03c-11e5-8728-1af6af208198_story.html.

21. Reflections on Brooklyn Bridge Park

1   A notable U.S. example of a park on an industrial site is the Gas Works Park in Seattle, a twenty-acre expanse created around a tower and other features of the former Seattle Gas Light Company. Designed by landscape architect Richard Haag, who won awards for it, the park opened in 1975.

2   Nicolai Ouroussoff, "The Greening of the Waterfront," *New York Times*, April 1, 2010, http://www.nytimes.com/2010/04/02/arts/design/02bridge.html.

3   "2009 Professional Awards: Analysis & Planning Category: Honor Award, Brooklyn Bridge Park," *American Society of Landscape Architects*, https://www.asla.org/2009awards/011.html.

4   "MAS to Award 23rd Brendan Gill Prize to Brooklyn Bridge Park Landscape Architect," *Municipal Art Society of New York*, January 18, 2011, http://www.mas.org/mas-to-award-23rd-brendan-gill-prize-to-brooklyn-bridge-park-landscape-architect/.

5   Rey Mashayekhi, "Jehovah's Witnesses Marketing Three Downtown BK Properties," *The Real Deal*, December 3, 2015, , http://therealdeal.com/2015/12/03/jehovahs-witnesses-marketing-three-downtown-bk-properties.

Patrick Bunyan, *All Around the Town: Amazing Manhattan Facts and Curiosities, Second Edition*

Salvatore Basile, *Fifth Avenue Famous: The Extraordinary Story of Music at St. Patrick's Cathedral*. Foreword by Most Reverend Timothy M. Dolan, Archbishop of New York

Andrew J. Sparberg, *From a Nickel to a Token: The Journey from Board of Transportation to MTA*

New York's Golden Age of Bridges. Paintings by Antonio Masi, Essays by Joan Marans Dim, Foreword by Harold Holzer

Daniel Campo, *The Accidental Playground: Brooklyn Waterfront Narratives of the Undesigned and Unplanned*

John Waldman, *Heartbeats in the Muck: The History, Sea Life, and Environment of New York Harbor, Revised Edition*

John Waldman (ed.), *Still the Same Hawk: Reflections on Nature and New York*

Gerard R. Wolfe, *The Synagogues of New York's Lower East Side: A Retrospective and Contemporary View, Second Edition*. Photographs by Jo Renée Fine and Norman Borden, Foreword by Joseph Berger

Joseph B. Raskin, *The Routes Not Taken: A Trip Through New York City's Unbuilt Subway System*

Phillip Deery, *Red Apple: Communism and McCarthyism in Cold War New York*

North Brother Island: The Last Unknown Place in New York City. Photographs by Christopher Payne, A History by Randall Mason, Essay by Robert Sullivan

Kirsten Jensen and Bartholomew F. Bland (eds.), *Industrial Sublime: Modernism and the Transformation of New York's Rivers, 1900–1940*. Introduction by Katherine Manthorne

Richard Kostelanetz, *Artists' SoHo: 49 Episodes of Intimate History*

Stephen Miller, *Walking New York: Reflections of American Writers from Walt Whitman to Teju Cole*

Tom Glynn, *Reading Publics: New York City's Public Libraries, 1754–1911*

Craig Saper, *The Amazing Adventures of Bob Brown: A Real-Life Zelig Who Wrote His Way Through the 20th Century*

R. Scott Hanson, *City of Gods: Religious Freedom, Immigration, and Pluralism in Flushing, Queens*. Foreword by Martin E. Marty

Dorothy Day and the Catholic Worker: The Miracle of Our Continuance. Edited, with an Introduction and Additional Text by Kate Hennessy, Photographs by Vivian Cherry, Text by Dorothy Day

Pamela Lewis, *Teaching While Black: A New Voice on Race and Education in New York City*

Mark Naison and Bob Gumbs, *Before the Fires: An Oral History of African American Life in the Bronx from the 1930s to the 1960s*

Robert Weldon Whalen, *Murder, Inc., and the Moral Life: Gangsters and Gangbusters in La Guardia's New York*

See www.empirestateeditions.com for a complete list.